The Irish Diaspora

Also by D.H. Akenson

SOCIAL AND RELIGIOUS HISTORY

God's Peoples: Covenant and Land in South Africa, Israel and Ulster
Occasional Papers on the Irish in South Africa
Half the World from Home. Perspectives on the Irish in New Zealand
Small Differences: Irish Catholics and Irish Protestants, 1815-1922.
    An International Perspective
Between Two Revolutions: Islandmagee, Co. Antrim, 1798-1920
    The United States and Ireland
The Church of Ireland: Ecclesiastical Reform and Revolution

BIOGRAPHY

A Protestant in Purgatory: Richard Whately: Archbishop of Dublin
Local Poets and Social History: James Orr, Bard of Ballycarry
    (with W.H. Crawford)

HISTORY OF EDUCATION

A Mirror to Kathleen's Face: Education in Independent Ireland, 1922-60
Education and Enmity: The Control of Schooling in Northern Ireland,
    1920-50
The Irish Education Experiment: The National System of Education in
    the Nineteenth Century
The Changing Uses of the Liberal Arts College: An Essay in Recent
    Educational History. (With L.F. Stevens)

NORTH AMERICAN STUDIES

Colonies. Canada to 1867 (With David J. Bercuson et. al.)
Being Had: Historians, Evidence and the Irish in North America
The Irish in Ontario: A Study in Rural History
(Editor) *Canadian Papers in Rural History*, 9 vols.

FICTION

At Face Value. The Life and Times of Eliza McCormack/John White
The Edgerston Audit
The Orangeman. The Life and Times of Ogle R. Gowan
Brotherhood Week in Belfast
The Lazar House Notebooks

The Irish Diaspora

A Primer

Donald Harman Akenson

P.D. Meany Company, Inc., Publishers
Toronto

The Institute of Irish Studies
The Queen's University of Belfast

Canadian Cataloguing in Publication Data

Akenson, Donald Harman, 1941-
    The Irish Diaspora: a primer

Co-published by the Institute of Irish Studies,
Queen's University Of Belfast.
Includes bibliographical references and index.
ISBN 0-88835-038-4 (bound) ISBN 0-88835-001-5 (pbk.)

1. Irish - Migrations - History - 19th century.
2. Irish - Migrations - History - 20th century.
3. Ireland - Emigration and immigration - History -
19th century. 4. Ireland - Emigration and immigration -
History - 20th century. I. Queen's University of
Belfast. Institute of Irish Studies. II. Title.

JV7711.A43 1993   304.8'099415   C93-094305-

Legal deposit, fourth quarter 1996

Published in the United Kingdom by
The Institute of Irish Studies
The Queen's University of Belfast
8 Fitzwilliam Street,
Belfast,
Northern Ireland.

ISBN 0-85389-499-X (bound)   ISBN 0-85389-663-1 (pbk.)

British Library Cataloguing-in-Publication Data. A
catalogue record for this book is available from the
British Library.

Design by Glen Patchet

Printed and bound in Canada
for
P.D. Meany Company Inc., Publishers
Box 118, Streetsville, Ontario, Canada L5M 2B7

Contents

Maps

Figures

Tables

Dedicated to:

John, David, Sean, Cormac, Jim, and Patrick

Acknowledgements

I am grateful for financial support in the research and writing of this primer to the Social Sciences and Humanities Research Council of Canada and to the Advisory Research Council of the School of Graduate Studies and Research of Queen's University, Kingston, Ontario. Earlier research was funded in part by the Australian National University, by the Stout Research Centre of Victoria University, Wellington, New Zealand, and by the Institute of Social and Economic Research of Rhodes University, Grahamston, Republic of South Africa.

This volume is dedicated to those scholars to whom I have an especially deep intellectual debt: John V. Kelleher, David Fitzpatrick, Sean Connolly, Cormac Ó Gráda, James Donnelly Jr., and Patrick O'Farrell. They are all good friends and equally good critics. In dedicating this book to them, I do so in the full confidence that my doing so will not in the slightest degree keep them from continuing to set me straight.

Part I

Clear Themes

Chapter 1

Introduction:
The Fabergé Egg

(I)

One of the most dazzling objects that one can enounter is a Fabergé egg. These gold and enamel creations, fashioned for the imperial Russian court, are masterpieces of detail. Yet, for all their fine craftsmanship, characterized by delicate handwork done millimeter-by-millimeter, they succeed as pieces of art because of the way the details relate to each other and, most importantly, the way each object works as a whole. Each is a unity.

If one had money to burn and a philistine heart, one could take apart a Fabergé egg. It would be possible to cut away a section, like slicing the skin of an orange, and then to flatten this section on to a two-dimensional surface so that the result resembled the way that a satellite photograph provides a two-dimensional image of a section of our three-dimensional earth. In so doing we certainly would learn something about the way that the Fabergé egg is constructed. Conceivably, we could do this to a whole set of the priceless objects and thus come to some comparative conclusions about the variety and type of these creations.

Now in many ways, the Irish diaspora is similar to a Fabergé egg. It is a marvellously complex phenomenon. Details, though fascinating in themselves, are subordinated to the larger picture, since they all interrelate and all are subject to the whole. And, like a Fabergé egg, the diaspora has to be viewed as a three-dimensional object if it is to be appreciated. One has to look at the phenomenon from all sides and to rotate it 360° in every plane to grasp its full character. In fact, the same is true of several other major cultural constellations — for example, the remnants of the world-circling Spanish empire, the French-derived cultures worldwide, and the dispersions of the several Oriental cultures. Yet, we almost never look at these marvellous ethno-cultural patterns as a whole. Instead, we slice them up.

One of the admirable developments of recent decades is the widespread interest throughout the English-speaking world in what is usually labelled "multiculturalism." At its best, multicultural books and university courses increase the understanding and tolerance of persons of a given group for the persons and culture of other ethnic and religious groups. Typically, this is achieved by studying how the values of each group and its cultural practices fit into the overall scheme of American (or, as the case may be, Canadian, British, Australian, or New Zealand) society.

This understanding is gained only at some cost. Examining, say, the Irish, or the Polynesians, or the Chinese or the Spanish-American cultures only as they exist in (for example) the United States is very much like severing homologous segments from several Fabergé eggs and then laying them side by side. Undeniably, it is a valid comparative exercise, but dealing with the Francophones, or the Spanish or the Chinese or the First Nations, only within the context of some modern nation-state means that one relegates to secondary importance anything that does not have to do with that particular modern nation.

So, as a supplement to the traditional multicultural approach, (and, emphatically, not as a rejection of that approach) it seems obvious that there should be books and university courses upon the subject of, for example, the Spanish cultures worldwide, on the Original Peoples throughout the western hemisphere, on Francophone cultures around the world, and upon the Polynesian cultures considered as a transnational phenomenon. So too, should there be an appreciation of the Irish diaspora as a worldwide fact.

That explains why this volume takes the shape that it does. I wish to speak primarily (but not solely) to persons in

Ireland whose family members have migrated overseas, and to persons of Irish descent in the United States. My belief is that one cannot understand very much about the Irish in the United States if one knows only the Irish who migrated to the States. The migrants to America (both historically and in the present day) are part of a larger pattern. Like constellations of enamelled pearls on a gilded egg, they cannot be interpreted on their own. The story of the Irish in America makes sense only within the context of a world-circling history.

There is also a practical aspect. Because, as I will indicate later, the information on the Irish in the United States is severely limited in many aspects, one needs to deal with the Irish in Australia, New Zealand, Great Britain, and South Africa in order to learn things that (with appropriate and careful methods) can be translated to the U.S. This will allow us to fill in some of the holes in the history of the Irish in the U.S. and to correct historical errors that have been the result of prejudice. Thus, paradoxically, to know very much about the Irish in America, one must first learn a good deal about the Irish elsewhere.

More than any other European nation, Ireland in the nineteenth and twentieth centuries was characterized by emigration. In relation to its size, it lost more of its population through out-migration than did any other major nation. Most young Irish men and women who came into adulthood from 1815, the end of the Napoleonic Wars and the effective start of the great outward flood, until the present day, have had something in common: they have considered whether or not to leave Ireland. Over the years most stayed home, but so deeply has the possibility of migrating been woven into the fabric of Irish social life that for most young people staying in Ireland has been just as much a matter of conscious choice as, for others, has been the decision to leave. As David Fitzpatrick, the leading modern student of Irish emigration patterns, has noted, "growing up in Ireland meant preparing oneself to leave it."[1]

The magnitude of the Irish diaspora of the nineteenth and twentieth centuries can be described in three ways: in absolute terms, as a proportion of the Irish-born population, and as a proportion of the population of the various New Worlds to which the Irish moved. These matters will be dealt with in detail in the chapters that follow, but here are salient examples of each mode of measurement. First: between 1815 and 1870, a total of 4.0 to 4.5 million persons migrated from Ireland.[2] Second: in 1890, when nearly three million Irish-born persons were living overseas, this represented nearly 40 percent of all of those living persons who had been born in Ireland.[3] And third: in certain jurisdictions around the world (states, provinces, territories which had their own legal codes and constitutional structures), the Irish-born and their descendants became the largest ethnic group and thus had a very strong impact on the character of the emerging New World societies. For example, when, in 1871, the first census of the dominion of Canada was taken, the Irish were found to be 24.3 percent of the entire population, making them the largest English-language ethnic group.[4] In Ontario, the heartland of English-speaking Canada, persons of Irish ethnicity were 34.5 percent of the population, by far the largest ethnic group.[5] What is misleadingly called the "English-Canadian" cultural identity is more Irish than anything else.

The overall pattern of the Irish diaspora was sequential. Up to 1845, the two places most frequently chosen as new homelands by Irish migrants were Great Britain (that is, Scotland and England and Wales) and British North America (which later became Canada). Then, from the mid-1840s until the First World War, most migrants from Ireland went to the United States of America. From World War I until the present day, the first choice has been Great Britain and especially England. Though sequential, these stages overlapped, and in every period there have been many secondary rivulets in the migration patterns, as well as the dominant streams.

(II)

Any discussion of so complex and world-circling a phenomenon as the Irish diaspora must have an agreed vocabulary. And the hardest portion of that vocabulary to pin down is the term "Irish."

The task becomes somewhat easier if one casts aside any metaphysical notions of Irish nationality and searches instead for a simple operational definition. Given that the heart and hearth of the Irish diaspora was the homeland, it makes sense to ask who in, say, 1815 (or in 1845, or in 1895) was an Irish person? The answer is clear: anyone who lived permanently within the social system that was the island of Ireland. This includes both Catholics and Protestants, Kerrymen, Ulstermen, descendants of Norman invaders and of Scottish planters as well as of earlier Celtic invaders, speakers of English as well as speakers of Irish Gaelic. That there were during the nineteenth and early twentieth centuries complex political arguments about what was the proper definition of Irish nationality is here irrelevant. It matters not if an individual was (for example) a Catholic whose family during the penal times turned Protestant: he or she was Irish. It matters not if the person was the descendant of some Norman soldier whose family had Hibernicized and become more Irish than the Irish they conquered: he or she was Irish. It matters not if the individual came by descent from one of the Cromwellians or from the Confederacy soldiers whom Cromwell defeated: she or he was Irish. Ireland was a political and social system and Ireland formed everyone who lived in it. They could hate Ireland, love it, hate each other, it mattered not. They were of Ireland: hence Irish.

Consider the alternative to acceptance of this simple definition — which, among other things, has the virtue of sidestepping what James Joyce has called "the old pap of racial hatred." If one believes that only a portion of the population living in Ireland in, say, 1841 was "really" Irish, then what was the total population of Ireland? Would one subtract from the government's enumeration of population all those persons who had English-derived names? There would go, for example, the great nationalist leader Charles Stewart Parnell, and most of the old Catholic gentry families, with their Norman roots. Fortunately, no professional historian of Ireland would accept this way of proceeding. For Irish historians, the history of the Irish is the history of the people who lived in Ireland, simple as that.

Where the exclusivist mentality lunacy still has some currency is in enclaves of the Irish diaspora, where the accepted local definition of who is "really" Irish is this: it is someone like us, whoever "us" may be. This is both blinkered and historically unworkable. This way of operating would mean that (for example) in the Kati-Kati settlement on the North Island of New Zealand in 1890, "Irish" would have included only Irish Protestants; while in Lawrence, Massachusetts in the same era, only Irish Catholics would have been encompassed.

It follows from our inclusive definition of "Irish" in the homeland that the only historically defensible definition of an Irish migrant is: a woman or man, girl or boy, who either was born in Ireland or was a permanent resident of Ireland before embarking for some New World. There are practical as well as purely intellectual reasons for accepting this definition of an Irish emigrant. Even if one wishes to strike from the tally of emigrants all those who had a certain sort of name or a certain religious belief or a certain political outlook, one really cannot achieve this. None of the tallies of Irish out-migrants contains information that would permit one to do that sort of cultural filleting. If one is absolutely committed to the particularistic and exclusive view that not all the Irish emigrants in the tallies were "truly" Irish, then one can follow only one course: burn all the data on Irish emigration as being useless and thereafter wander into the historical darkness.

Notice where our logic train is leading. If an Irish emigrant is someone who was either born in Ireland or was a permanent resident of Ireland before emigrating, it follows that the same inclusive definition must be adopted when we discuss the recipient countries, the various New Worlds. Every migrant from Ireland is part of that great collective phenomenon, the Irish diaspora. One cannot erase from the history of the Irish in the USA, Canada, Australia, New Zealand or Great Britain, the life histories of persons who do not fit some pre-determined (and, clearly, prejudiced) definition of who is Irish.

Does this mean that I believe that we should delete from the history of both the Irish homeland and of the several New Worlds the deep religious differences that historically have divided the Irish from each other? Quite the opposite. As Sean Connolly has suggested, sectarian divisions were the very marrow of nineteenth-century Irish life, and one notices only partial abatement in the present century. Connolly mentions a situation that is a perfect metaphor for the distance between Catholics and Protestants: in the southeast of Ireland in the pre-Famine years there were separate Catholic and Protestant inns, and separate stage coaches plied the same routes, duplicating each other's path. Thereby they precluded the need for merchants and gentry of one faith to travel alongside those of the other.[6] Two sets of inns, two coaches, separate and each undeniably Irish. Far from ignoring sectarian differences of all sorts, political, economic, and social, one should deal with them directly, for they were central to the physics of the Irish social system.

Similarly, when one deals with Irish migrants to new lands, one must recognize not only that the Irish were both Catholic and Protestant, but also that sectarian hostilities brought from the Old World frequently had a continuation in the New. Sad to say, to study Irish history either of the homeland or of any part of the diaspora without considering sectarian divergencies is not to study the Irish at all.[7]

(III)

There are other matters, less emotionally volatile ones, which require the reader's tacit consent.

It is crucial that our agreed vocabulary asserts that the *migrant generation* and the *entire ethnic group* are two different things. The migrants often are referred to as the *Irish-born* or, within the context of their new homeland, as the *first-generation*.

In contrast, the Irish ethnic group is a *multigenerational* phenomenon. In historical discussion it includes not only the migrant generation but their direct offspring and, often, subsequent generations of descendants.

What exactly an ethnic group is and what constitutes a sense of ethnicity are matters that have been fought about among social scientists and historians for at least the past two generations, without agreement. For the present purposes, a person is accepted as being of Irish ethnicity if she or he, when asked "what is your primary ethnic background?" responds by saying "Irish." Such self-definition and self-declared ethnic affiliation should be taken at face value. (That in individual cases, a person who is of Irish ancestry may declare that he or she is English, or that someone whose background is English may declare himself or herself to be Irish, is not important when dealing with

9

large numbers of cases, as such errors cancel out each other). In countries which have accrued a bank of data upon ethnicity (Canada is the best example), this acceptance of self-definition makes matters simple: a person is part of the Irish ethnic group — whether he or she is of the first generation or the fifth or anything in between — as long as his or her primary sense of ethnic identity is Irish.

Where difficulties arise is in jurisdictions (and these include most of the English-speaking world) wherein such ethnicity questions have not been asked by official statisticians or have been asked so badly as to be untrustworthy. One cannot ignore ethnicity in some country just because the official enumerators did so. This is particularly important in the case of the U.S., for American census officials have never asked a question concerning primary ethnic identification. But though primary ethnicity has never been mentioned on the census forms, that does not mean that there is not a robust sense of ethnicity among Americans.

There are ways around such dead ends and this book is designed to illustrate them. The crucial point is that in no nation should historians and social scientists collect information about the migrant generation (the Irish-born) and then generalize about "the Irish." That term — "the Irish" — should be employed when dealing with the new homelands only to refer to the entire multigenerational ethnic group. The greatest single source of error in Irish diaspora studies is caused by floating terminology, especially by scholars who study the first generation, and then misleadingly refer to "the Irish" as if their conclusions could automatically be transferred from the migrant generation to the several generations of the Irish ethnic group.

To successive twentieth-century Irish governments, emigration has been a very touchy topic, a symptom of national failing. In the late 1940s and early 1950s, the government of the Republic of Ireland engaged in a major study of how to deal with the "problem" of out-migration from Ireland.[8] At about the same time, a group of intellectuals from Great Britain, the U.S. and Ireland contributed to a book entitled *The Vanishing Irish* whose keynote question was "are the Irish going to vanish from this earth?"[9] There is an emotionally rich literature, based largely upon anecdote, that sees the Irish diaspora as tragedy and as having been largely an involuntary movement. Therefore, the Irish in the USA, Australia, Great Britain and elsewhere are depicted as "exiles." As I will argue later, this viewpoint is condescending to the migrant generation (who have for the most part been capable of strong and conscious decision-making, and were not mere passive bits of flotsam on some alleged historical tide). The emigration-as-exile perspective is also unconsciously demeaning to the various new homelands in which the Irish migrants settled, for it treats the New Worlds as a set of Elbas where no one would settle by choice.

In order to avoid the hyper-emotionalism that sometimes misleads students of the Irish diaspora, this book uses numbers: big numbers. Personally, I loath dealing with figures. I much prefer to write novels, biographies, and community studies. Numbers are not much fun. But before one becomes engaged in the enjoyable aspects of chronicling the Irish diaspora (things such as the heroics of individual migrants, the flash of sectarian riots, the machinations of ambitious politicians) one needs to know where within the big picture the individual story is situated. Numbers are our most accurate adjectives and adverbs, if not the most entertaining. Instead of saying that "most," "few," or "some" of the Irish had a certain characteristic, it is much better to be able to give an accurate percentage. Although I will here be presenting generalizations that are based on the collection of several million datum points, only simple arithmetic will be used. No regression analyses, no beta-weights, nothing complicated. Anyone who has passed primary school arithmetic can deal with this material.

Numbers, even big numbers (by which I mean numbers drawn from large-scale and representative data bases) are only as accurate as the mode by which the basic data were collected. Ideally, we would have basic information on every migrant who left Ireland and on every Irish immigrant into a new land. But we do not. Therefore, at points, we will have to pay close attention to the character of the evidence that comes to hand, for a misreading of the basic evidence inevitably produces inaccurate generalizations. "Data" should not be a turn-off word. It simply refers to what one points to when someone says "Prove it."

The reason that attention must be paid closely to the nature and extent of the available data bases is that the two places to which Irish migrants most often moved during the nineteenth and twentieth centuries — the USA and Great Britain — are the very jurisdictions that have the weakest sets of information. Therefore, one of our major tasks is to find ways around the great empty spaces in the American and British data. The trick is to turn away-games into home-games. (One is reminded of Yogi Berra's aphorism, that "home openers are always exciting whether they're home or on the road.") That is, because there was a common nodal point in the entire Irish diaspora, namely the Irish homeland, it is possible to learn fundamental things about (for example) Tipperary migrants to the United States by studying the characteristics and behaviour of Tipperary migrants to central Canada, a group that, through the work of Bruce Elliott, is particularly well documented.[10]

Obviously, there is a danger of false translation as between national jurisdictions. Unless one is careful, translating results from one country to another can produce results analogous to the following English language encountered in a Belgrade hotel elevator:

> To move the cabin, push button for wishing floor. If the cabin should enter more persons, each one should press a number of wishing floor. Driving is then going alphabetically by national order.

What one requires to avoid solecisms is rigorous "experimental design." This is a modern term for a very old concept, tight reasoning. One reads with attention the words taken from The Wisdom of Jesus the Son of Sirach (chapter 27:6-7). "The fruit discloses the cultivation of a tree; so the expression of a thought discloses the cultivation of a man's mind. Do not praise a man before you hear him reason, for this is the test of men."

The temporal focus of this primer is similar to a spotlight. At the centre are the years 1815-1920. The great Irish out-migration began at the end of the Napoleonic Wars and continued in its classic form until the Partition of Ireland in 1920. Most Irish migration from the Tudor conquest to the present day occurred in those years, 1815-1920.

However, just as a stage spotlight has a penumbra in which dramatically important actions sometimes occur, so there are peripheral time periods in the history of the diaspora that deserve notice. Migration from Ireland before 1815 is given some attention, especially in its effects on colonial America. Further, even though it becomes difficult to obtain accurate data on all-Ireland migration patterns once the Partition Act of 1920 comes into effect, post-1920 emigration from Ireland is not ignored. Whenever possible, I have continued data-series up to the mid-twentieth century. Anecdotal material is included up to the present day.

In the compressed space of a primer, it is impossible to talk about the Irish in South America or Latin America even though several countries (especially Argentina and Mexico), have had significant Irish populations. Nor can one deal with the various Irish enclaves in the Caribbean and in Asia, nor with the extensive missionary work of Irish nuns and clerics in virtually every nation on earth. Effectively, this is a primer on the Irish diaspora in the English-speaking world. Although that probably comprehends 99 percent of the diaspora, this does not mean that other topics are not potentially important and fruitful.[11] Overwhelmingly, however, the Irish migrants settled in two empires (and their constitutional derivatives), the British and the American.

Neither, in our limited space, can we discuss three peripheral but fascinating aspects of the Irish diaspora. One of these is the matter of migration into Ireland from outside. In earlier eras (through the thirteenth to seventeenth centuries, especially) in-migration was consequential.[12] However, in the nineteenth and twentieth centuries in-migration was minor. Most of those who did move to Ireland from outside were governmental employees: British civil servants, coast guards, police and military officers, an interesting, but not demographically important group. A second matter had more import, namely "return migration." That is: migration back to Ireland by individuals who had left it or whose parents had done so. (In the historical literature this is sometimes called "reverse migration.") The available studies of this matter are very limited, but they suggest that the Irish were less apt to return home than were persons of most other European groups. Responsible estimates of the return migration from the USA to Ireland in the second half of the nineteenth century range from 6 to 10 percent of the number of out-migrants.[13] This is an especially sharp contrast to the other major Catholic group to migrate to the U.S. — the Italians — 58 percent of whose emigrants are estimated to have returned home. Even so, the number of Irish reverse–migrants was not small and any full study of the Irish diaspora would require a long chapter on those individuals. A third matter that cannot here be discussed fully is what might be called "intra-diaspora migration." This refers to the fact that many Irish migrants did not merely go immediately to a final destination, but moved from one new homeland to another before settling down. I have encountered in the records young men who left Munster and first became miners in the Great California gold rush and then moved on to mine in Australia, before fetching up in the gold fields of the west coast of the South Island of New Zealand. And it has been noted in R.A. Burchell's history of the Irish in San Francisco, that more than half of the first arrivals in that city were not from Ireland, but came from Australia.[14] The one aspect of intra-diaspora migration that will receive attention in this primer is the very large flow of Irish migrants within North America. Hundreds of thousands of Irish migrants who eventually settled in the USA migrated first to Canada. Conversely, significant numbers of the Canadian Irish had moved north after spending part of their odyssey in the USA.

Carl Sandburg once remarked that "an expert is nothing but a damn fool a long ways from home," and that is a salient caution when reflecting on the Irish diaspora. For each of us, the Irish diaspora must in part be forever foreign: spanning as it has done the globe, the diaspora is therefore not comfortably within any single ambit. There is no possibility of any one person, or even any team of scholars, capturing it all. It can only be approached with humility, as an extremely complex, often unfathomable, frequently awe-inspiring, collective human creation.

Chapter 2

The Homeland and the Outflow

(I)

When, on 3 December 1990, Mary Robinson assumed the post of president of Ireland (a ceremonial post, the real power being held by the Taoiseach, that is, the prime minister), she gave an inaugural address that was aimed well beyond the borders of the Irish homeland. "There are over seventy million people living on this globe who claim Irish descent," she asserted. "I will be proud to represent them."[1] The new president probably meant not that there are seventy million persons with a drop or two of Irish blood in their veins, but that there are seventy million who, if asked what their primary national heritage was, would have replied, "Irish." Her estimate is entirely plausible. Good authorities have estimated that between 1801 and 1921, at least eight million Irish men, women and children left Ireland.[2] Given normal fecundity and continuing emigrations since 1921, there easily could be seventy million persons of primarily-Irish ethnic descent scattered throughout the world in the 1990s.

Most of President Robinson's seventy million persons are by now the third or fourth generation to live outside of Ireland. To most of them being in some sense "Irish" is not a primary focus of their lives, merely one of the many aspects of their conscious self-definition. These individuals of course have multiple identities. They are Australian, Canadian, or American in terms of loyalties to a state, and Catholic, Baptist, Anglican, Presbyterian or Agnostic in terms of religious identity. But being in some way "Irish" is

15

important, even though secondary for most individuals. And ethnicity can influence an individual's behaviour even when she or he has lost all conscious sense of ethnic affiliation.

One of the points at which the usually-flaccid sense of ethnic identity among the Irish in the English-speaking world becomes tauter is where the great nineteenth-century outflow from Ireland is memorialized and especially when the Great Famine and its flood of migration is depicted. That, more than anything else, touches a communal nerve, and it does so equally in the homeland. So, this is the very point at which they (and we) are most apt to lose our critical judgement and to be fooled. So keen are we to be told emotionally compelling stories from those catastrophic times, that we are apt to believe anything, provided it is sufficiently vivid.

Thus, as a cautionary parable, we should heed the story of *The Voyage of the Naparima*, published in Canada in 1982. This book is purported to be based on the diary of a Famine emigrant, one Gerald Keegan, and it is gripping indeed: the chronicle of the course of the Famine and of the horror of migration to Canada by way of the infestuous Grosse Isle. Now anyone with a knowledge of Irish history could tell that this book was a fiction (a perfectly legitimate historical form, after all), if badly done fiction. However, when the book was re-published in Ireland (by a leading publisher, Wolfhound Press), the obvious-fiction became transposed into fact. The volume became a best-seller, acclaimed as an eye witness account of the great Irish Famine tragedy. Parts of it were serialized in *The Irish Times* and read on the Irish state radio network. It was great and true history, almost everyone agreed. In fact not only was the work a fiction, but it was the creation of a Scottish-born Canadian Orangeman and it had twice been published in book form before its 1982 Canadian edition.[3]

The lesson here is clear: the hunger for knowledge about certain aspects of the Irish diaspora is so great that one must guard strenuously against credulity, especially when the information that comes to hand is evocative, emotionally gripping, and fits with pre-existent stereotypes.

Map 1
Ireland, post-1920

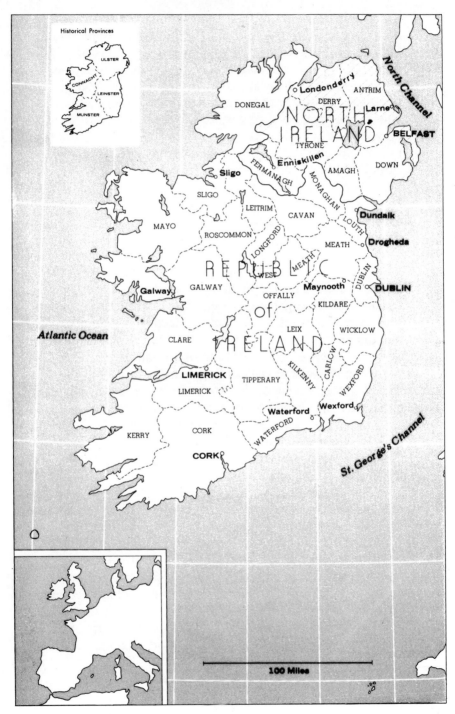

Historical Provinces

ULSTER

CONNACHT

LEINSTER

MUNSTER

North Channel

Londonderry

ANTRIM

DONEGAL

DERRY

Larne

NORTH
IRELAND

BELFAST

TYRONE

Enniskillen

FERMANAGH

AMAGH

DOWN

Sligo

MONAGHAN

SLIGO

LEITRIM

CAVAN

Dundalk

MAYO

ROSCOMMON

LONGFORD

LOUTH

MEATH

Drogheda

REPUBLIC

MEATH

WEST

DUBLIN

Galway

GALWAY

OFFALY

Maynooth

DUBLIN

KILDARE

Atlantic Ocean

of

CLARE

LEIX

WICKLOW

IRELAND

LIMERICK

TIPPERARY

KILKENNY

CARLOW

WEXFORD

LIMERICK

KERRY

CORK

Waterford

Wexford

WATERFORD

St. George's Channel

CORK

100 Miles

(II)

Within the field of Irish history, one of the long-running debates concerns the question of how important was the Famine of 1845-49 in determining the social history of the country? Up to the mid-1950s, the Famine was used to explain almost everything that occurred in nineteenth and twentieth century Irish social history. Then scepticism arose, and it was argued that despite the Famine's horrific short term effects, it really changed nothing: the social re-ordering that occurred in the second half of the nineteenth century actually was already in progress before the Famine, and these changes would have continued, even if there had not been a Famine. Today the pendulum has swung back towards seeing the Famine as a major causal event, although not *the* cause.[4]

If we take the modern era in Irish history as dating from 1690 (the final defeat of Gaelic-Catholic Ireland), and lasting to the present day, the Famine is the most suitable fulcrum upon which to organize a discussion of Irish social history. That is not to say that the Famine razed everything, but that our thinking is cleared if we use the Famine as our primary agreed reference point. It is the one point of reference that the emigrants of the last century would share with those of us who are studying the Irish diaspora from our own perspective at the end of the twentieth century.[5]

What the Great Famine was in human terms is easily said, if impossible fully to comprehend. It was first, death: the most recent modern estimate set one million deaths as a minimum figure, and one-and-a-half million as a possible maximum. And second, the Famine was dispersal: roughly one million Irish persons migrated overseas in the Famine years and an additional, unknown, number to Great Britain.[6]

Equally, in order that we use the Famine properly as a reference point, we should understand what it was not. The Famine was not inevitable. This conclusion has been convincingly argued by Cormac Ó Gráda, a leading economic historian of Ireland. His point is that although there were previous smaller famines in (1740-41 and in 1822 in particular) as well as other years of food scarcity, the Great Famine was totally beyond prediction. The fungus that caused the Great Famine, *Phythopthora infestans*, was *infestans*, was completely new to Ireland and no one could have foreseen its sudden appearance. At the time this fatal fungus hit, potatoes were the main food of more than half of the Irish population. Thus, as Ó Gráda says, "in the end, the Irish were desperately unlucky."[7]

Neither was the Great Famine unique, horrific though it was. An estimated nine to thirteen million persons died in the great Chinese Famine of 1877-78, and ten million died in the Bengal famine of 1940-43. [8]

The fact that massive famines have occurred in the twentieth century (and, indeed, smaller ones are raging through parts of Africa in the 1990s), indicates that they are phenomena that will not go away through their being approached with a simple mixture of good intentions and social engineering. Famines are not the occasion for blame-casting. In the Irish case, blame-casting has taken two forms. One of these is "Malthusian." It is argued that the Irish Famine was caused by "over-population." A less polite way of summarizing this view is to suggest that the Irish starved because they did not have the good sense to limit the size of their families — in other words, that they procreated themselves to death.

An equally ahistorical form of blame-casting is the view that the Famine was in some way part of a British conspiracy to wipe out the Irish nation. In a scholarly *tour de force*, Patrick O'Farrell has demonstrated how in the 1860s the tragedy of the Great Famine was turned into an anti-British political myth.[9] The fountainhead of the myth is the artistic and fictional masterpiece of John Mitchel, *The Last Conquest of Ireland (Perhaps)*. The 1860 volume has essentially the same character structure as does nineteenth-century melodrama, with virtuous Irish peasants on one side and hard-hearted British officials on the other. The power of Mitchel's masterpiece has flavoured popular writing about the Famine right to the present day.[10] Never mind that the Famine relief, inadequate though it was, more efficiently provided in Ireland in the last century than at present the United Nations is able to provide in Eritrea and the Sudan. And never mind that Mitchel's capacity for moral self-delusion always had been remarkable: he had supported the southern side on the American slave question. Although serious historical writing now eschews such blame-casting, the myth is still alive in popular culture, especially among the diasporate. This trivializes as mere conspiracy a truly great tragedy.

And, finally, the Famine was not the cause of the Irish diaspora. Heavy emigration from Ireland began well before the Famine. Numbers in the 1830s were particularly high. In the case of some nations (the USA, Australia and Canada) the basis of the Irish as an ethnic group was set down well before the Famine. What the Famine did was confirm and accelerate the Irish predisposition to leave the homeland.

(III)

Given that the Famine is our primary chronological reference point, we can now acquire four basic and fundamental demographic points of reference. These are the total population curve, the geographic distribution of the population within Ireland, the basic gender ratio, and the age structure of the entire population.

The first population census of Ireland was conducted in 1821 and it underestimated the population; that for 1831 overestimated. The figures are much better, however, than those available before 1821. For that earlier era, one must rely on Kenneth Connell's estimates of total population based on his calculations from the hearth tax returns. The population of Ireland from 1687 to 1971 is presented in Table 1. The sharp break at the Famine is obvious. At the time of the Famine, the population was roughly 8.5 million persons. Thereafter, alone among European countries Ireland experienced a century-and-a-quarter of population decline. When at mid-twentieth century it was learned that the population had once again begun to increase, the news was greeted as a sign of renewed national confidence.

In consonance with the usual pattern for European societies, there were slightly more women than men in Ireland, although not so large a difference as to create a serious case of what, in the nineteenth century, was called "surplus women."

TABLE 1

**Irish Population
1687-1971**

Year	Population

Basis, 1687-1791: K.H. Connell's estimates

Year	Population
1687	2,167,000
1718	2,894,000
1732	3,018,000
1772	3,584,000
1781	4,048,000
1791	4,753,000

Basis, 1821-1911: United Kingdom census authorities

Year	Population
1821	6,801,827
1831	7,767,401
1841	8,175,124
1851	6,552,385
1861	5,798,967
1871	5,412,377
1881	5,174,836
1891	4,704,750
1901	4,458,775
1911	4,390,219

Basis, 1926-71: United Kingdom census authorities (for Northern Ireland data) and authorities of what is now the Republic of Ireland (southern Ireland data):

Year	Southern Ireland	Northern Ireland	All-Ireland
1926	2,971,992	1,256,561	4,228,553
1936-37	2,968,420	1,279,745	4,248,165
1951	2,960,593	1,370,921	4,331,514
1961	2,818,341	1,425,042	4,243,383
1966	2,884,002	1,484,775	4,368,777
1971	2,978,248	1,536,065	4,514,313

Source: W.E. Vaughan and A.J. Fitzpatrick (eds.) *Irish Historical Statistics, Population, 1821-1971* (Dublin: Royal Irish Academy, 1973), pp. 2-4.

TABLE 2

**Number of Males and Females in the Irish Population
1821-1971**

Year	Males	Females
1821	3,341,926	3,459,901
1831	3,794,880	3,972,521
1841	4,019,576	4,155,548
1851	3,190,630	3,361,755
1861	2,837,370	2,961,597
1871	2,639,753	2,772,624
1881	2,533,277	2,641,559
1891	2,318,953	2,385,797
1901	2,200,040	2,258,735
1911	2,192,048	2,198,171
1926	2,144,977	2,113,576
1936-37	2,143,608	2,104,557
1951	2,174,416	2,157,098
1961	2,110,773	2,132,610
1966	2,172,916	2,195,861
1971	2,250,436	2,263,877

Source: Vaughan and A.J. Fitzpatrick (eds.) p.3.

The Irish age structure was the oldest in the British Isles. That is: Ireland in the post-Famine era. Ireland had proportionately fewer young people and more older ones than did Scotland, England and Wales. The Irish situation is shown in Table 3.

TABLE 3

Percentage of Irish Population under Specific Ages
1861-1946

Ireland (32 counties)
(Percentage)

Male	1861	1871	1881	1891	1901	1911
10	23.4	24.7	24.0	21.5	20.6	20.2
20	45.8	46.7	47.2	45.5	41.9	39.9
30	63.4	61.5	62.6	61.7	59.8	55.9
40	73.4	72.5	72.8	72.1	71.7	69.5
50	82.9	81.2	82.3	81.4	81.1	80.0
60	91.1	89.4	89.6	89.7	89.1	87.7
All Ages	100.0	100.0	100.0	100.0	100.0	100.0

Female						
10	21.7	22.9	22.4	20.2	19.5	19.6
20	43.2	43.8	44.6	43.0	40.0	38.6
30	61.0	59.9	60.5	59.3	58.4	54.8
40	71.5	71.4	71.7	70.4	70.3	68.2
50	81.9	80.6	81.7	80.7	80.3	78.3
60	90.3	89.1	89.3	89.3	89.0	86.0
All Ages	100.0	100.0	100.0	100.0	100.0	100.0

	Southern Ireland				Northern Ireland			
Male	1926	1936	1946	Male	1926	1937	1946	1960
10	19.3	17.9	19.1	10	20.4	18.5	19.9	20.8
20	39.0	36.5	36.6	20	40.1	37.4	37.9	37.8
30	54.3	52.8	51.4	30	56.3	53.4	54.3	55.1
40	66.3	65.3	64.9	40	68.4	67.1	67.9	68.5
50	77.8	76.1	76.4	50	79.3	78.0	78.5	79.1
60	87.9	86.3	85.6	60	89.0	87.2	87.2	87.6
All	100.0	100.0	100.0	All	100.0	100.0	100.0	100.0

Female				Female				
10	19.2	18.3	18.8	10	18.6	16.9	18.1	19.1
20	38.7	36.9	36.1	20	37.0	34.6	34.5	34.8
30	54.0	52.3	51.0	30	54.0	50.9	51.2	51.2
40	66.2	65.1	64.4	40	67.1	65.2	65.3	65.2
50	77.5	75.8	75.8	50	78.5	76.7	77.0	77.1
60	86.7	85.6	85.1	60	87.9	86.3	86.2	86.4
All	100.0	100.0	100.0	All	100.0	100.0	100.0	100.0

Source: N.H. Carrier and J.R. Jeffery, *External Migration: A Study of the Available Statistics, 1815-1950* (London, HMSO, 1953), p. 109.

Ireland being a profoundly regionalized country, one should recognize the geographic shifts in the population over time. (See Table 4)

TABLE 4

Irish Population by Province
1871-1971

Year	Leinster	Munster	Ulster	Connacht
1821	1,757,492	1,935,612	1,998,494	1,110,229
1831	1,909,713	2,227,152	2,286,622	1,343,914
1841	1,973,731	2,396,161	2,386,373	1,418,859
1851	1,672,738	1,857,736	2,011,880	1,010,031
1861	1,457,635	1,513,558	1,914,236	913,135
1871	1,339,451	1,393,485	1,833,228	846,213
1881	1,278,989	1,331,115	1,743,075	821,657
1891	1,187,760	1,172,402	1,619,814	724,774
1901	1,152,829	1,076,188	1,582,826	646,932
1911	1,162,044	1,035,495	1,581,696	610,984
1926	1,149,092	969,902	1,556,652	552,907
1936-37	1,220,411	942,272	1,560,014	525,468
1951	1,336,576	898,870	1,624,173	471,895
1961	1,332,149	849,203	1,642,566	419,465
1966	1,414,415	859,334	1,693,078	401,950
1971	1,498,140	882,002	1,743,269	390,902

Source: Derived from Vaughan and A.J. Fitzpatrick (eds.) pp. 15-16, 24. For purposes of continuity, I have defined "Ulster" after 1920 as the historical nine provinces of Ulster, not the area under the government of Northern Ireland.

Behind these four set of dispassionate numbers lies a virtual social revolution. One part of this revolution was what David Fitzpatrick has termed a "class collapse." By this he refers to the fact that in the half-century after the Famine male farm workers, previously the largest group employed in the society, declined sharply in number. Between 1841 and 1911, the number of male farm workers fell by two-thirds. This means that the rural working class was severely compressed, and in a predominantly agricultural nation that was tantamount to a class collapse.[11]

One could explain this class collapse by suggesting that it was part of a larger development, the switch in Irish agriculture from tillage to pasturage, but that is an unsatisfyingly technical explanation.

Instead, it is more accurate to see the class collapse among the rural proletariat as merely a small part of a massive set of changes that had begun before the Famine, but which the Famine confirmed, accelerated, and deepened. These involved nothing less than a redefinition of the Irish family. At the risk of burlesquing a complex debate, the dominant view of the pre-Famine situation is as follows: that (1) in common with the dominant pattern in western Europe, the family was nuclear, not extended. Although on occasion two generations shared the same house (and masters and servants did so also), the building blocks of the Irish family were the father, mother, and unmarried children; (2) marriage occurred most frequently in the mid-twenties. That is, the common European pattern of relatively late marriage prevailed; (3) because most small farmers were willing to subdivide their land among their children, the economic constraints against marriage, while significant, were not crippling; (4) there was, in comparison to other European countries, relatively little in the way of "illicit love" by which is meant sexual activity resulting in either illegitimacy or prenuptial pregnancy; and (5) within marriage there was a high fertility rate.[12]

By the time of the Great Famine, a demographic shift was in train.

The post-Famine family structure may be summarized as follows: (1) the Irish family remained nuclear and, indeed, became more so, for "stem family" ideology became overwhelmingly dominant. Under the stem family system, only one child per generation inherited the family's main economic interest, be it farm or small town shop. Consolidation, not division of farms, became the rule;[13] (2) the age of marriage rose, so that in the Irish Free State by the year 1926 (the first date for which data are available) it was thirty-five years of age for men, far above the European average;[14] (3) the Irish became the most celibate people in the western world. "Celibacy" in this case refers not to the renunciation of sexuality in the theological sense, but is a demographer's term for spinsterhood and bachelorhood;[15] (4) by European standards there was very little illicit love, and, if anything, less than in pre-Famine times;[16] (5) as a result of the restrictions on marriage and on non-marital love, Ireland became the most sexually repressed society in the modern world and some scholars tie this to Ireland's extremely high rate of mental illness, particularly schizophrenia;[17] (6) within marriage the fertility rate was amazingly high;[18] (7) the combination of the stem family system (which precluded subdivision of small farms), the absence of an industrial sector outside of Ulster, and the high rate of marital fertility meant that a very high rate of emigration was induced; (8) uniquely in Europe, Ireland underwent an absolute decline in population from the mid-nineteenth century until the mid-twentieth.

Thus, Ireland's family history in the nineteenth century is so striking that it is easy to think of it as totally unique. Yet one should not be so taken by the character of Ireland's post-Famine population decline and by the extreme form of frequent celibacy and late marriage as to forget that the Irish simply were exhibiting a national version of an international pattern, the "European marriage pattern." In common with the rest of western Europe — and in contrast to most of the rest of the world — Ireland was adopting a social template that consisted in a late average age of marriage and the acceptance of a fairly large number of persons in each generation as unmarried.[19]

The shift from the pre-Famine to the post-Famine family pattern can be seen as part of a general western phenomenon that is usually denominated as "the demographic transition." This is a set of changes in family life, the result of which was the replacement of a society characterized by high birth rates and high death rates, by one

26

with low birth rates and low death rates. The Irish reached the same demographic result as did most western nations — although, admittedly, they took an unusual route in getting there. (While it is necessary to generalize about Ireland's demographic family pattern, it is well to remind oneself continually that the overall pattern subsumes many striking sectorial variations — that is, variations of class, geography, and local culture.)

That the Irish were among the first (after the French) to successfully control their birth rate,[20] obviously had something to do with emigration, but one should not jump to hasty conclusions about what that relationship may have been. For example, the practice of limiting marriage opportunities well may have caused some individuals to migrate to other lands so as to be able to have a normal family life. On the other hand, the same limitations preserved Ireland's limited agricultural resources against population pressure and therefore permitted the production of enough of an agricultural surplus so that even though they had not inherited land, spinsters and bachelors could remain in Ireland, albeit at a modest level.

(IV)

One central aspect of the Irish social structure must be recognized — the more so because it usually is cut out of discussions of the Irish diaspora: this is the fact that sectarian religion was the hub around which the most important of Irish cultural beliefs and social practices revolved. Irish people lined up on either side of a great divide: they were either Catholic or Protestant. And, within Protestantism, there were denominational differences, some of which had general cultural and social implications. Crucially, neither Irish Catholics nor Irish Protestants can be discussed adequately without reference to the other. The two major religious groups were part of a dialectical system. It was the existence of the Irish Protestants that helped to make the Irish Catholics so distinct a group within the Roman Catholic world; and it was the Irish Catholics who helped to form the mentalities of the Irish Anglicans and Irish Presbyterians, two very unusual groups within the worldwide Protestant communion. It was virtually impossible for any individual to have experienced the Irish religious system and not to have been profoundly influenced by it. Even persons who were avowedly unbelievers (a very small group until recently), nevertheless defined their unbelief as being the rejection of the Irish religious-cultural system.

The first Irish religious census was conducted in 1834, the second in 1861. Thereafter information was collected at intervals, most often ten years apart. The religious breakdown of the major denominations is given in Table 5. (In that table only the three major denominations are included, and so the totals are somewhat less than the total population at any given census).

These and related information dictate four important inferences. The first of these is the confirmation of the obvious point, stated earlier, that the Protestants cannot be ignored. Not to include them in any study of the Irish diaspora would be the statistical equivalent of dropping both the African-Americans and the Hispanic-Americans from a study of ethnicity in the USA. Aside from the rebarbative prejudice such an action would imply, the numbers are in any case too big to avoid. Secondly, notice that an equation which runs through much of the New World conventional wisdom about the Irish diaspora is wrong: the identification of "Irish Protestant" with "Irish Presbyterian." The Anglicans (that is, adherents of the Church of Ireland), not the Presbyterians, were the largest Protestant denomination. Thirdly, the Anglicans were dispersed more widely than were the Presbyterians, who were overwhelmingly in the north. Therefore, one cannot equate "Protestants" with residence in Ulster. In particular, the assumption in much American immigration history that Irish Protestants were overwhelmingly of "sturdy Ulster stock" (or some variant of the phrase) is mistaken.

A fourth point relates to religious distributions within Ulster. Not only can one not equate Irish Protestants with Ulster Presbyterians, one cannot even identify Ulster residents (or, within the context of the Irish diaspora, Ulster emigrants) with Irish Presbyterians. What was the dominant religious denomination in Ulster? Roman Catholicism and by a large margin. And, significantly, the Anglicans (identified, roughly, with "Anglo-Irish" origin), were not far behind the

TABLE 5

Irish Religious Composition
1834-1971

(A) In the Formerly-United Ireland

Year	Number of Catholics	% of Pop.	Number of Anglicans	% of Pop.	Number of Presbyterians	% of Pop.
1834	6,427,712	80.9	852,064	10.7	642,356	8.1
1861	4,505,265	77.7	693,357	12.0	523,291	9.0
1871	4,150,867	76.7	667,998	12.3	497,648	9.2
1881	3,960,891	76.5	639,574	12.4	470,734	9.1
1891	3,547,307	75.4	600,103	12.8	444,974	9.5
1901	3,308,661	74.2	581,089	13.0	443,276	9.9
1911	3,242,670	73.9	576,611	13.1	440,525	10.0

(B) In Post-Partition Ireland

Year	Number of Catholics	% of Pop.	Number of Anglicans	% of Pop.	Number of Presbyterians	% of Pop.
1926	3,171,697	75.0	502,939	11.9	425,803	10.1
1936-37	3,202,210	75.4	490,504	11.5	418,998	9.9
1946(SI) and 1951(NI)	3,257,493	75.3	478,074	11.1	434,085	10.0
1961	3,171,020	74.7	448,816	10.6	432,066	10.2
1971	3,273,517	72.5	432,059	9.6	421,771	9.3

Sources: Derived from D.H. Akenson, *Being Had: Historians, Evidence, and the Irish in North America* (Toronto: P.D. Meany Co., 1985), pp. 62-63; Vaughan and A.J. Fitzpatrick (eds.), pp. 49-50.

Presbyterians. Given in Table 6 are the major religious percentages for Ulster, from the year 1861, the first for which they are available, until 1971. (The post-1920 figures are for the historical province of Ulster, not for the six counties of Northern Ireland). And, further, the Anglicans were not much behind the Presbyterians in numbers. What this means is that when one sees the number of Ulster emigrants tallied, one must not automatically assume that they were Protestant, or even in those cases where they certainly were Protestant, that they were Presbyterian (the Ulster-Scots or the "Scotch-Irish" of American history). Almost equally often, they may have been Anglo-Irish.

TABLE 6

Ulster Religious Percentages
1861-1971

Year	Catholic	Church of Ireland (Anglican)	Presbyterian
1861	50.5	20.4	26.3
1871	48.9	21.5	26.1
1881	47.8	21.8	25.9
1891	46.0	22.4	26.3
1901	44.2	22.8	26.9
1911	43.7	23.2	26.6
1926	42.8	23.7	26.6
1936-37	42.5	23.8	26.2
1961	41.8	21.9	25.9
1971	38.1	20.2	24.1

Note: "Other denominations" and "no religion" varied considerably year by year, and in 1971 refusals to answer the query were frequent.

Source: Compiled from Vaughan and A.J. Fitzpatrick (eds.), pp. 51-73.

Figure 1

Occupations Grouped by Percentage of Protestants and Catholics
Employed, 1861

% Protestant		% Catholic
100		0
	needle makers, linen thread makers, damask designers, artisans in pearl	
90		10
	nobles, barons, knights, baronets, cotton weavers, army surgeons, flax yarn makers	
80		20
	land agents, teachers of Irish, bankers, insurance agents, photographers, army officers, druggists, factory overseers, surgeons, authors, barristers	
70		30
	house agents, judges, physicians, linen and damask weavers, attorneys and solicitors, engravers, saddlers, merchants	
60		40
	watch makers, landed proprietors, portrait painters, artists, gunsmiths, weavers, poor-law clerks, coast guards, mill workers, prison officers, apothecaries	
50		50
	embroiderers, excise officers, rent collectors, postmasters, engineers, hotel keepers, clerks, drapers, flax dressers, grocers, parish clerks, factory workers	
40		60
	milliners, shirt makers, pawnbrokers, leather dealers, sculptors, pensioners, painters, glassers and decorators, constabulary and metropolitan police, saddlers and harness makers, process servers	
30		70
	gate keepers, letter carriers, stewards, dressmakers, shopkeepers, skilled weavers, coat makers, carpenters, farmers, loaders, housekeepers	
23		77
	brick layers, rope and twine makers, carters, seamstresses	
20		80
	flax spinners, tanners, bootbinders, musicians, publicans, bakers, blacksmiths, tailors, knitters, stablemen, domestic servants, prostitutes, waiters, butchers, thatchers, basketmakers, slaters, charwomen, farm laborers, fishermen	
10		90
	tobacconists, peddlers, cattle dealers, wool weavers, masons, chimney sweeps, old clothes dealers, carriage brokers, brogue makers	
0		100

Source: Adapted from A. Hume, *Results of the Irish Census of 1861* (London: Rivingtons, 1864), 51.

Figure 2

Religion and Occupation, Adult Males, 1861

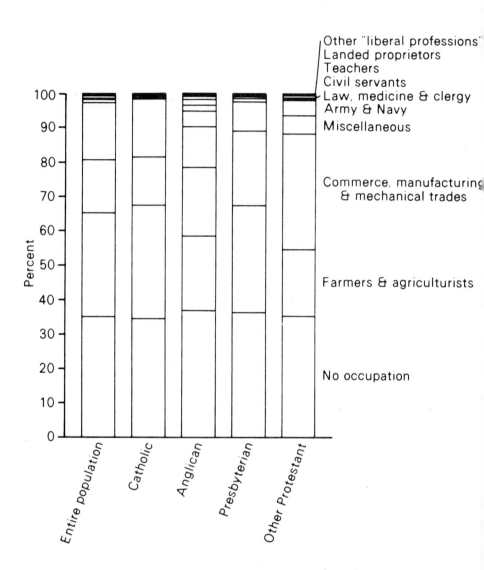

Source: D.H. Akenson, *Small Differences. Irish Catholics and Irish Protestants, 1815-1922. An International Perspective.* (Kingston and Montreal: McGill-Queen's University Press, 1988), pp. 21, 159.

The most obvious fact in modern Irish religious history is also the hardest to interpret: that the Catholics were economically disadvantaged. Figures 1 and 2 make clear that there were many poor Protestants and also a sizeable Catholic middle class. It is easy to forget that in the countryside there were many poor Protestant tenant farmers who were scarcely (if at all) better off than their Catholic counterparts.

Nevertheless, there was clearly a gradient, and when nineteenth-century Irish society is considered as a whole, there is no doubt that in general the Protestants were better off. This relatively privileged position of the Protestants has continued throughout the twentieth century, albeit on a greatly diminished basis. That the Protestants' position in Northern Ireland after the Partition Act of 1920 was augmented by a discriminatory governmental structure, which lasted into the 1970s, is too well known to require comment. What does bear note is the residual privilege of the Protestants in the Republic of Ireland. For instance, as late as 1971, the average size of Protestant farms was noticeably larger than that of Catholic farms.[21]

Farm Size	1926		1971	
Acres	Catholic	Anglican	Catholic	Anglican
1-14	27.5	11.1	4.2	11.6
15-29	29.0	20.7	11.8	22.8
30-49	19.5	19.6	20.5	26.8
50-99	15.1	22.2	30.5	26.1
100-199	5.8	13.9	21.6	9.9
200+	1.7	10.1	10.6	2.2
Not stated	1.4	2.4	0.8	0.6
Total	100	100	100	100

Similarly, Protestants in the Irish Republic remained over-represented in professional occupations and in the upper levels of commerce.[22]

How does one explain the advantaged position of the Protestants and the disadvantaged position of the Catholics?

— again, always taking into account that many individuals were exceptions to the general pattern. In my opinion the answer is so simple as not to require much elaboration. In the eighteenth century, the Irish Catholics experienced the impact of the "penal code," which for much of the century barred them from most professions and civic offices and which, by 1775, had reduced the proportion of Irish land owned by Catholics to about 5 percent of the national total. Although the penal code was mostly removed by the start of the nineteenth century, its effects lingered and had not yet disappeared by the time Ireland was partitioned in 1920. In the new jurisdiction of Northern Ireland, systematic discrimination was re-introduced, although on a much less severe basis than had existed in the eighteenth century. In the south, Catholic disadvantages after Partition were quickly reduced, for the new government became in practice (if not in theory) strongly pro-Catholic. However, since the new Irish Free State preserved private property rights, Protestant advantages, though reduced, continued.

The reader should understand that there is an alternative school of thought on Catholic disadvantages. Simply put, this school holds that Catholicism in general, and Irish Catholicism in particular, was a cultural-social system that handicapped the Irish Catholics as they encountered the modernizing world. In other words, Catholicism was a causal agent in Irish economic "backwardness." Conversely, it is held that Protestantism in general, and Irish Protestantism in particular, was much more adapted to economic initiative and to entrepreneurship, characteristics that were an advantage in the nineteenth and twentieth centuries especially. I have argued strongly against this school of thought (in a book entitled *Small Differences*)[23] but in fairness I must emphasize that the opposing view has a long and distinguished academic history. Its genealogy goes back to Max Weber's *The Protestant Ethic and the Spirit of Capitalism* (1904). The same sort of thinking was the backbone of R.H. Tawney's massively influential *Religion and the Rise of Capitalism* (1926) and was central to David McClelland's *The Achieving of Society* (1961). In Irish studies it has had its most recent reincarnation in Kerby Miller's *Emigrants and Exile. Ireland and the Irish Exodus to North America* (1985).

Obviously, it makes a great deal of difference as to how one understands Irish migrants and their descendants if one starts with the assumption that Irish Catholicism was inherently a handicap for the migrants and that, by implication, Irish Protestantism was inherently a relative advantage. By "inherent" one means that it was something so tightly wrapped into Irish culture that Irish emigrants took the disadvantage or advantage with them as part of their cultural baggage.

So dangerous is it to impute inherent backwardness (whatever its cause may be thought to be) to any cultural, ethnic, religious, or racial group, that one should resist such a theory unless there is very strong evidence confirming the claim. In my view, there is no systematic evidence for the theory of Catholic backwardness as it involves the Irish. (One, of course, can find anecdotal evidence to support almost any claim in human history; it is systematic evidence that is important here). Moreover, I believe that there is strong systematic evidence which one can garner from throughout the Irish diaspora that disproves through positive evidence the contention that Irish Catholicism was a cultural system that implied technological, economic, and social backwardness. Emphatically, this is not to deny that in many cases there was strong discrimination against the Irish in general and the Catholic migrants in particular, the worst being in the United States. However, to see Irish Catholicism as the cause of this situation is to blame the victim for the crime. Thus, the reader should understand that the remainder of this primer is based on the assumption (one that is provable, I believe, but in any case is non-racist), that the Irish Catholic emigrants from Ireland did not leave the homeland with any inherent cultural disadvantages.

(V)

"The difference between lakes and rivers," a primary pupil wrote, "is that rivers are always in a hurry to get somewhere else." Emigrants, like rivers, are both substantively similar to their origin and in many ways different. Emigrants are in many ways special. Sometimes because they are especially good (witness the brilliant Jewish scientists who migrated to the USA just before World War

II), and sometimes because they are especially bad (as some of the criminals sent into exile for felonies) but, undeniably, as a group emigrants are selected. They are not merely a replica of the larger population from which they are drawn.

There have been various attempts at developing models of migration in order to explain why some sorts of people migrate and others do not. The most venerable goes back to the 1880s when E.G. Ravenstein worked out a set of "laws" of migration. In folk culture, explanations abound. Probably, most members of the Irish diasporate would probably agree that the able and the ambitious were the ones who emigrated, while those who were left behind believe it was the restless and undisciplined who left. We do not know enough about migration out of Ireland as yet to be able to suggest any but the most tentative hypotheses, and certainly no "laws."

Fundamentally, there are only two sorts of migrations, those that are forced and those that are volitional. Forced migrations are those such as occurred when Josef Stalin relocated at bayonet point several of the ethnic groups within the Soviet Union, such as have happened during wartime in the last two decades in South East Asia and in Sub-Saharan Africa, or as when human beings have been captured and sold into slavery. Volitional migration occurs when individuals choose to migrate. Their choice never is totally free, for they are always reacting to the constraints that surround their lives. But they have the choice of staying or leaving. In Irish history there has been very little forced emigration. The chief exceptions in our time period were the common criminals and political nationalists who were sent to Australia.

Curiously, there long has been an interest in avoiding this fact. Karl Marx's essay "Forced Migration" (1853) is the classic statement of the position that "compulsory emigration" took place from Ireland because of landlordism and improved farming techniques. "It is not the want of productive power which creates a surplus population; it is the increase of productive power which demands a diminution of population, and drives away the surplus by famine or emigration."[24] While Irish historians have eschewed Marx's vocabulary, many of them have adopted the implications of his analysis — that the Irish emigrants were passive flotsam on the fast-running tide of modern history.

This viewpoint is fundamentally misguided in that it robs the migrants of one of their chief historical characteristics: their dignity as intelligent, self-aware responsible persons, each of whom made a conscious decision to leave Ireland (excepting, of course, young children brought out by their parents). The emigrants made heroic decisions. This does not mean that I am letting the landlords or the British government off easy, but to see those two traditional bogeymen as the active causal agents in the migration-decision is to make the historical mistake of disempowering emigrants. The emigrants were not the truly poor, the near-starving, for such persons did not have the resources to leave Ireland. Those who emigrated, however poor they may appear to our modern eyes, were, by definition, in command of surplus economic resources — enough in any case to allow them to reach a seaport and to pay passage away from Ireland. These resources could have been used to maintain the emigrants in Ireland, but they *chose* to go. Even though this seems a simple decision to us, for an individual caught in a frightful economic system, to chart out for him or herself a series of alternative futures and then to decide upon one and to act upon the choice is something that we should not treat condescendingly, by claiming that such individuals were passive and non-responsible.

Of course this demand, that we grant integrity and authenticity to the decisions of millions of Irish emigrants, is based on an assumption: namely, that individual human beings seek their own best interests and that they prefer happiness to unhappiness and better conditions to worse conditions. It also assumes that they are intelligent enough to collect information, to weigh it, and to decide for themselves about alternative futures. This is a position that can only be asserted, not proved, but it certainly makes more sense of the world than to assume either of the main alternatives: that human beings prefer unhappiness to happiness, or that they have no idea of their own self-interest and that their actions are determined by circumstances of which they can have no conscious appreciation.

The emigrants chose to leave Ireland and in each case that was a matter of behaviour. That behaviour usually left a mark or two upon the historical record. What the emigrants did not leave (except in the rarest and least-typical of instances) was a record of what considerations internal to their own hearts eventually produced this behaviour. Usually, whether someone decided to leave Ireland because his family had been evicted from a small holding and there was nothing suitable available nearby, or left because he had just had a fight with a tyrannical old father, or because he had received a letter from a cousin in the USA telling how wonderful life there was, the result was the same: one person was added to the tally of those who had decided to leave Ireland. Given that we can only know the behaviour — the emigrant walking up the gangway and leaving Ireland — we should not mystify the emigration process. In particular, we should avoid the temptation to provide psychological explanations of emigration, ones that claim to peer into the hearts of several million Irish men and women and purport to tell why they did what they did. Even the good-old-fashioned heuristic technique of thinking of emigration as being caused by a mixture of "push" and "pull" factors is an arrogance, given the paucity of information we have on the Irish emigrants. To determine to what degree any set of persons was influenced by push or pull is patently impossible. All that we have is behaviour, the external embodiment of an internal chemistry that is forever unknowable.

Therefore, instead of trying to guess the psychological, emotional, and intellectual processes that preceded all of the millions of individual decisions to leave, we should concentrate on understanding the context within which the behaviour that was emigration occurred.[25]

An obvious contextual matter is that the Irish diaspora, though singular in Europe in its relative dimensions, was not a unique process. Anyone who remembers his or her grade 10 history will recall the process called "the expansion of Europe," that often awe-inspiring, often disquieting process, whereby western European civilization became dominant over most of the globe. More directly, one scarcely should forget that what might be termed the "British Isles diaspora" involved many more Scots and English and Welsh in a world-encircling outflow, than it did Irish. Between 1815 and 1914, an estimated twenty-plus million persons sailed from the British Isles to destinations beyond Europe, thirteen million of these to America, roughly four million to Canada and approximately four and a half million to Australia and New Zealand.[26] The Irish did not go in significant numbers anywhere that the British had not gone first. From the eighteenth century onward, the Irish mingled with the British flow. Frequently they were on the same ships. They passed through the same foreign ports and went on to settlements in the same New Worlds. It is hardly an accident that the overwhelming bulk of the Irish diaspora went to points in the English-speaking world.[27]

Within that context, the Irish migrants had a considerable set of advantages as compared to migrants from other countries (and this despite their frequently being worse off than other migrants in financial terms). The Irish migrants' advantages stemmed from the fact that well before their move to other lands, most individuals had been "anglicized." This was the process in which most of the Irish population came to adopt the language, commercial practices, and many of the cultural values of the dominant culture of the English mainland. The process is not one that enthusiasts for the older Irish culture can be very happy about; however, one must accept that it was an historical reality. Indeed, anglicization, and the conquest of Australia, New Zealand, Canada and America was by a culture that was primarily Anglo-Celtic in nature. Oliver MacDonagh has aptly summarized the process in Ireland: "in this context, 'anglisation' does not mean the crude and total displacement of one culture by another, but rather the steady modification and attenuation of what was distinctly Gaelic, with language perhaps the leading sufferer."[28]

MacDonagh's emphasis upon the centrality of language is well taken. Long before the Famine, most Irish people were able to speak English. In 1851 (the first year for which figures are available), only 4.9 percent of the Irish population could not speak English, and only 23.3 percent could speak "Irish" (the accepted term for the version of Gaelic spoken in Ireland).[29] Precisely when English replaced Irish as the primary language of Ireland is something scholars argue about. A reasonable estimate is that by roughly the year 1800, English was ascendant. Among young people, knowledge of English was more common than among their elders and (as will be established in a moment) it was the younger people who most often chose to emigrate. Despite the odd bit of legend about Gaelic-speaking emigrants who knew no English, such persons were rare. A knowledge of English was one of the most important assets that Irish emigrants took with them. Thus, while one can grant that the decline and near-extinction of the indigenous Gaelic tongue of Ireland was a tragedy, there was a trade-off: Irish emigrants started off with a great advantage over continental European migrants to the new English-speaking homelands. This held true both before and after the Famine.

Further, as compared to the bulk of nineteenth-and early-twentieth century emigrants from various European countries, the Irish were well educated: not in the sense of higher education, but in terms of functional literacy being relatively widespread. This may at first seem surprising, because our view has been tinctured by the anti-Irish prejudice of many nineteenth and early twentieth-century observers. In fact, however, as Joel Mokyr has pointed out, the one area in which pre-Famine Irish society invested heavily was in "social overhead capital," particularly in schools. A "national system of education" was begun in 1831, but even before that, investment in education was substantial by European standards. Mokyr suggests that even if one assesses Irish investment in education conservatively, the proportion of children receiving basic education on the eve of the Famine was well ahead of that in comparable countries, such as Italy and Spain, and on a level closer to that of France.[30] The illiteracy rate in Ireland in 1851 was 47 percent. That is, most persons could either read or read and write a bit. In 1841, the illiteracy figure had been 53 percent.[31] These figures covered the entire population aged five years of age and above. Older people in the population were less likely to have had the advantage of primary education, for the national school system still was growing in the 1840s from its very modest beginnings in the previous decade. Because emigrants tended to be less well off than the general population, the migrants were somewhat less apt to be literate than the general population. Still, it is clear that from the 1870s onward most Irish emigrants indeed were literate and in English.[32] Throughout Irish society the rate of illiteracy dropped sharply during the second half of the nineteenth century and perforce the proportion of illiterate emigrants dropped. A good indication of the relative advantage Irish migrants had over other Europeans is found in data collected for the U.S. senate in 1911. Surveying all immigrants in the U.S. fourteen years of age and older for the period 1899-1910, the investigators found that 26.7 percent were able neither to read nor write. The illiteracy rate ranged from 0.4 percent for the Scandinavian-born to 68.2 percent for the Portuguese-born. Significantly, the illiteracy rate of Irish-born immigrants was only 2.6 percent. The only groups more apt to be literate than the Irish-born were the other groups from the British Isles, the Finns, the Scandinavians, the Bohemians and the Moravians.[33]

That the Irish diaspora was mostly a movement of anglicized Irish persons who could speak and read English before they migrated to various corners of the English-speaking world was, in fact, what David Fitzpatrick has called "preliminary acculturation."[34] So too was the Irish emigrants' awareness of how political games were contested in a democratizing world. It is easy to forget that in the 1820s Ireland had the first mass-based extra-parliamentary political movement in the English-speaking world, in the form of the Catholic Emancipation movement led by Daniel O'Connell. One should not romanticize the political involvement of the Irish population during the nineteenth and early twentieth centuries, but if one compares the political experience of the generality of Irish people to that of, say, the generality from southern Europe, the Irish advantages become apparent: they learned in their homeland, before emigrating, the basic rules of democratizing politics, what the vocabulary of political argument was in the English-speaking world, and how to mess up political systems when it was to their advantage to do so.

(VI)

Given that the emigrants were a selected population, it is useful to describe the character of the emigration flow in terms of the same social variables that we employed earlier to describe the general Irish population: gender, age, geographic distribution, occupation, and religion. In using the available data on emigrants (which is much more limited than one would wish), we should look at the information both in absolute and in relative terms. We must avoid making either of two errors that are very common when historians are making comparisons, namely (1) the acceptance of a "false converse" and (2) falling into "false relativism." An example of the first of these would be to infer that, since most Presbyterians lived in Ulster, most persons who lived in Ulster were Presbyterian. That is a conclusion which I already have demonstrated is false; yet this particular false converse actually has been accepted by many historians of the Irish diaspora. The point here is not the specific factual issue, but the necessity of avoiding a fallacious mode of thinking, a method of making errors.

An example of the second mode of fallacious thinking, false relativism, is as follows: (a) people in the province of Connacht in the 1870s had a higher propensity to emigrate than did persons in the province of Leinster, so (b) therefore, more people emigrated from Connacht than from Leinster. This does not follow, for it may be either true or untrue: the accuracy of the conclusion can be determined only if the actual absolute population of each place is known, as well as the propensity to emigrate of each population. As comparisons become more complicated and more mathematically abstruse, the likelihood of falling into false relativism increases.

The most striking thing about Irish emigration patterns for all the years for which we have data is that women left Ireland in numbers approaching those for males. This is very unusual in European history. Most societies sent out many more males than females. Given below is the gender ratio of recorded emigration by Irish persons in the six decades after the Famine. It is expressed in terms of the number of emigrating females per 1,000 emigrating males.[35]

1852-60	951
1861-70	809
1871-80	823
1881-90	950
1891-1900	1,151
1901-10	1,008
1911-21	1,025

Although the form of the post-1920 data is not quite comparable to the above series, it is clear that the proportion of female migrants stayed roughly at parity with the male from the 1920s at least to 1950,[36] and probably down to the present day. The difficult question is: did this hold true for the pre-Famine era of the Irish diaspora? No one really knows.

Unlike the matter of gender, in which the out-flow was similar to the gender structure of the entire Irish population, the age structure of the migrants was very different from that of the overall population. As Table 7 makes clear, the migrants were sharply selected by age. Most were under twenty-five years of age and, after thirty, emigration was relatively infrequent: under one-fifth of the total were over thirty in most years. Notice in Table 7 that the age profile of emigrating females is very similar to that of emigrating males. Again, the symmetry in emigration patterns as between men and women is very unusual by European standards. This pattern of gender symmetry continued at least to mid-twentieth century.[37] and probably has to the present day. And again, when one focuses on the pre-Famine era, and asks "Did the same pattern hold for early years?" the answer comes back that no one at present knows for certain, and that, given the limited nature of available records and their unfortunate flaws, the answer probably is unknowable.

Where in Ireland did the emigrants come from? The answer is "everywhere," but that their origins varied over time and, further, that there was some regional specialization according to the countries to which the migrants moved.

That said, we must accept the fact that at no time in the history of the Irish diaspora do we have accurate information on the absolute number of persons who left Ireland according to their place of residence. From mid-1851 onwards, however, there are counts of the number who left Ireland from Irish ports, and from 1876 fairly detailed data exist. The big problem is that the data represent a serious undercounting. In part this is because the persons who went to England as transients and then later migrated permanently overseas are not found in these returns, which include only Irish persons sailing overseas from Irish ports. Further, the Irish migration to Great Britain was in any case seriously undercounted. Then, after 1920, annual figures for migration from Ireland were not collected (although there were occasional studies of the whole matter), and direct data on migration according to region of origin were not annually collated.

TABLE 7

Percentage of Age Distribution of Emigrants from Irish Ports 1852-1921

	0-14	15-19	20-24	25-29	30-34	35-54	55 and over	Not specified	Total
Males:									
1852-54	22.6	14.7	28.1	21.2		12.2	1.1	0.1	100.0
1861-70	13.7	8.4	33.7	20.1	9.0	9.9	0.9	4.3	100.0
1871-80	13.5	10.2	31.7	20.9	10.5	11.8	1.3	0.1	100.0
1881-90	13.7	15.0	38.3	15.5	6.6	9.5	1.3	0.1	100.0
1891-1900	8.5	11.0	41.6	23.4	6.2	7.9	1.4	0.0	100.0
1901-10	9.0	11.6	42.1	21.3	7.8	7.2	1.0	0.0	100.0
1911-21	9.3	12.7	41.6	28.1		7.5	0.8	0.0	100.0
Females:									
1852-54	22.0	18.8	28.4	16.8		12.6	1.3	0.1	100.0
1861-70	16.1	13.1	34.0	13.3	6.9	10.9	1.2	4.5	100.0
1871-80	15.7	17.8	33.8	13.6	7.6	10.0	1.4	0.1	100.0
1881-90	13.9	26.0	35.5	10.0	4.8	8.5	1.2	0.1	100.0
1891-1900	7.3	22.1	44.1	14.1	4.6	6.7	1.1	0.0	100.0
1901-10	8.8	25.2	39.5	14.0	5.1	6.2	1.2	0.0	100.0
1911-21	8.7	26.5	39.5	18.2		6.1	1.0	0.0	100.0

Source: Commission on Emigration and other Population Problems, 1948-1954 (Dublin: Stationery Office, 1954) Table 91, p. 122.

There are two ways around the problem, neither of which is fully satisfactory, but both are better than having no information at all. One of the methods is to affirm the fact that the information on emigration was indeed untrustworthy as a set of absolute numbers, but to suggest that one should pay attention nevertheless to the proportions that it contains. That is, perhaps we can use the post-1851 material as a sample of the origins of total migration. This seems sensible, for there is no reasons to think that the undercounting of emigrants affected those from one province more than those from another.

A more sophisticated means of dealing with the incomplete information is to estimate "cohort depletion." This is technically complicated, but in essence is quite simple. The method consists of noting how many people existed in a certain census age group (say, the group 15-25 years of age, inclusive) and then noting the size of the cohort ten years later (25-34 years, inclusive). If one has an accurate idea of how many persons died in that period, then the number of persons who have otherwise disappeared from the cohort should equal the number who emigrated from Ireland. Conceivably, this technique could be used to provide an accurate measure of total Irish emigration, as well as of the geographic origin within Ireland of the migrants. Thus far, however, the technique has been employed to show the comparative rates of out-migration as between regions, rather than to project absolute numbers of emigrants. When employed comparatively, the cohort-depletion method indicates that for the period 1821-41 Ulster had the highest emigration rate. From 1841-51, Connacht was highest; from 1851-61, Munster; and from 1861-71, Connacht.[38] (Remember that these are rates and that the province with the highest rate did not necessarily send the most emigrants).

Throughout the historical literature on the Irish diaspora, there are frequent suggestions that certain geographic regions were associated with certain overseas destinations. This undoubtedly is true and is worth noting, as long as the fact is kept in perspective. The early (seventeenth- and eighteenth-century) ties of the counties of Waterford and Wexford with Newfoundland are well known. These ties were unique in that in the early stage of the relationship, fishermen from Waterford and Wexford spent part of the year living in Newfoundland and returned home for part of the year. Later many of these became permanent residents of Newfoundland.[39]

TABLE 8

Emigration from Irish Ports, by Region, 1851-1920

	Leinster	Munster	Ulster	Connacht	Total
1 May 1851-31 March 1861	235,460	434,338	341,261	138,059	1,149,118
	20.5	37.8	29.7	12.0	100.0%
1 April 1861-31 March 1871	149,838	304,105	201,240	113,676	768,859
	19.5	39.5	26.2	14.8	100.0%
1 April 1871-31 March 1881	110,619	181,370	240,110	86,551	618,650
	17.9	29.3	38.8	14.0	100.0%
1 April 1881-31 March 1891	49,552	177,236	86,455	117,750	430,993
	11.5	41.1	20.0	27.3	100.0%
1 April 1901-31 March 1911	42,638	110,903	106,587	84,960	345,088
	12.4	32.1	30.9	24.6	100.0%
1 April 1911-end 1920	22,952	36,221	57,978	33,605	150,756
	15.2	24.0	38.5	22.3	100.0%
Total 1851-1920	749,341	1,496,253	1,250,155	735,820	4,231,569
	17.7	35.4	29.5	17.4	100.0%

Source: Derived from Vaughan and A.J. Fitzpatrick (eds.), pp. 344-53. Emigration to Great Britain is included.

Immigration lists for the USA for the period 1820-34 reveal that about 40 percent of the Irish incomers were from Ulster and 47 percent from Leinster.[40] Such relationships changed over time. Studies of the period 1887-1914 indicate that persons with Connacht origins were over-represented in the flow to the USA, and that Ulster people were proportionately higher in the migrations to Canada and New Zealand. Origins in the southwest and the north midlands of Ireland were over-represented in the Australian migration of the same era. Persons with origins in the northeast were over-represented among those who migrated permanently to Scotland, and eastern and southern coastal origins were proportionately higher among those who moved permanently to England.[41] In viewing such relationships the perspective to adopt is that such "over-representation" is a relative concept and it should not be confused with absolute numbers, nor should it obscure the fact that in the case of each of the significant national destinations, migrants came from all over Ireland.

When we turn to an examination of how the Irish emigrants were selected by occupation, we immediately are bedeviled by the same problem that we encountered when discussing regional origins: all available figures are undercounts and, further, we know virtually nothing systematic about the occupational profile of pre-Famine emigrants. The only remotely useful data are inferior. The one thing that is clear is that from earliest times until at least 1950, the majority of Irish emigrants came from the agricultural sector. At least from the Famine onward, and certainly until the mid-twentieth century, the overwhelming bulk of the emigrants (whether of rural or of urban origin) were unskilled.[42] That is what one would expect, given the general occupational profile of Ireland that we examined earlier.

What is unclear is whether or not any specific class was over-represented in the outflow. My own guess (and all anyone can do is guess) is that if one considers the entire Irish diaspora for the years 1815-1950: (a) the very poor, such as the long-term unemployed, were strongly under-represented among the emigrants; (b) landless male agricultural labourers and their female counterparts were over-represented; (c) skilled artisans, the so-called "aristocracy of the working class," and small farmers (holders of under thirty acres) emigrated in numbers roughly proportional to their total numbers in the Irish population; (d) while there was considerable middle class emigration, especially after 1920, over the entire time span 1815-1950 the middle class was somewhat under-represented among emigrants; and (e) the upper class migrated in disproportionately high numbers, the reasons being, first, that in the nineteenth century they took advantage of the opportunities the expanding British empire opened to their younger sons and, second, that after the land legislation of 1903 came into effect, they took the opportunity of getting out of Ireland with as many of their resources intact as possible.

The one period for which we have partial information about the occupation of emigrants is 1876-1920, when there was an interesting sorting of emigrants according to skill levels and country of destination. At one end of the spectrum were the migrants to the United States of America. Put simply, America received the "worst" of the Irish migrants, considered in terms of economically useful skills. This is what one would expect, given the skewing of their geographic origins. David Fitzpatrick has observed: "Analysis for the period 1876-95 shows that the American-Irish tended to come from counties that might be termed 'backward.'" These counties had many Irish-speakers, few Protestants, large agricultural populations and low farm valuations per capita. Even more emphatically than for Irish emigrants as a whole, those choosing America tended to leave counties which had lost unusually large numbers of agricultural labourers over the thirty years of economic adjustment which followed the Famine.[43] The inference drawn from geographic information is confirmed by direct occupational data compiled for 1912-13, as found in Table 9. This makes it clear that on the eve of World War I, the USA received the least-skilled of the Irish emigrants.

If the USA represents one end of the spectrum, South Africa represents the other. Alone among the countries that received significant numbers of Irish migrants, South Africa drew mostly persons from the skilled professions, the commercial class, and the skilled trades. This of course was because the racial structure of southern Africa meant that there was little need for unskilled Irish labourers. In the middle of the spectrum were Australia and New Zealand. Indeed, as will be argued later, the emigration to Australia in most respects was the most "normal," the most dead-centre in the Irish diaspora. In terms of relative quality, in this period Canada received just slightly above the average, but it was basically at the centre of the spectrum.

TABLE 9

Occupational Distribution of Irish Male Migrants, 1912-1913, to Various Locations from all United Kingdom Ports ("No Information" excluded) (Percentages)

Occupation	To South Africa	To U.S.A	To Canada	To Australia & New Zealand
Commerce, Finance, Professions	48.7	8.3	17.3	16.1
Skilled Trades	32.1	9.9	14.2	15.3
Agriculture	17.0	33.6	24.0	54.5
Labourer (including agriculture & transport)	2.2	48.2	44.5	14.1
Total	100.0	100.0	100.0	100.0

Source: Derived from Carrier and Jeffery, pp. 116-23.

Those data cover only a small period of time. Probably the pattern remained the same at least until 1950.[44] However, if one moves back in time towards the pre-Famine period, the picture becomes less clear. Probably the pattern held as far back as the early 1850s (save for the fact that before 1870 there were few migrants of any sort to southern Africa.)[45] Before that is *terra incognita.*

Finally, in considering the emigrants as a group selected from the general population (self-selected, but selected nonetheless), we must approach the problem of religion. There are no direct data of any sort on out-migration according to religious faith, and no one has yet developed a set of indirect measures that are entirely satisfactory. However, the logic of the situation is compelling. Notice that Table 5 clearly indicates that all of the Irish religious denominations experienced a drop in numbers, from (one infers) the outset of the Great Famine until the 1960s. What this means is that Protestants (both Ulster-Scots and Anglo-Irish) must have made up a considerable portion of the Irish diaspora. Now, if one wanted to keep the Protestants out of the picture, one could argue that they had smaller families and a lower birthrate than did the Catholics, so that their decline was through family limitation, not emigration. However, the available information suggests that the differentiation between Protestant and Catholic styles of life was a matter of the twentieth century, not the nineteenth.[46] And we also know from occupational data, that Protestants were less likely to have been caught in the poverty-trap and to be therefore too poor to emigrate. Thus, if anything, Protestants were apt to be a larger proportion of the emigrant stream than they were of the general population. Certainly they were present at least in proportion to their population numbers.

This inference is confirmed by various non-systematic sources collected for the pre-Famine era.[47] The only systematic study of emigration-by-religion was done for the post-Famine period by Robert E. Kennedy Jr. and it indicates that until 1911 Protestant and Catholic emigration rates were essentially the same.[48]

After Partition in 1920, Ireland broke into two separate emigration systems, tied together by a mirror-like symmetry In the north, Catholics emigrated at a higher rate than did Protestants: this is well indicated by the fact that although the Catholics had a much higher birthrate in the mid-twentieth century than did Protestants, they remained a remarkably stable population.[49] Which is to say, the Catholics in Northern Ireland had a higher propensity to emigrate than did the Protestants. Exactly the opposite was true in the south. After 1920, the Protestant population in southern Ireland dropped sharply.[50] Even when one compensates for the departure of British garrison forces and also for Protestants having a lower birthrate in the mid-twentieth century than Catholics, one still has to conclude that the Protestants had a much higher propensity to migrate out of southern Ireland than did the Catholics. Most of these Protestants were Anglicans.

The general reason that the Catholics in the north and the Protestants in the south had a relatively high propensity to emigrate is that each of them was a minority group. In the north, the Catholics faced a strongly discriminatory state, particularly in economic and political terms. In the south, the Protestants encountered not only a majority culture that was alien, but a political system that effectively excluded them as a group from any significant power (a few individuals had influence, but these were exceptions).

There was more, however. In each case there was a good deal of nastiness towards minorities. 1922 marks not only the independence of the twenty-six counties of southern Ireland, but the close of a very tense period in the relations of Irish Protestants and Irish Catholics, and two sets of violent events.

One of these was the "Belfast pogroms" of 1920-22. These are misnamed, for they were not pogroms in the full European sense of the word, but they were nasty and long lasting periods of riot and intimidation. Each side bloodied the other, but the Catholics, being the weaker of the parties in Belfast, suffered most of the consequences. Roughly 200 Catholics were killed by Protestants and about 100 Protestants by Catholics. No count was kept of the number of persons maimed or of the houses burned, but it was estimated that 9,000 Catholics were driven from their jobs between mid-1920 and early 1922, many of them in the skill-intensive and well-paid Belfast shipyards.[51]

There was a parallel campaign in the south of Ireland and that against Protestants. Unlike the northern episode, this was mostly a rural affair. It consisted of hectoring, intimidating, burning, and murdering isolated Protestants, most but not all of whom were owners of small town businesses or of relatively large farms. These actions were not part of the considered policy of the Irish national movement of the time, and republican leaders, Michael Collins especially, tried without success to stop them. The atrocities were for the most part spontaneous and local and derived not from political ideology but from the deep and free-flowing stream of sectarian hatred that runs through Irish history of that era. A precise tally of Protestant victims of these outrages for the entire period 1920-22 is not available, but between early December 1921 and late March 1923, 192 residences belonging to the Protestant minority in southern Ireland were destroyed.[52] The real effect of anti-Protestant intimidation and of the pinching-in upon Protestants in cultural and employment matters by the new Free State government (particularly in educational policy and in hiring in the new civil service) became clear in 1926 when the first census of southern Ireland was taken. It revealed that thousands of Protestants had decided they had no future in Catholic Ireland and had left: in 1911 there had been 327,000 Protestants in what eventually became the Irish Free State, but by 1926 there were only 221,000.[53] This, and not the events in Belfast in 1920-22, or, indeed in 1969-72, represents the biggest movement of population in twentieth-century Irish history.

The sum of all of these religiously conditioned matters as they affected the diaspora is as follows. They dictate that any discussion of the Irish diaspora must recognize (1) that the Protestants were a significant proportion of the out-flow, at least as large a proportion as they were of the home population (that is, one-fifth to one-quarter, depending on the time period), and that in some eras, such as the 1920s, they were considerably more; and (2) that over the entire period 1815-1950 there was as great a propensity for the Anglo-Irish (roughly, the Anglicans) to emigrate as for the Ulster-Scots (roughly the Presbyterians) to do so. After 1920, the Anglo-Irish left in proportionately higher numbers.

(VII)

Because the Irish diaspora is a worldwide phenomenon, involving both the Irish homeland and several New Worlds, it is a complicated matter, and therefore presents a great temptation: to simplify it by paying attention to only one country (the USA, Canada, Australia, or whatever) and to assume, without saying so explicitly, that the country in question is the norm. That will not do. What we need is an "ideal type" (in the sociological sense) of the Irish emigrant population so that we can then assess what happened in each nation that received significant numbers of Irish-born immigrants. This ideal type is the equivalent of a yardstick, with the centre marked; from that point one can indicate how far the characteristics of each nation's portion of the Irish diaspora deviated from the norm.

A simple ideal-type of the Irish diaspora would suggest that a country would be near the centre of the spectrum — the norm — if:

(1) the Irish-born immigrants to its shores were mostly young: under twenty-five years old for the most part and overwhelmingly under thirty;

(2) the numbers of men and women were roughly equal;

(3) the age profiles of the males and females were quite similar;

(4) unskilled labourers predominated, but with a strong infusion of skilled and middle class migrants. (Here recall the spectrum implied by Table 9, with the USA and South Africa at the extremes of the skills-spectrum, Australia and New Zealand at the centre, and Canada and Great Britain near the centre, albeit slightly beyond the norm);

(5) in the immigrant generation in the new land, Catholics predominated, but with Ulster-Scots forming roughly 10 percent of the in-migrants, and the Anglo-Irish roughly 10 percent;

(6) the immigrant flow, considered by religious persuasion, was steady over time, so that the entire multi-generational ethnic group in the new homeland had approximately the same characteristics as the migrant generation: approximately 80 percent Catholic, 10 percent Ulster Scots, 10 percent Anglo-Irish.

This six-point yardstick is a simple instrument. It can be transported from country to country. Of course one could construct a more complex instrument, but that would be counter-productive. Getting basic perspectives clear is job enough.

(VIII)

The reason for keeping things simple is that we know so little about many facets of the diaspora. Doubtlessly the reader

TABLE 10

Permanent Residence of Irish-Born Persons, 1841-1921 (in thousands)

Year	Population of Ireland (32 counties) including non-Irish born	Irish-born living in Ireland	Irish-born living in U.S.A., Canada, Australia, and G.B. Total Irish-born§	Irish-born persons living outside Ireland			Great Britain			Persons living outside Ireland as % of total of Irish-born§
				U.S.A.	Canada	Australia	England and Wales	Scotland	Total Great Britain	
1841	8,175	8,141	537 *	8,678	N/A	122	N/A	289	126	415	6.2
1851	6,552	6,502	1,916 +	8,418	962	227	N/A	520	207	727	22.3
1861	5,799	5,721	2,703 +	8,424	1,611	286	N/A	602	204	806	32.1
1871	5,412	5,307	2,854 +	8,161	1856	223	N/A	567	208	775	35.0
1881	5,175	5,062	3,035	8,097	1,855	186	213	562	219	781	37.5
1891	4,705	4,581	2,901	7,482	1,872	149	227	458	195	653	38.3
1901	4,459	4,327	2,533	6,860	1,615	102	184	427	205	653	36.3
1911	4,390	4,233	2,134	6,367	1,352	93	139	375	175	550	27.5
1921	4,354 (est.)	N/A	1,759	N/A	1,037	93	105	365	159	524	N/A

Source: Derived from *Commission on Emigration and Other Population Problems, 1948-1954* (Dublin: Stationery Office, 1954), Table 95, p. 126.

* excluding U.S.A., Australia   + excluding Australia   § with exclusions noted in column 3

will have noticed one major omission in the discussion thus far: I have not given a time series on the actual number of Irish emigrants. I shall do so, but the reader must understand that we do not know (and are not even close to knowing) the actual dimensions of the Irish diaspora. So, although the best available numbers for Irish emigration are given in Table 11, they should not be taken literally. They are like the pale shadows in Plato's cave: an intimation of a reality that will not ever be known fully. Why should that be?

Because, in part, before 1852 (when procedures were improved), customs authorities did not do a creditable job of counting the out-flow. There are few external sources that permit one to redact the existing numbers. (For example, the USA conducted its first tally of the place of birth of everyone in the population only in 1850). Despite heroic efforts at correcting the Irish emigration data (especially by William Forbes Adams)[54] we are at a loss for the pre-Famine period. As Cormac Ó Gráda notes, "There are no reliable estimates of even total emigration during the years between Waterloo and the Famine."[55] A quantum jump in accuracy was made in 1852 and another in 1876, but even so, comparison figures (such as the number of Irish-born that show up in the census of the various countries to which the emigrants moved), lead to the conclusion that even the best estimates of Irish overseas migration (that is, to every place but Great Britain) for the second half of the nineteenth century are as much as one-quarter too low.[56] After Partition, neither the authorities of the new independent government of the south of Ireland nor the authorities of northern Ireland kept accurate overseas emigration records. Up to 1936 United Kingdom officials made an effort to keep an annual record of emigration from both parts of Ireland. (The year 1935 was the last full year of their effort; they made estimates for 1936, and then quit, as southern Ireland withdrew from the British Commonwealth).

But the overseas migration data are not even half the problem. A much worse one has to do with a form of emigration not included in Table 11: emigration to Great Britain. The counting of migrants from Ireland to Scotland and England and Wales was done so inefficiently that the official figures on the matter in the second half of the nineteenth century are probably off by an amazing 100 percent. While the official estimate for between 1850 and 1911 of the total migration from Ireland into Great Britain was about one-half million, the real flow probably was about one million.[57]

TABLE 11

Emigration from Ireland (32 Counties), 1825-1935 (excluding emigration to Great Britain)

Period	To U.S.A.	% of total	To Canada	% of total	To Australasia	% of total	Other overseas countries	% of total	Total overseas emigration (note exclusions)
1825-30	50,040	38.7	79,142	61.3	N/A	N/A	N/A	N/A	129,182
1831-40	171,087	39.1	262,004	59.8	4,662	1.1	N/A	N/A	437,753
1841-50	908,292	70.0	362,738	27.9	22,825	1.8	4,539	0.3	1,298,394
1851-60	989,880	81.4	118,118	9.7	101,541	8.3	6,726	0.6	1,216,265
1861-70	690,845	84.4	40,079	4.9	82,917	10.1	4,741	0.6	818,582
1871-80	449,549	82.8	25,783	4.8	61,946	11.4	5,425	1.0	542,703
1881-90	626,604	85.3	44,505	6.1	55,476	7.5	7,890	1.1	734,475
1891-1900	427,301	92.7	10,648	2.3	11,448	2.5	11,520	2.5	460,917
1901-10	418,995	86.3	38,238	7.9	11,885	2.4	16,343	3.4	485,461
1911-20	172,490	75.3	32,857	14.3	15,429	6.7	8,463	3.7	229,239
1921-25	109,911	69.7	29,400	18.7	12,105	7.7	6,168	3.9	157,584
1926-36	121,408	70.6	37,387	21.8	13,051	7.6	N/A	N/A	171,846
1931-35	3,004	46.6	1,881	29.1	1,568	24.3	N/A	N/A	6,453

Sources: The basic data for the table are taken from *Commission on Emigration and other Population Problems, 1948-1954* (Dublin: Stationery Office, 1954), p. 124, as is the data for 1851-1920. However, for the years before 1851, this commission's report left several holes which are filled in by N.H. Carrier and J.R. Jeffery, *External Migration: A Study of the Available Statistics, 1815-1950, being No. 6 In the General Register Office's "Studies on Medical and Population Subjects"* (London: HMSO, 1953), p. 95. In turn, the Carrier and Jeffery material has been corrected for under-counting for sailings to the U.S.A. and to British North America according to the work of William Forbes Adams. *Ireland and Irish Emigration to the New World from 1815 to the Famine* (New Haven: Yale University Press, 1932), pp. 413-14. For 1836, for which Adams made no estimate, I have interpolated the data myself. For the years 1846-50 (for which Adams made no correction for under-counting) I have used his formula. See D.H. Akenson, *The Irish in Ontario*, pp. 14-15, 29-30. Post 1920 figures are compiled from *Commission on Emigration . . .*, Table 93, p. 124 and from Carrier and Jeffery, Table D/F/G(1), p. 96.

Perhaps the casualness about migration into Great Britain was understandable up to Partition, for until then Ireland was part of the United Kingdom and movement between the nations was in some sense internal migration. The curious thing is that after southern Ireland became independent, the level of record keeping became worse. This was occurring just at the time that Great Britain replaced the USA as the new homeland most frequenly chosen by Irish emigrants. One wonders if these developments were related: if the details of the heavy outflow to Britain were something that the authorities in the newly-independent twenty-six counties did not want to know.

As this point, if we wish to learn more about the nature of the Irish diaspora, the most efficient strategy is to turn to the individual countries which received significant numbers of Irish emigrants. Each country of course has an integral story of its own; each new nation has its own history. But we should remember always that the Irish diaspora was a set of related events and that knowledge of how the migrants behaved in one new setting may help us to understand how they acted in another, thousands of miles away.

Irish Diaspora

Chapter 3

New Zealand:
A Complete and Distant World

(I)

John Kelleher, the doyen of Irish scholars in North America, once told me of his grandfather and two great-uncles, three brothers who individually migrated to Massachusetts between 1859 and the mid-1870s. Two of the brothers were convinced Irish nationalists; the third could not have cared less. In fact, he had succumbed to the blandishments of the recruiting sergeant at the fair at Macroom and served a twelve-year enlistment in the British army. Then he emigrated to Massachusetts, only to find that his two brothers would not speak to him. So eventually he moved on to New Zealand, where he had a successful and uneventful life. However, so ashamed was the nationalist side of the family of his having served the Crown, that John's father did not learn that his own father had a brother in the Antipodes until he turned twenty-one and, being of legal age, now presumably could deal with such shame.

Actually, that sort of settlement pattern (although not the animus) was very common. When one goes through the printed summaries that genealogists do of their family trees, among Irish families one frequently finds that an entire generation dispersed worldwide, one member to the USA, another to Canada, one or more to South Africa, Australia, or New Zealand. This is not merely a sidebar to history. It hints at the possibility of a new sort of research that someday will unlock many of the secrets of the Irish diaspora - namely, that someone will do the equivalent of the "matched twin" studies that have been conducted at the University of Minnesota and which have virtually reshaped the thinking of social scientists about the interplay of generative and environmental factors in human development. A large-scale comparative study of family members who went to the USA for instance, and of others who went to other nations, would be one of the best ways to help historians learn what characteristics of Irish emigrants were the result of their Irish background, and what other characteristics were the product of their experience in North America.

We do not have to wait for such a study, however, before utilizing information on the Irish migrants and their descendants in a given nation to teach us useful things about the Irish elsewhere. New Zealand is a particularly good place to start. It is relatively small, has excellent records on some matters (especially on the social and economic characteristics of the migrants of the 1870s and 1880s) and reasonably good records on other things, such as occupational and residential patterns in the new land. Most importantly, it is a relatively clean laboratory. In particular, New Zealand did not have the great source of pollution that makes the USA in the nineteenth century such a difficult place to study ethnic history: slavery and its aftermath.

Notice that New Zealand's relatively small size is not a disadvantage. It would be easy to suggest that it is unimportant because only a small percentage of the Irish diaspora went there. That is not how laboratories work. Only a minute percentage of the world's electrons pass through a cyclotron during a given experiment, but if the laboratory is clean, the results reveal something about electrons everywhere. What we observe in New Zealand (and later in Australia, South Africa, and Canada) may well be the clear and clean version of basic facts that we are unable to observe directly amongst the hubbub of the bigger reception areas, especially Great Britain and the USA. The chief limit to the use of New Zealand as a laboratory is that the overwhelming majority of its Irish immigrants arrived well after the Famine, so any inference we draw from the New Zealand story should not be projected back into the period before mid-nineteenth century.

To return to John Kelleher's family, split as it was in the last quarter of the nineteenth century by emigration to the USA and to New Zealand. Near the end of World War II, a descendant of one of the two stoutly nationalist brothers who had stayed in Massachusetts was on furlough from the U.S. Marine Corps and was on the North Island of New Zealand. He made contact with the descendants of the man who had soldiered for the Crown. Even after separation by more than half a century and by half the circumference of the globe, the two halves of the family were mirror images of each other. Each side had valued education, had settled into governmental and managerial jobs, and had done well. They could have exchanged jobs with each other, or churches, or schools, and within a fortnight have fit in perfectly. The two sides of this diaspora family had taken different paths around the world only to arrive at the same place.

(II)

To use the vocabulary of the social sciences and the criteria for Irish migrants developed in Chapter Two, the Irish migrants to New Zealand in the second half of the nineteenth century and the early twentieth century were close to being "ideal types."[1] The migrants were mostly young, primarily unskilled, but there was a tincture of skilled and middle class migrants and, indeed, a few capitalists and gentry. Catholics predominated among the immigrants. This religious flow remained constant over time, so that the multi-generational ethnic group had nearly the same religious composition as did the first generation. The only skewing from dead-centre normal occurred during the gold rush days of the 1860s, when Catholics were slightly over-represented and women were markedly outnumbered by men. Census figures for the early twentieth century indicate that both these matters had settled down to normal, and indeed probably had been in the "ideal type" range since the early 1870s. Overall, what this means is that the Irish migrants to New Zealand and their descendants were a fairly representative slice of the entire Irish diaspora in the late nineteenth and early twentieth centuries.

One of the first impressions that strikes one about Irish migrants to New Zealand is that they knew what they were doing. The amount of information that Irish migrants

NEW ZEALAND

Bay of Islands

Firth of Thames

AUCKLAND

Coromandel Peninsula

Thames

BAY OF PLENTY

Ngaruawahia

WAIKATO

TAURANGA

HAMILTON   Cambridge

ROTORUA

AUCKLAND

GISBORNE

Lake Taupo

Poverty Bay

Waitara

TARANAKI

NEW PLYMOUTH

Inglewood

WELLINGTON

HAWKE BAY

NAPIER

Hastings

Hawera

Patea

WANGANUI

MANAWATU

HAWKES BAY

Waipawa

Feilding

Woodville

PALMERSTON Nth

Foxton

HUTT

WAIRARAPA

Masterton

Golden Bay

Tasman Bay

Picton

COOK STRAIT

NELSON

BLENHEIM

WELLINGTON

Karamea

MARL-BOROUGH

WESTPORT

NELSON

GREYMOUTH

HOKITIKA

WESTLAND

CANTERBURY

Rangiora

CHRISTCHURCH

LYTTELTON

Banks Peninsula

Akaroa

Ashburton

Temuka

TIMARU

OTAGO

OAMARU

Palmerston

DUNEDIN

SOUTH-LAND

N

INVERCARGILL

FOVEAUX STRAIT

Stewart Island

.... PROVINCIAL BOUNDARIES

0   100
Miles

collected, from newspapers, from cousins who had gone before, from governmental emigration literature, was impressive. Despite newspapers, from cousins who had gone before, from governmental emigration literature, was impressive. Despite New Zealand's relatively small size having precluded its being a major host for the Irish, the migrants had reasonably well-informed views of the opportunities it offered and of the price, in monetary and physical terms, of getting there. In the everyday case, this knowledge came from letters sent from earlier migrants to family and friends at home.[2] It was supplemented by reports in literary journals and in newspapers and by evidence collected by United Kingdom parliamentary commissions which looked into conditions of emigration. *The Dublin University Magazine* was a fair representative of educated Irish opinion. An article in the October 1845 issue noted that New Zealand was "the most recent, remotest, and least civilized of our colonies."[3] In subsequent years, the periodical showed an increasing interest in these islands. At first it was drawn to the more exotic details of Maori culture,[4] but increasingly it evinced an informed awareness of the emerging settler society:

> We cannot omit a brief examination of the main attractive features of New Zealand as a place of residence for Englishmen. Favoured with a climate that shames that of Australia, and with a soil exuberant in the highest degree, presenting also many alluring young settlements with vast and fertile plains on their skirts, those islands are every year more largely engaging the attention of emigrants.[5]

The favourable comparison of New Zealand to the Australian colonies was common in the Irish emigration literature. It had taken form as early as the 1847 House of Lords select committee on colonization from Ireland. "Do you think that it [New Zealand] is better adapted for an agricultural population than the province of Sydney?" a gentleman who had resided both in New South Wales and in New Zealand was asked. "I think it is much more so," he replied and went on to explain his reasons. "New South Wales I consider is a very badly watered country, and it is also subject to droughts. New Zealand again is one of the best watered countries in the world and it has always an abundant supply of moisture for the growth of crops."[6] That the New Zealand climate resembled that of Ireland was a benefit not lost on potential Irish migrants, most of whom were small farmers and agricultural labourers.[7]

If the Irish were favourable to New Zealand, the government of New Zealand was much less keen on them. In part this was because most Irish immigrants would be Roman Catholics. But that was not all: an endemic, if low temperature, xenophobia was directed at all the Irish, Protestant and Catholic alike. William Pember Reeves's assessment was: "Not only by its founders, but for many years afterward, Irish were avowedly or tacitly excluded" from the immigrants sent to New Zealand.[8] Yet, New Zealand needed settlers, so from the very beginning one discovers mixed attitudes. For example, although high officials of the New Zealand Company were opposed to Irish migration, the company set up three agencies in Ireland to attract migrants, one at Belfast, one at Dublin, and one which dealt with the rest of the country.[9] Later, during the 1870s, when immigration from the British Isles was strongly encouraged, the government both stimulated Irish migration — there were forty-six New Zealand emigration agents in Ireland in 1873[10] — and worried that it might get out of hand. One aspect of this "Vogel scheme" of immigration (named after Sir Julius Vogel, its chief proponent) involved allowing new residents to nominate friends or relatives in the Old World for assistance in migration, which was a great boon to the Irish: they, more than any other group in the British Isles, were noted for what is today called "chain migration."[11] The New Zealand government tried to limit the dangers (whatever those might have been) in large-scale Irish immigration by putting as many of its agents as possible in the north of Ireland, which was predominantly Protestant. In the later 1870s, governmental officials decided that the degree of Irish immigration into New Zealand should be in the same proportion of the total flow from the British Isles as the Irish represented in the total population of the home islands. A quota system was drawn up based on this formula, but it proved impossible of enforcement.[12]

One reason that the New Zealand government never put its heart fully into restricting the Irish was that, like all new colonial ventures, New Zealand was desperately short of women, and single Irish women were much more willing to emigrate from their homeland than were unmarried English, Scots, or Welsh women. As the minister of immigration explained in 1883: "Of the [1,941] Irish, 1,124 are single women; and the Government have not deemed it desirable to exclude any of these, by endeavouring to maintain the proportions as strictly as was originally contemplated."[13] Thus, whether or not New Zealand's governmental officials liked the fact, the tide of Irish emigration washed over New Zealand, as it did over the entire English-speaking world.

When one tries to discover the exact number of Irish migrants to New Zealand, one at first bogs down in an evidentiary quagmire. Until 1920, the government of New Zealand did not define what an immigrant to its shores was, and pass-through travellers were tallied alongside permanent settlers. The information from the Irish side of the journey is not much better, because most persons who emigrated from Ireland to New Zealand did so from Scottish and English ports and were therefore lost from the Irish port statistics on emigration. Further, a large number of Irish-born persons arrived in New Zealand after a sojourn in Australia or some other intermediate point.

That said, the reader is saved from a long paper-chase through the migration records: elsewhere I have worked out estimates for the number of Irish-born migrants into New Zealand.[14] Taken together, Tables 12 and 13 provide the flow pattern of Irish migrants up to mid-twentieth century.

The number of Irish immigrants living in New Zealand in any given census year is given in Table 14. As is the case in most lands of the Irish diaspora, the number of the Irish-born reached a peak in the last quarter of the nineteenth century and declined thereafter, as the out-flow from Ireland tailed off. More revealing is Table 14's indication of the size of the entire Irish ethnic group and its size in relation to New Zealand's Pakeha (that is, white) population. From the late 1860s onward, and until mid-twentieth century, persons of Irish ethnicity were between one-fifth and one-sixth of the country's Pakeha.[15] This means that although they were a minority (every ethnic group was a minority, actually), they were too large to be treated as insignificant. The Irish had sufficient numbers to be able to defend whatever collective interests they had.

TABLE 12

Irish Immigration
1871-1920

Year	Hypothetical Irish Gross Immigration	Year	Hypothetical Irish Gross Immigration
1871	2,087	1896	1,711
1872	2,220	1897	1,808
1873	2,809	1898	1,793
1874	9,101	1899	1,793
1875	6,570	1900	1,767
1876	3,812		
1877	2,688	1901	1,928
1878	3,366	1902	2,346
1879	4,959	1903	2,370
1880	3,137	1904	2,641
		1905	2,503
1881	1,938	1906	3,062
1882	2,189	1907	2,940
1883	3,843	1908	3,523
1884	4,004	1909	3,460
1885	3,240	1910	3,010
1886	3,220		
1887	2,738	1911	3,452
1888	2,721	1912	3,789
1889	3,078	1913	3,877
1890	3,006	1914	3,220
		1915	1,940
1891	1,563	1916	1,586
1892	1,830	1917	1,099
1893	2,557	1918	810
1894	2,507	1919	1,454
1895	2,161	1920	3,775

Source: D.H. Akenson, *Half the World from Home. Perspective on the Irish in New Zealand, 1860-1950* (Wellington: Victoria University Press, 1990), pp. 24-25.

TABLE 13

**Permanent Irish Migration (32 Counties)
to New Zealand, 1922-1950**

Year	Irish Migration
1922	900
1923	707
1924	851
1925	1,443
1926	1,900
1927	940
1928	496
1929	493
1930	491
1931	173
1 Jan.-31 Dec. 1932	49
1 Jan. 1932- 31 Mar. 1934	97
1934-35	71
1935-36	81
1936-37	78
1937-38	245
1938-39	303
1939-40	286
1940-41	45
1941-45	N/A
1945-46	34
1946-47	189
1947-48	213
1948-49	478
1949-50	640

Sources: Derived from: *Statistical Report on External Migration . . . 1932*, p. 9; and from *Statistical Report on Population and Buildings . . . 1933-34*, p. 34; *1934-35*, p. 24, *1935-36*, p. 19; *1936-37*, p. 28; *1937-38*, p. 21; *1938-39*, p. 21; *1939-40*, p. 21; *1940-41*, p. 22; *1944-45* and *1945-46*, p. 32; *1946-47*, p. 31; *1947-48*, p. 32; *1948-49*, p. 34; *1949-50*, p. 37.

TABLE 14

Notional Ethnic Origins of Persons of British Isles Background, New Zealand, 1858-1951
(data base exclusive of Maori)

Year	Immigrants	Imigrants as % of N.Z. population	2nd gen. & ff.	Ethnic total	Irish ethnic group as % of N.Z. population
1858	4,554	7.7	2,738	7,292	12.3
1861	8,831	8.9	4,160	12,991	13.1
1864	20,317	11.8	7,909	28,226	16.4
1867	27,955	12.8	12,153	40,108	18.3
1871	29,733	11.6	17,863	47,596	18.6
1874	30,255	10.1	23,589	53,844	18.0
1878	43,758	10.6	33,549	77,307	18.6
1881	49,363	10.1	43,073	92,436	18.9
1886	51,408	8.9	57,550	108,958	18.8
1891	47,634	7.6	69,716	117,350	18.7
1896	46,037	6.5	85,390	131,427	18.7
1901	43,524	5.6	100,853	144,377	18.7
1906	42,460	4.9	123,487	165,947	18.7
1911	40,958	4.1	142,312	183,270	18.2
1916	37,380	3.4	157,642	195,022	17.7
1921	34,419	2.8	178,240	212,659	17.4
1936	25,865	1.7	227,347	253,212	17.0
1945	18,615	1.2	252,976	271,591	17.1
1951	17,172	0.9	306,770	323,942	16.7

Note: The Irish-born population was distributed as follows, 1936-51:

	Northern Ireland	Southern Ireland	Ireland undefined
1936	1,788	747	23,330
1946	9,024	7,249	2,342
1951	8,817	6,423	1,932

Source: Akenson, *Half the World*, pp. 40, 62-63.

In Table 15 I have calculated the religious breakdown of the Irish ethnic group. Simply put, once the abnormal flow of the 1860s gold rush was over, the Protestants comprised about one-quarter of the Irish ethnic group, which is just what one would expect, given their proportion in the Irish homeland.[16]

TABLE 15

**Irish Ethnic Breakdown as a Proportion of the
New Zealand Population (exclusive of Maori) 1858-1951**

Year	Irish Ethnic group as % of total population	Irish Catholics as % of total population	Irish Protestants as % of total population
1858	12.3	11.1	1.2
1861	13.1	11.0	2.1
1864	16.4	12.5	3.9
1867	18.3	13.9	4.4
1871	18.6	13.9	4.7
1874	18.0	13.5	4.5
1878	18.6	14.2	4.4
1881	18.9	14.1	4.8
1886	18.8	13.9	4.9
1891	18.7	13.9	4.8
1896	18.7	14.1	4.6
1901	18.7	14.2	4.5
1906	18.7	14.3	4.5
1911	18.2	13.9	4.3
1916	17.7	13.8	3.9
1921	17.4	13.4	4.0
1936	17.0	13.1	3.9
1945	17.1	13.2	3.9
1951	16.7	12.9	3.8

Source: Akenson, *Half the World*, p. 67.

(III)

All of this is important, but very dry. Let us briefly encounter some real migrants, persons we get to know from their correspondence with friends at home or through their diaries and journals.[17] Here is Minnie Williams: she left Ireland in 1881 in the company of her mother and father, three sisters, and a brother. They travelled on the *Zealandia*, an iron clipper ship of 1,116 tons that had been built specially for the long distance migrant trade and was operated by Shaw, Savill and Co., one of the British Isles' largest emigration firms. The vessel carried nine first class passengers, seventeen second class, and fifty-six third class. The Williamses were in third class. For the total of eighty-two passengers, there were a captain and forty-three crew members, including a medical doctor. Although Minnie Williams's journal does not make the point, almost certainly her family was one of the family groups of "assisted emigrants" that the New Zealand government strove to attract. The family was representative in that it was going to New Zealand as part of a process of "chain migration." Another son had travelled to Auckland earlier and had set up house. The family was to join him. Young Minnie began her travel diary as follows:

> *Thursday 23rd June 1881.* Left Ballymena 20 minutes past one. Arrived at Larne, crossed to Stranraer. Sea very calm; all sick except Papa and Tom who had fine work attending on us ...[18]

Like almost all emigrants from Ireland to New Zealand, they were headed for a British port, as very few vessels sailed from Ireland to the Antipodes. A few journeys originated in Scottish ports, but most vessels sailed from the south of England:

> *Friday, 24th.* Arrived at Euston Station at 8:00 a.m., almost done up. Agent waiting for us with bus and van for luggage. Drove 7 miles to B'wall. Made very comfortable at agent's house. Had breakfast, went to bed, got up. Dinner: roast beef, green peas and new potatoes. Papa's sister and Aunt Emma spent the day with us. Went over the vessel. Found things better than we expected; we have lots of room for our boxes in cabins. Our hearts all failing us at the thought of 3 months.

Four days later the long voyage began:

> *Tuesday, 28th.* Awoke about 4; sailors all singing as they hoisted the sails. It sounded very nice. Up about 7 and were amazed to find that we had nothing for breakfast but coffee and hard biscuits. After some work we managed to get a loaf, cooked some bacon (which we brought with us) and soon were very comfortable. Sat on deck and worked, soon felt rather queer, lay down on deck till tea. Went to bed; some got better after tea. Had a nice walk. A beautiful night, rather cold. Just opposite the Isle of Wight.

The mixture of pleasure and, in this case, physical pain was indicated in the following entries:

> *Thursday, 30th.* Up at half past seven. Breakfast: rice pudding and coffee. All better and enjoying ourselves. Dinner: salt pork and baked potatoes. Took our last look at the English coast. The sailors said they never had finer weather going up the Channel; passed the Eddystone lighthouse.
> *Friday, 1st July.* All sick except Papa and Tom. Stomachs soon settled and shipboard routine took over.

On the ships of the New Zealand emigrant run, it was usual to have weekly divine services.

> *Sunday, 10th.* Up about 8. After breakfast we have to muster and pass before the Captain, the Doctor reading out our names to see that none were missing. Church in the saloon about 1/2 past 10 a.m. the Doctor reading the lessons. Dinner 1/2 past 11, some mutton pies which were very good. After dinner on Sundays the Captain gives the children nuts and raisins.

Third class passengers did their own cooking:

> *Monday, 11th.* Emma and I have to cook this week and began by making two huge rice puddings which looked much better than they tasted as the rice would not get soft. We had pea soup and salt pork for dinner.

The tropics proved a difficult experience:

> *Wednesday, 20th.* Up at 6, even this is very hot... We live now nearly on rice as the salt food makes us so thirsty. We get a bottle of lime juice every week when in the tropics.

Minnie summed up her family's outlook after a time at sea:

> *Saturday, 23rd.* A month out. Are not sorry, we have enjoyed ourselves very much.

and:

> *Monday, 1st August.* Up about 7. Ladies are not expected on deck till nearly 8 as the gentlemen have their baths under the pump. The finest days we have had. All in excellent health and good spirits ... Saw another Booby. I never saw such a beautiful sky and sunset in my life. Had a concert by moonlight, sailors doing their share. Some of them are very good singers.

Not that everything was perfect:

> *Monday, 8th.* ... Can't make our stores last the week, they generally run down about Friday and Saturday and Sunday we are half starved. All the people in the 3rd cabin signed a petition to the Captain that we might get some more flour, but it was no use.

Yet they can scarcely have been undergoing great privations:

> *Wednesday, 10th.* We are all in great spirits. We generally pair off every evening and walk up and down, Papa and Mama and all. Mr. Smith's birthday, a 2nd class passenger. We four girls were invited to the party, had a very pleasant evening.

And so it went until finally they sighted their destination.

> *Wednesday, 28th September.* Pass the Barrier in the night, in view of Auckland. I can't describe the scenery. It is something beautiful. Gentlemen's houses and gardens, churches and windmills, all surrounded by the sea. It is worth coming thousands of miles to see.

But the pleasure is a mixed one:

> *Friday, 30th.* Alongside the wharf, can go on shore when we like. Busy packing all morning. Go on shore about 3:00 p.m. Kate, Emma and I are disgusted with the place, would give anything to be back again. All the rest are delighted.

Thus, in the innocent prose of Minnie Williams one hears many of the themes that run through the New Zealand emigrants' experience: a mixture of excitement and of apprehension, a sense of opportunity to be seized, a voyage of great length, of some discomfort, but of considerable interest for anyone with an alert intelligence.

In a sense, the Williamses were prospectors, although not for mineral wealth. Like most migrants to New Zealand, they were looking for a better livelihood for themselves. The son, Sam, who had come earlier to Auckland, had acted as a scout and the family was moving along a well-tested, governmentally-supervised route, one about which the Williamses were well-informed.

Many of the prospectors for good fortune who came to New Zealand were part of a "Tasman connection," that is, of a pattern of migration and friendships and family alliances that ran back and forth across the Tasman Sea. The clearest example of the Tasman connection found in New Zealand emigrant letters is provided by the Quinn brothers, William and Patrick. They were from a Catholic family whose members' movements were part of a general process occurring in the north of Ireland in the nineteenth and early twentieth centuries, the drift from small towns to Belfast. The boys had been raised in Newry, but at some time in their youth the family had moved to the Falls Road, Belfast. The Falls Road, close by the railway terminus where the rural and small town migrants entered the city, had become a Catholic ghetto early in the nineteenth century. Although the Quinns' mother lived for the rest of her life in the Falls Road and another brother stayed in Belfast, William and Patrick spent a life prospecting in various ways. William arrived in New South Wales, Australia, some time in the 1880s and took up mining. He was a witness to the great mine strike of 1890 and was still at Broken Hill in 1892. William was in and out of work and moved from mine to mine, eventually rising from being a labourer to the position of underground manager. In 1905 one finds him with an injured leg, unable to mine, and now in New Zealand. His correspondence home shows that earlier in his career he had moved back and forth from Australia to New Zealand at least twice. In retirement in New Zealand in 1907, he was a person seemingly of substantial assets and with a pompous consciousness of hard-won middle class social position.[19]

What about Patrick? He was much less successful. In a sense, he was the real prospector, for he took up gum digging in New Zealand. Unlike mining, which, by the

1890s, was a large scale corporate activity in the usual case, gum digging was solitary and involved little in the way of equipment save a long pole, a swag, and an ability to stand one's own company. Throughout his career in mining in Australia and in his later retirement in New Zealand, William Quinn was conscious of the activities of his brother and found him an embarrassment, though worthy of brotherly concern. In 1890 William made a visit to New Zealand ("things are very dull there"), and he told his mother in a letter that "I have not heard anything of Pat; he is still carrying on his old game, drink."[20] Five years later, William was sending home similar information, now with vocational details. "The last word I heard of Pat," he told his mother, "he was drunk about 100 miles from Auckland." He continued:

> He is what we call a bush man, they are men that goes away in the backwoods and works at saw mills and stops twelve months without coming to a township and then perhaps 20 or 30 of them will start together to the first public house they come to; there they stop till the money is done, so that is how Pat spends his money.

He added gloomily, "If I hear of his death I will let you know."[21]

Pat may not have been doing well, but he was far from being the broken reed that William implied. Almost a full five years after William had implicitly predicted his demise, Patrick was writing from near Auckland to his brother John at home in Ireland. He was not getting rich, certainly:

> Dear brother I am at the gum digging and I don't average 2s. a week; it is no good; if there is one man making wages there is 20 barely make "tucker" and only for the pension I would be very badly off. Now when I am not digging gum I am mending and washing my clothes and getting firewood."[22]

Yet Patrick was doing better than he sounded and his mention of the pension is the key to this fact. New Zealand had the most advanced system of social welfare in the English-speaking world at that time, and Patrick was receiving ten shillings a week. In Ireland at his age he would not have been receiving a farthing and that helps to explain why, although he manifestly did not get on in the New

World, he had no lachrymose ideas of returning to his homeland. The real separation in the Quinn family was not between the family members in Ireland and those in Australasia, but the distance between the brothers Patrick and William. They lived for at least four years in the autumn of their lives within a day's journey of each other (they were both in the vicinity of Auckland), but they communicated only by infrequent letters. William, the substantial citizen, was loath to embrace the less-successful Patrick. They had come half way around the globe, only to be worlds apart.

The Quinns' family relationships bring to the fore the point that the Irish diaspora was a phenomenon embedded deeply in the matrix of family relationships. Each such relationship was unique and generalizations are dangerous, but in the most simplistic terms there were two, seemingly contradictory, themes. One of these themes is evoked by the columns that are frequently encountered in nineteenth- and early twentieth-century newspapers throughout the former British Empire and the United States of America: the Lost Persons column, in which the names and circumstances of individuals who have been "lost" by their relatives and friends (usually those in the Old Country) are sought. Undeniably, families often were rent asunder by emigration. This seems to have been especially frequent in the case of single unmarried men and women (a large proportion of the Irish diaspora), who never wrote home and who became part of the great anonymous horde that was lost forever to their families in the homeland.

Even when migrants kept in touch with their families in Ireland, the relationship should not be romanticized. Take the case of Oliver McSparron, who came to New Zealand in the 1860s. A native of rural County Londonderry, he was by turns a labourer, a small carting contractor, and a gold miner. From his early days in New Zealand he was under pressure from his father, a widower, to return home, presumably to take over the family holding. In a series of letters home, Oliver adopted two ploys. One of these was to send short letters, his excuse being that "the mail is closing, so I have not time to write anymore" or a version of that phrase. And, second, he continually stalled about going home:

[1865] I am doing nothing at present as I have sold my team of five horses and waggon for 200 a few days ago. I have not made up my mind as yet as to what I shall do next. The last time I wrote to you I was intending to be home in six months after, but I did not realize my expectations.[23]

[1869] I have left the part that I was in before and am now on the digging. I have always had a great wish to try my luck at the gold digging and I am determined to try my luck at last ... I had a great notion of going home this some time back but I could not bring my mind to as I think I could not stop if I went home.[24]

In 1880, Oliver was still delaying.

You need not expect me home before 12 months as there is money owing to me that I cannot get at present and it will not do to leave it. There is very hard times here at present for everybody. Oats sells at 8p to one shilling per bushel of 40 lbs. We get 3/3d. per bushel of 60 lbs. General farm servants get from 10/- to 15/- and 20 shillings per week and scarcely any work to be got at that rate. In Government are employing men on the railways at 21/- per week ... to keep them from starvation. There is nothing but farmers selling out and insolvencies on all sides.[25]

This last letter had begun with a peevish notice by the younger McSparron that "I was not a little surprised to see an advertisement in the Otago Witness for me to go home as you were quite alone." To be advertised for like some lost spalpeen offended young McSparron, the more so because he learned about the advertisement from an acquaintance. That indignity and an unpaid debt from the old days before he had left his father's farm rankled, and in 1882 he wrote a most surprising letter to his father:

Dear Father,
    I write this to remind you that when I left there I left twenty-five pounds with you for a certain purpose. You did not put it to that use, but wrongfully converted it to your own use. You never even offered to send it to me. I now claim payment of the sum with ten per cent compound interest added, which now amounts to £176.10 sterling. If the above is not paid per draft on Union Bank of Australasia, Oamaru, within six months from date I will be forced to adopt other measures for recovery of same.[26]

There, not surprisingly, the father-son correspondence ends.
    One way that families kept in touch across vast oceans

was to send money. "Remittances" home to Ireland were common throughout the Irish diaspora, but evidence of this in the surviving New Zealand letters is scant. William Quinn sent money home frequently to his mother in the Falls, Belfast. This was in the form of bank drafts of £10 roughly every three or four months. After he retired, he sent his brother John £110 in gifts to distribute to the family at home.[27] There is some irony in this, however, for while William Quinn was sending money to Ireland, his estranged brother Patrick, living near Auckland, was receiving money from the Falls Road, Belfast, sent by the same brother John to whom William sent funds from New Zealand. "Dear brother, I am very thankful of your consideration in sending me a Christmas box," a grateful Patrick wrote home. "I didn't expect it for you have a large family and will want all that you have."[28]

One suspects that the matter of remittances always was more complex and ironic than usually it has been painted. Remittances home were a source of pride to the homefolk (indeed, virtual local competitions in the comparison of bank drafts from abroad were carried on) and they were a source of pride to those who sent them.

These remittances to Ireland were remembered. But money sent abroad from Ireland was less a matter of pride and largely has slipped from the historical record except for tales about well-off "remittance men" who received £100 or £200 annually from the Old Country. In the usual event, I suspect it was the poor taking care of the poor that was more common: that is, scrimping Irish parents, brothers, and sisters, sending money they could ill afford in reply to begging letters from unsuccessful offspring in some New World.

How much grief was shown at the departure of so many able-bodied persons from Ireland? In the letters to hand, not much was shown on the part of the emigrants themselves. The real sense of grief was evinced by those who stayed home, for they experienced the loss of loved ones without having the compensation of new opportunities. Elizabeth McCleland of Dunronan, County Londonderry, wrote to her daughter Ann in October 1840:

> ... [I] suffered after you went away, grieving night and day about you. I hoped you would have perhaps rued and changed

your mind, when you would go to Liverpool, but alas to my sorrow you went on leaving me ... I am now so strong in body, and enterprising in spirit ... that if you see the place would answer me, that I would readily and fearlessly undertake to go to you, but if the place don't answer me I can live at home and you might yet come to see me in your native land ... As soon as possible write to me everything about you, both by sea and land, how you are fixed and if you met with friends since you left me. Oh, I have a vast enquiries to make, but your own good sense will direct you to write as fully and satisfactorily to us as you can.[29]

Doubtlessly, many emigrants regretted for a time their decision to leave home, but those feelings are expressed in the surviving letters in a very muted form. For example, in 1905 Hugh Rea wrote from Otago to his brother-in-law in Seaford, County Down, enquiring about economic conditions at home. Clearly, he was considering a return:

When you write you mention what rent is charged for the labourers cottage in Ireland and how much land is in with the cottage and what wages is paid in Ireland per day or per week and how many hours you work in each day; the wages in this country is good but in a great many cases you cannot get steady employment so that when you calculate your earnings for the year it comes to be a very small average; in fact I know that the[re] are hundreds of people in this country that came here 20 or 30 years ago and if the[y] could pay their passage to thire natife country they would to tomorrah. You have no knowledge of how some people are situated here; the labouring class in particklar you would think it strange in Ireland to see working men traveling on the roads in 1/2 dozens carr[y]ing theire blankats and a little can in their hand to make thire tea together with a little bread in a bag slung on theire shoulder; if you were here you could see this every day in the year.[30]

Notice here that Rea's complaint was economic, not cultural. It was low wages and high prices that bothered him, not any sense of being lost in an alien land. In fact he stayed in New Zealand, where he died in 1916.

The most direct expression of regret in the correspondence that is to hand has nothing to do with leaving Ireland, but with the writer's not having applied himself while still at home. "My time for reading and study of any kind is rather limited," J.N. Armstrong, a new farmer and part-time militia officer, wrote to his sister in Dublin. "A settler's life is not favourable for the pursuit of knowledge. I often regret that I did not give my mind a little more up to it when it was unoccupied with other matters; however, I know whom to blame for my not doing so and it is certainly neither mother nor any of you; in other words, no one but myself."[31]

If there is one dominant quality that runs through the surviving emigrant letters from New Zealand, it is their matter-of-fact tone. These are practical letters written by practical people. They contain lots of information on day-to-day concerns; affection is expressed for relatives and friends at home, but grief, depression, and hyper-emotionality of any sort are absent. The flat, reasonably self-confident tone of J.N. Armstrong as he waited in 1865 to see if he would be able to obtain a block of Taranaki land is representative. "I shall be glad to get anything to do rather than remaining stagnating any longer, although for some months it is not likely to be pleasant work," he wrote home to Dublin. "Still there will be something to look forward to and with that one can rub through a great deal."[32]

(IV)

Where did these matter-of-fact people come from in Ireland? How many were single? How many had families? What was their economic background?

For most destinations in the Irish diaspora, one cannot answer such questions, because of the poor quality of the historical records. However, for New Zealand, there is a window. This is provided by the ships' registers of the "assisted immigrants" who came to New Zealand during the "Vogel scheme" of the 1870s and 1880s. The government of New Zealand, having put good money into helping these people migrate to New Zealand, kept better records than it otherwise did.

We can use the year 1876 as a sample year.[33] That is a good year to chose because it was during the midst of the high era of immigration into New Zealand and because the shipping records are more complete for 1876 than for any other year in the nineteenth century. Assisted immigrants comprised the overwhelming majority of migrants to New Zealand at this time, and included the middle classes and persons of means who paid their own passage. The chief skewing in our sample year occurs through the exclusion from the data of those persons who came to New Zealand after staying for a time in Australia. We have direct information on 2,191 Irish persons who sailed from the British Isles to New Zealand in 1876.

For Irish migrants to New Zealand there were four basic strategies and the migrants sorted themselves out into distinct groups associated with each one. One came (a) as part of a family with children, or (b) as a member of a childless couple, or (c & d) as a single person, male or female. Married migrants (including those without children) were older than the unmarried. The average age of married men and women migrants from Ireland was above thirty, while single men and women were on average twenty-two or twenty-three years old.

TABLE 16

Average Age of Assisted Irish Migrants, 1876
(N=2, 191)

Male heads of household travelling with spouses.	31.0
Females travelling with spouses.	28.3
Male heads of household travelling without spouses.	34.9
Male heads of household travelling with no other adult.	36.1
Single men.	22.5
Single women.	22.4

Source: Derived from *National Archives of New Zealand, IM/15*, pp. 260-86.

Strikingly, more than one-third of the Irish married couples (34.4 percent) had no children. Those that did have children had fairly large families: an average of 3.23 children per Irish immigrant couple, as compared to the average of 2.8 children per couple for all assisted immigrants with children. In one sense, migrating with children was a handicap. Given the social practices of the time, only the man was available for full-time employment and the woman for only casual jobs, such as taking in washing, doing mending, and the like. Thus, in the first year or two, the larger Irish families inevitably were a handicap. With time, however, they turned to being a benefit. If the family continued in wage labour, the children as they became adolescents could be sent out to earn money. And, if the family acquired a holding of land, then the children became part of the economic unit, at first doing small jobs and eventually taking on adult farm tasks. The point here is that Irish married couples had two very different strategies of migration, depending on whether or not just the male or both the male and female would be wage earners. Each strategy made sense, but each demanded a very different set of behaviours in the new land.

TABLE 17

Family Attachments of Assisted Irish Migrants, 1876
(N=2, 191)

	No.	%
Male heads of household travelling with spouses.	186	8.5
Females travelling with spouses.	186	8.5
Male heads of household travelling without spouses.	7	0.3
Female heads of household travelling with no other adult.	15	0.7
Children, travelling with adults.	465	21.2
Single men.	890	40.6
Single women.	442	20.2
(Sub-total, unmarried adults.)	(1,332	60.8)
Total	2,191	100.0

Source: Derived from *NANZ, IM/15*, pp. 260-86.

Most immigrants, as Table 17 indicates, were single. The high proportion of unattached persons, especially young men, explains in large part why the Irish immigrants had a reputation for being noisy, mobile and frequently troublesome. Those are characteristics that have nothing directly to do with being Irish and a lot to do with being single, particularly single and male.

Most of the Irish migrants were unskilled, having been in the homeland either farm labourers or general unskilled labourers. This held true for both married and unmarried persons. However, as Table 18 indicates the skill levels of

TABLE 18

Occupation of Adult Male Assisted Migrants from Ireland, 1876
(N=1, 083)

| | Heads of Household | | Single Males | |
	No.	%	No.	%
Labourer (undefined)	22	11.4	108	12.2
Domestic servant	2	1.0	5	0.6
Farm servant and agric. labourer	104	53.9	626	70.3
Skilled farm labourer	34	17.6	96	10.8
Farmer	10	5.2	8	0.9
Artisan and semi-skilled	19	9.9	42	4.7
White collar	0	0	1	0.1
Army, navy, merch. marine	1	0.5	0	0
Capitalist	0	0	0	0
Gentry	1	0.5	1	0.1
None of the above	0	0	1	0.1
No information	0	0	2	0.2
Totals	193	100.0	890	100.0

Source: Derived from *NANZ, IM/15*, pp. 260-86.

married men tended to be slightly higher than those of single men. So, one had a set of overlapping disjunctures amongst Irish migrant males: one group consisting of very young single men, almost universally unskilled, the other comprised of married men mostly in their thirties, with a slightly higher occupational skill level.

Most Irish women of adult age among the migrants were single. Because, under the custom of the time, women who travelled with their husbands were not recorded as having a trade or profession, we have less information on women than on men. Table 19 indicates the occupations of Irish single female migrants and also includes the relatively small number of women (widows and unmarried mothers) who migrated to New Zealand as heads of their own households. Basically, the Irish female migrant was (by the definitions of the era) unskilled.

In choosing 1876 as our sample year for examining the profile of Irish migrants to New Zealand, we are in rhythm with the historical records: that is the year in which the Registrar General for Ireland began keeping accurate statistics about the geographic origin of every person who migrated from Ireland by way of an Irish port. These records were kept until Partition in 1920. In a sense, even these figures for 1876-1920 are a sample, rather than a complete data set, for people migrating to New Zealand from ports outside of Ireland and from Australia are not included. Still, a reasonable suggestion is that the persons who went directly to New Zealand from Irish ports were not fundamentally different from those who went via other ports, and so the information collected by the Registrar General for Ireland is probably representative of the entire larger group. As Table 20 indicates, there were two very different geographic foci of Irish migration to New Zealand: Ulster and Munster (together with its neighbouring county of Galway). Munster was undergoing a "class collapse" in the last quarter of the nineteenth century. As the subdivision of farms sharply diminished, the landless agricultural labourers virtually ceased to exist as a class. They migrated to Dublin, Great Britain, and overseas. The band of single males that we observed in the 1876 data must have been the sons of small tenant farmers, young lads who, with no hope of acquiring enough land in Ireland to support a family, decided to chance life elsewhere. The flow of migration from the south and west of Ireland diminished radically after 1891, when assisted passages ceased. This indirectly confirms the inference that the bulk of the assisted migrants from Ireland had been poor landless labourers.

TABLE 19

**Occupations of Adult Females from Ireland,
Assisted Migrants, 1876 (N=457)**

	Heads of Household		Single Females	
	No.	%	No.	%
Servant (undefined)	6	40.0	194	43.9
Domestic servant	5	33.3	150	33.9
Farm servant and agric. labourer	0	0	18	4.1
Skilled farm labourer	1	6.7	59	13.4
Farmer	0	0	0	0
Artisan and semi- skilled	2	13.3	4	0.9
White collar	0	0	9	2.0
Army, navy, merch. marine	0	0	0	0
Capitalist	1	6.7	0	0
Gentry	0	0	0	0
None of the above	0	0	0	0
No information	0	0	8	1.8
Totals	15	100.0	442	100.0

Source: Derived from *NANZ, IM/15*, pp. 260-86.

TABLE 20

**Geographic Origin of Natives of Ireland who
Emigrated to New Zealand, from Irish Ports,
1876-1920, Inclusive**

	1876-90	1891-1900	1901-10	1911-20	Total
Province of Ulster					
Antrim	1,573	97	428	402	2,500
Armagh	413	15	37	23	488
Cavan	397	32	23	13	465
Donegal	288	6	40	36	370
Down	745	53	188	136	1,122
Fermanagh	263	11	14	14	302
Londonderry	843	43	135	97	1,118
Monaghan	248	12	31	11	302
Tyrone	746	35	50	66	897
Sub-total: Ulster	5,516	304	946	798	7,564
Province of Leinster					
Carlow	78	15	11	10	114
Dublin	335	47	25	6	413
Kildare	55	14	9	4	82
Kilkenny	331	10	14	15	370
King's	127	22	5	6	160
Longford	77	5	6	2	90
Louth	17	1	3	8	29
Meath	98	7	3	0	108
Queen's	87	10	6	8	111
Westmeath	102	13	3	0	118
Wexford	95	14	26	30	165
Wicklow	97	10	5	4	116
Sub-total: Leinster	1,499	168	116	93	1,876

Irish Diaspora

TABLE 20 (Continued)

	1876-90	1891-1900	1901-10	1911-20	Total
Province of Munster					
Clare	1,682	46	15	8	1,751
Cork	1,167	62	27	73	1,329
Kerry	1,308	86	24	33	1,451
Limerick	1,252	41	15	5	1,313
Tipperary	1,219	36	20	16	1,291
Waterford	397	23	37	15	472
Sub-total: Munster	7,025	294	138	150	7,607
Province of Connacht					
Galway	743	33	1	1	778
Leitrim	88	8	3	4	103
Mayo	100	10	5	1	116
Roscommon	323	14	1	0	338
Sligo	100	10	4	0	114
Sub-total: Connacht	1,354	75	14	6	1,449
Total	15,394	841	1,214	1,047	18,496

Sources: Compiled from: *Emigration statistics of Ireland for the year 1876*, p. 12, [C1700], H.C. 1877. *1877*, p.12, [C2066], H.C. 1878, lxxvii. *1878*, p. 12, [C2221], H.C. 1878-9, lxxv. *1879*, p. 12 [C2501], H.C. 1880, lxxvi. *1880*, p. 12, [C2828], H.C. 1881, xciv. *1881*, p. 12, [C3170], H.C. 1882, lxxiv. *1882*, p. 12, [C3489], H.C. 1883, lxxvi. *1883*, p. 12, [C3899], H.C. 1884, lxxxv. *1884*, p. 12, [C4303], H.C. 1884-5, lxxxv. *1885*, p. 12, [C4660], H.C. 1886, lxxi. *1886*, p. 12, [C4967], H.C. 1887, lxxxix. *1887*, p. 12, [C5307], H.C. 1888, cvii. *1888*, p. 12, [C5647], H.C. 1889, lxxi. *1889*, p. 12, [C6010], H.C. 1890, lxxix. *1890*, p. 12 [C6295], H.C. 1890-1, xcii. *1891*, p. 12, [C6679], H.C. 1892, lxxxviii. *1892*, p. 12, [C6977], H.C. 1893-4, cii. *1893*, p. 12, [C7288], H.C. 1893-4, cii. *1894*, p. 12, [C7647], H.C. 1895, cvii. *1895*, p. 12, [C7959], H.C. 1896, xciii. *1896*, p. 12, [C8366], H.C. 1897, xcix. *1897*, p. 12, [C8740], H.C. 1898, ciii. *1898*, p. 12, [C9193], H.C. 1899, cvii. *1899*, p. 12, [Cd111], H.C. 1900, cii. *1900*, p. 12, [Cd531], H.C. 1901, lxxxviii. *1901*, p. 12, [Cd976], H.C. 1902, cxvi, pt ii. *1902*, p. 12, [Cd1489], H.C. 1903, lxxxii. *1903*, p. 13, [Cd2030], H.C. 1904, cvi. *1904*, p. 13, [Cd2467], H.C. 1905, xcviii. *1905*, p. 13, [Cd2868], H.C. 1906, p. 13, [Cd3376], H.C. 1907, xcvii. *1907*, p. 13, [Cd3987], H.C. 1908, cxxii. *1908*, p. 13, [C4550], H.C. 1909, ciii, 169. *1909*, p. 15, [Cd5088], H.C. 1910, cix, 479. *1910*, p. 15, [Cd5607], H.C. 1911, lx. *1911*, p. 15, [Cd6131], H.C. 1912-13, cv. *1912*, p. 15, [Cd6727], H.C. 1913, lv. *1913*, p. 15, [Cd7313], H.C. 1914, lxix. *1914*, p. 15, [Cd7883], H.C. 1914-16, lxxx. *1915*, p. 15, [Cd8230], H.C. 1916, xxxii. *1916*, p. 13, [Cd8520], H.C. 1917-18, xxxvii. *1917*, p. 10, [Cd9013], H.C. 1918, xxv. *1918*, p. 10, [Cmd77], H.C. 1919, li. *1919*, p. 5, [Cmd721], H.C. 1920, l. *1920*, p. 5, [Cmd1414], H.C. 1921, xli.

The Ulster stream was quite different, although one should not overstate the contrast. After the period of assisted passages, Ulster became the largest source of Irish migrants to New Zealand. This does not mean that most of the migrants were Presbyterians or even Protestant. (Remember that the largest single denomination in Ulster was Roman Catholic). The loading of New Zealand migration towards Ulster migrants after 1890 is a complex matter and does not simply imply a transfer of Ulster-Scots culture to a New World.

What we have in New Zealand, then, is something old and something new. The something old is that the New Zealand migration followed a pattern that we already know: it was dead centre normal in the spectrum of characteristics of Irish migrants in the diaspora. The something new is that we have learned that behind the tallies of migrants lie at least four major distinct emigration strategies: those of single females, of single males, of married couples with children and of married couples without children. These are not merely historical categories. They represent different groups in terms of age, and of their skill profile, as well as whether or not they had partners and whether or not they had dependants. How they approached their lives in their New Worlds was heavily conditioned by these matters.

(V)

One more set of new things that we would like to learn: how did the Irish immigrants stack up against the rest of the New Zealand population? How well did the entire multigenerational ethnic group do? And were there observable handicaps among the Catholics that would make one think that their Catholic cultural background was a handicap?

To answer these questions, one needs to wait until the Irish migrants had time to settle into their new homeland. This is crucial, because too often in studies of the Irish diaspora, things that are actually a function of the relative recency-of-arrival of the migrants are mistaken as being ethnic characteristics. By the time of World War I, such recency-effects had worn off and any differences between the Irish-born and the rest of the population were real. Look first at the urban-rural breakdown for 1921 for the entire New Zealand population:[34]

Entire population	56%/44%
All foreign-born persons	62%/38%
English-born	64%/36%
Scottish-born	59%/41%
Irish-born (includes both Catholics and Protestants)	55%/45%
Native-born New Zealanders	54%/46%

Never mind that the New Zealand definition of urban was extremely broad and that it included large areas of bush within town boundaries: the same definition of urban and rural held for all groups, so comparisons are valid. The obvious point is that the Irish immigrants settled in the same urban-rural pattern as did everyone else, so that it is highly unlikely that they were ghettoized. This probability becomes a virtual certainty when one examines the settlement-by-region data for 1916.[35]

Region	Distribution of Entire Population	Distribution of the Irish-born
Auckland	28.1	27.2
Taranaki	5.1	4.1
Hawke's Bay	4.9	5.3
Wellington	20.4	17.7
Marlborough	1.5	1.3
Nelson	4.4	3.5
Westland	1.3	2.1
Canterbury	16.3	20.1
Otago	12.0	12.3
Southland	5.4	5.9
Other	0.6	0.5
	100.0	100.0

The clear inference is that the Irish immigrants were not forced by their cultural background to arrange themselves in tight communities that protected them against the larger society. In New Zealand, the Irish immigrants were virtually typical of the entire population in settlement pattern. Of course, there were exceptional areas, small towns and city neighbourhoods that had an over-representation of the Irish migrants, but in fact the same observation could be made about every immigrant group in New Zealand. These over-representations should not be confused with ghettoes. The overall distribution of the Irish immigrants is clear and its implications undeniable. The pattern is based on evidence provided not by a few anecdotal references, but by every Irish immigrant living in New Zealand in the years surveyed.

Unfortunately, the New Zealand census authorities never collected information on the various multigenerational ethnic groups. However, because between 1870 and 1940, the overwhelming (indeed, almost the sole) source of adherents to the Catholic church consisted of Irish immigrants and their descendants, we have a *surrogate* for the multigenerational Irish Catholic ethnic group, namely the census category "Catholic." So, let us examine the occupational profile of the Catholics in 1921, keeping in mind that we are viewing the occupational profile of the Irish Catholic male ethnic group:[36]

Occupational	Catholics	Entire male population%
Professional	4.72	4.78
Domestic service	2.13	1.43
Commercial	6.94	9.39
Transport and communications	9.97	8.45
Industrial Primary producers (mostly farmers)	14.38	15.82
Other	22.01	22.90
Dependent upon others for livelihood (mostly children)	4.39	4.11
	35.46	33.12
Total	100.00	100.00

Notice that the Irish Catholics as an ethnic group had an occupational profile so similar to that of the general population that one has to stretch hard to find significant differences. Especially important is the fact that the most common occupation of Irish Catholic men was farming, just as it was for the entire population. These data are systematic and they cover every adult male in the population, so they cannot be treated as accidental. What they suggest is that there was nothing in the cultural background of the Catholic migrants from Ireland to New Zealand that prevented them and their children from prospering as much as anyone else in New Zealand, a country that was largely agricultural and more of a frontier society than was the USA in the same time period. Irish Catholics could, and did, survive and prosper on an open agricultural frontier.

That is the value of using New Zealand as our first case study. It is a clean and easily comprehended laboratory that tells us something important about the Irish diaspora in the post-Famine years and most particularly from the 1870s onward: that neither Irishness nor Catholicity can be viewed as impediments to success in a New World.

Chapter 4

Australia: Coming Attractions

(I)

If there were a Coming Attractions board for studies of the Irish diaspora, it would read, "Watch for Australian Developments." My prediction is that in the next decade Australian historical writing will produce a major breakthrough relating not only to the Irish in Australia, but worldwide. This is for two reasons. One of these is that although the group of historians working on the history of the Irish in Australia is not large, the quality of their work is extremely high. The basic framework for modern Irish-Australian historiography has been established by the prodigious research of Patrick O'Farrell.[1] No other historian of Irish settlement and evolution in any diaspora country has done as much, or as at high a level, as has O'Farrell. Recently, the most gifted scholar of Irish emigration, David Fitzpatrick, has focused his attention on Australia. In addition, two other outstanding scholars, Eric Richards and Richard Reid have each begun to produce major work.

This ties in with a second fact: Australia, alone among the nations to which Irish migrants moved in significant numbers, has records of individual migrants that permit the tracing of large numbers to their precise home backgrounds in Ireland. This is extraordinarily promising. The situation for every other country is that we have fragmentary records of the emigrants as they make their way out of Ireland and, in the new homelands, we have records (of varying quality) of immigrants getting off the boat and dispersing. In most cases, these records are in the form of aggregate numbers, although in a few instances (Canada being the most important of these), there is solid documentation of the life-courses of individual Irish migrants in their new homeland. The trouble is, that the people we see making their way towards emigration ports and the individuals we observe getting off the boat are not the same. Only for Australia is there the possibility of trans-oceanic linkage. This linkage offers the possibility of actually recreating for large numbers of individuals a collective biography, one that starts with the home parish, religion, occupation, and family situation of each migrant and follows each one as he or she leaves Ireland, then continues to chart the life of the migrant as he or she settles in Australia. This is possible because most emigration from the United Kingdom in the nineteenth century (including that from Ireland) to Australia was governmentally assisted. For example, 79 percent of those who landed in Sydney between 1838 and 1864 had government assistance.[2]

Because the Australian colonial governments were spending money, they kept very good records, better even than those the government of New Zealand collected for the 1870s, and they, as we have seen, were very useful indeed. Studies of the Australian records now are in train. When they are complete, literally tens of thousands of Irish migrants to Australia will have been traced to their point of origin in Ireland and for the first time true trans-oceanic social history on a large scale will become possible for Irish migrants.[3]

Even now the history of the Irish in Australia suggests some crucial points about the Irish diaspora. Australia is an even more useful laboratory than is New Zealand. Like New Zealand, it received a group of migrants who (with the exception of those who were forcibly transported during the convict period) were in the centre of the spectrum of Irish migrants as far as age, occupation, religion, and gender distributions were concerned. As was the case with New Zealand, the Irish in Australia were a "charter group," which means that although they faced some discrimination it was relatively minor and its impact was limited by the fact that they arrived early and in large numbers. What makes Australia even more revealing than New Zealand as a social

Map 3

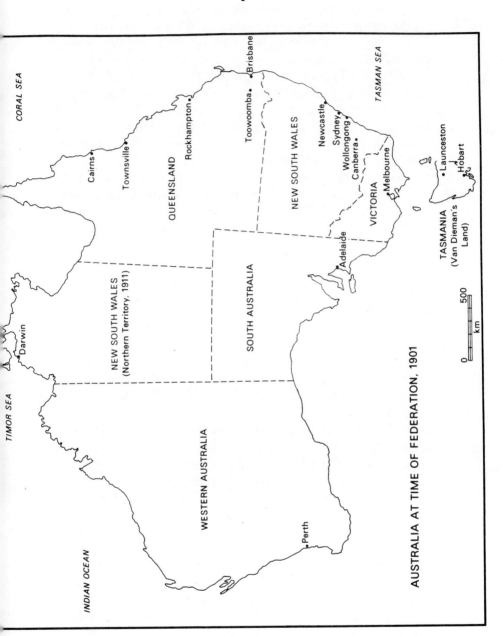

AUSTRALIA AT TIME OF FEDERATION, 1901

laboratory is that a significant proportion of the Irish ethnic group had its origins in the pre-Famine era. The great bulk of the Irish migration to Australia occurred in the years 1788-1901, so that one can sum up its collective nature through the use of early twentieth-century social data. The critical point is that the picture we draw at the end of the Victorian age is of a population that is comparable to that of the USA or of Canada, in having its foundation set down before the Great Famine of mid-nineteenth century.

Nevertheless, amongst the Australian historical literature, one must move critically. In one of his tart and memorable phrases, Patrick O'Farrell noted that until recently the history of the Irish in Australia "had been particularly bedeviled by what happens when historians fail to do their job: the growth in the place of serious scholarship of myths, prejudices, bigotries, stupidities, hagiography and fables."[4] What he had in mind in particular was a widespread misreading of the character of the Irish during the convict period and, in later eras, an emphasis upon "larikanism" (that is, upon the bad behaviour of "wild colonial boys" of whom Ned Kelly became the emblem). In contrast, as Geoffrey Bolton points out, good recent scholarship has rejected the idea that the Irish were an exceptional or a difficult group in Australian history. "The Irish in Australia," Bolton wrote in 1986, "are seen not as a branch of Australian history distinct from the mainstream nor as an advertisement for assimilation, nor as an aberrant element requiring explanation and perhaps apology, but as examples of social processes which may be identified in other societies.[5]

Because the image of the convict is such a potent one, two caveats must quickly be made. The first of these is that the Irish were not a disproportionate segment of the convict population. Quite the opposite: they were under-represented. They comprised roughly 25 percent of the criminals sent to the penal colonies; this at a time when the Irish share of the United Kingdom's population was roughly 30 percent.[6] Secondly, despite the popular mythology in the Irish homeland (found to this day in school texts in the Irish Republic), the Irish felons who were transported to Australia were not in substantial numbers political prisoners. Actually, from 1788 to 1853 (when transportation to the eastern Australian colonies was abandoned), fewer than 600 —

about 1¼ percent to 1½ percent — of the Irish felons had been convicted of political crimes.[7] Of course, it is possible to view all crime as a form of social protest against oppression, in which case all of those transported were political prisoners. But if one eschews that extreme doctrine, it seems more appropriate to view the overwhelming majority of Irish criminals as just that, criminals: thieves, highway robbers, the habitually violent, and minor felons (pickpockets and the like) who fell afoul of a harsh legal code.

What makes the story of the early Irish in Australia complicated is not merely that the treatment and status of the convicts varied considerably from colony to colony and according to the temper of the head of each colonial administration; nor that the emancipation of convicts who had served their time was uneven. The great complication is that free (that is, non-criminal) settlers began migrating to Australia at a very early date and therefore a society evolved in which the free community intertwined with the society of the convicts (many of whom worked for the free settlers). Ultimately, the two societies were fused together.

Estimates are that from 1788 to 1853, about 40,000 Irish criminals were shipped directly from Ireland to Australia. Another 8,000 Irish men and women were sent to penal exile in the Australian colonies from courts in England and Scotland.[8] (It is this group of persons, the 48,000 Irish prisoners, that provides a potentially salient comparison to the group of involuntary exiles who in the same period were sent to the United States: the black slave population. It is a commentary on the endurance of racist attitudes in western societies that the former criminals were assimilated for the most part by mid-nineteenth century, while the descendants of the American slave population experienced legal segregation until the middle of the twentieth century.)

Alongside this stream of involuntary Irish felons came voluntary settlers in ever-growing numbers. The colonies of New South Wales and the Port Phillip District (later renamed "Victoria") received approximately 12,000 Irish persons between 1837 and 1850.[9] In New South Wales in 1846, there were 47,457 Irish-born persons resident,[10] and in Victoria in 1857 there were 65,264.[11] Given that the total number of Irish convicts for the years 1788-1853 was

48,000 and that many of the convicts were long dead by the time of the 1846 and 1857 enumerations, it is clear that well before the middle of the nineteenth century most of the Irish-born population of the Australian colonies was composed of free immigrants, not convicts or former convicts.

If the existence of the convict strand in the background of the Irish ethnic group in Australia distinguished the Irish-Australians from their counterparts elsewhere in the Irish diaspora, a second characteristic made them different from their counterparts in North America and Great Britain: relatively few had their roots in the Famine. An estimated 15,000 Irish migrants came to Victoria during the six years, 1846-52.[12] That is not an insignificant number, but it is not anything like the huge swell experienced elsewhere. The real surge in Irish migration came instead during the Australia gold rush of the early 1850s. During the fifties, an estimated 84,000 Irish migrants arrived in the Australian colonies. The great majority of these migrants, mostly gold-seekers (an estimated four-fifths), stayed on to become permanent settlers.[13]

One other characteristic distinguished the Irish migrants to Australia from those to North America: during the nineteenth century, the era of their great move to Australia, most received some form of assistance from Australian colonial sources. The first governmental schemes of assisted migration were introduced in 1831 to New South Wales and to Van Dieman's Land. Thereafter a variety of schemes evolved (over a dozen by the end of the century), the details of which varied from colony to colony, as well as over time. After 1856, when the restrictions of the United Kingdom's Colonial Office were virtually removed, each of the four main colonies (New South Wales, Tasmania, Victoria, and South Australia) developed its own scheme and some had more than one (Queensland, when it was formed out of New South Wales in 1859 immediately became another strong competitor for migrants). Although assistance schemes were sharply reduced in the 1890s, those targeted on special groups continued as late as the 1970s.[14]

What proportion of Australia's total immigration in the nineteenth century was governmentally assisted? The available statistics are confusing. Recent studies indicate that assisted migrants composed 64 percent of all immigrants up to 1850, 34 percent in the gold rush era and 51 percent from 1860-1900. This clashes with contemporary official statistics compiled for New South Wales (the biggest recipient of immigrants), which state that between 1838 and 1864, the assisted migrants comprised 79 percent of the inflow.[15] What is clear, however, is that during the nineteenth century most immigrants were assisted by governmental funds.

It is also clear that the Irish were especially quick to understand the mechanisms of assisted migration and to use them. Although the Irish were only about 30 percent of the total population of the British Isles, they made up 52 percent of the assisted migrants to New South Wales and to the Port Phillip district (later Victoria) in the period 1837-50.[16] If one takes the time period 1847-72, the Irish made up 35 percent of the total assisted migrants to Australia.[17] During and immediately after the Famine, four-fifths of the Irish migrants were subsidized.[18] In 1872, when the United Kingdom Emigration Commissioners surrendered their powers to the U.K. Board of Trade, and thus a summary accounting was conducted, it was stated that up to that year, 140,000 Irish migrants had been assisted to the Australian colonies, in addition to the convicts who had been sent before mid-century.[19]

A question naturally arises: what does the fact that most Irish migrants were assisted by governmental grants indicate about the character of the migration? In the first place, undoubtedly the mechanics of assisted migration made for a somewhat more localized origin in Ireland for the migrants than otherwise would have been the case. That is because the caprice of emigration agents could lead them to concentrate their efforts on certain locales. Also, localization occurred because of the "nomination" schemes that operated during most of the nineteenth century, under which a person who had migrated to Australia could obtain reduced-price passages for specific individuals in the homeland. Chain migration to Australia, therefore, was especially strong. This means that many of the men and women who appear in the statistics as being unattached single migrants were not in fact moving into a foreign void, but usually were going to destinations in Australia where they had relatives or at least friends.

The hardest question is: what did the prevalence of assisted migration do to the collective social background of the Irish migrants to Australia? David Fitzpatrick has suggested that it "greatly broadened the social spectrum of potential settlers by reducing the cost of transit."[20] This is certainly true, for the fare to Australia was three to five times the fare to the USA and twenty-fold more expensive than a ticket across the Irish Sea to Great Britain.

Eric Richards has gone farther and has suggested that "although we are not yet in a position to make systematic comparisons of people going to North America and Australasia, it is likely that a higher proportion of those coming south were broadly proletarian in origin."[21] This idea — that the Irish migrants to Australia were more "plebian" (in Richard's phrase) than those who went to other destinations — is highly debatable, as Richards himself recognizes. The point to made here, however, is that the Irish migrants to Australia should not be thought of as having been privileged, or as having been sorted out by the various governmental authorities as being of an unusually high standard of occupational skill or of "better" socio-economic background.

If by virtue of its excellent records on individual migrants, Australia is the future cornucopia of Irish diaspora studies, at present it is a tantalus. One reason is that, surprisingly, there are no solid aggregate flow figures on permanent migrants from Ireland as they arrived year-by-year in Australia. In part, this is because the Australian colonies were not fused into a single state until 1 January 1901. But even after that, migration records were very slackly kept, and not until 1906 was a Commonwealth of Australia Bureau of Census and Statistics established. The new bureau immediately stirred about, rather like a busy school prefect strutting about the school yard, but in fact, it achieved little. The bureau honoured two pre-1901 precedents, much to its detriment: (1) every person leaving ship in an Australian port was counted as an immigrant, and (2) statistics upon nationality and upon place-of-birth employed categories under which the British Isles were defined as a single country, and thus the Irish, Scots, Welsh, and English were not separately tallied.[22]

So, for information on the migrant flow, we must turn to the other side of the process, the Irish shore. Here we have two sets of estimates. Those shown in Table 21 were compiled in the 1950s by officials of the Republic of Ireland.

TABLE 21

**Government of Ireland Estimates of Irish
Emigation to Australia and New Zealand
1841-1925**

Year	Estimated Number
1841-50	22,825
1851-60	101,541
1861-70	82,917
1871-80	61,946
1881-90	55,476
1891-1900	11,448
1901-10	11,885
1911-20	15,429
1921-25	10,355

Note: The figures for 1921-25 are for Australia only.

Source: Commission on Emigration and other Population Problems, 1948-54, Reports (Dublin: Stationery Office, 1954), Table 93, p. 124.

Those in Table 22 were put together at about the same time by demographic statisticians of the United Kingdom. Both of these estimates attempt to make corrections for the various sorts of under-counting that occur in nineteenth-century tallies. Both lump the migrants to Australia and those to New Zealand in a single total. That is inconvenient, because although it is certain that over the long haul the bulk of these persons went to Australia rather than to New Zealand, at certain times (such as in some years in the 1870s), most probably went to New Zealand. Therefore the figures are a rough indication of the flow characteristics of the Irish migrants to Australia, but not much more than that. (Incidentally, the reader will note that the figures from Irish governmental sources and those from United Kingdom sources, while following the same wave pattern, do not agree in detail; this is yet another instance of the vexing and age-old question, "Who is right, the British or the Irish?") No matter which source one uses, it is clear that the flood tide of Irish migration to Australia began to ebb sharply after 1880 — as did the Irish outflow, worldwide-and in the twentieth century it became a trickle.[23]

One way to escape from the untrustworthy statistics on migrant flow is to step back and to take a series of still pictures and then to infer what happened between snapshots. This, effectively, is what one does if one assembles the information on the number of persons of Irish birth who were living in Australia at various moments in the past. Table 23, which is essentially a series of snapshots, tell us three things. First, that the actual number of the Irish-born (that is, Irish immigrants) living in Australia reached its height in the last decade of the nineteenth century and declined fairly sharply after that. Secondly, as a percentage of the entire Australian population, the Irish immigrants were at their peak at the end of the goldrush (assuming that one sets aside the early convict period when everyone was an immigrant and when the Irish were about one-quarter of the entire population). And, thirdly, at the end of the third quarter of the nineteenth century, the Irish-born were roughly one-quarter of the foreign-born, a proportion that declined from the 1880s onward as Irish migration tapered off.

TABLE 22

United Kingdom Estimates of Irish
Emigration to Australia and New Zealand, 1830-1935

Year	No.	Year	No.	Year	No.	Year	No.
1830	0	1860	6,345	1890	2,794	1920	2,066
1831	135	1861	5,642	1891	2,539	1921	2,200
1832	0	1862	12,402	1892	1,732	1922	1,934
1833	523	1863	17,390	1893	932	1923	1,689
1834	0	1864	14,936	1894	725	1924	2,699
1835	0	1865	10,920	1895	616	1925	3,583
1836	822	1866	7,973	1896	458	1926	4,744
1837	419	1867	4,084	1897	633	1927	3,464
1838	1,060	1868	3,141	1898	916	1928	2,342
1839	1,703	1869	3,260	1899	1,398	1929	1,576
1840	0	1870	3,169	1900	1,499	1930	925
1841	4,420	1871	2,015	1901	1,239	1931	342
1842	937	1872	2,066	1902	1,181	1932	277
1843	509	1873	3,471	1903	975	1933	323
1844	520	1874	8,976	1904	1,087	1934	286
1845	0	1875	8,261	1905	863	1935	340
1846	0	1876	7,064	1906	948		
1847	0	1877	7,403	1907	888		
1848	0	1878	8,553	1908	1,246		
1849	0	1879	8,198	1909	1,622		
1850	0	1880	5,949	1910	1,836		
1851	0	1881	4,545	1911	3,553		
1852	367	1882	6,704	1912	1,894		
1853	12,746	1883	10,088	1913	2,802		
1854	16,202	1884	8,336	1914	2,365		
1855	15,500	1885	6,284	1915	1,024		
1856	8,359	1886	5,072	1916	532		
1857	15,426	1887	5,251	1917	79		
1858	9,356	1888	3,585	1918	58		
1859	8,254	1889	2,817	1919	362		

Source: Carrier and Jeffery, Table D/F/G(1), pp. 95-96.

TABLE 23

**The Irish-Born in Australia
1861-1981**

Year	Irish-born	% of total population	% of foreign-born
1861	177,405	15.4	24.5
1871	213,765	12.9	27.7
1881	214,771	9.5	26.0
1891	229,156	7.2	22.7
1901	185,807	4.9	21.6
1911	141,331	3.2	18.5
1921	106,274	2.0	12.6
1933	79,185	1.2	8.8
1947	45,066	0.6	6.1
1954	47,844	0.5	3.7
1961	50,327	0.5	2.8
1971	63,902	0.5	2.5
1981	69,917	0.5	2.3

Source: Derived from Charles A. Price, "Immigration and Ethnic Origin," in Wray Vam Plew (ed.) *Australians, Historical Statistics* (Sydney: Fairfax, Syme and Weldon, 1987), pp. 8-9.

TABLE 24

Provincial Origins of Irish Migrants to Australia,
via Irish Ports, 1876-1920

Province	1876-80		1881-90		1891-1900		1901-10		1911-20		Total: 1876-1920	
	No.	% of total	No.	% of total	No.	% of total	No.	% of total	No.	% of total	No.	% of total
Ulster	3,562	21.0	9,010	23.1	1,458	17.1	1,611	33.5	1,974	48.7	17,615	24.1
Leinster	2,504	14.8	8,244	21.2	2,802	32.8	1,824	38.0	1,211	29.9	16,585	22.6
Munster	9,027	53.3	17,856	45.9	3,166	37.1	1,008	21.0	738	18.2	31,795	43.4
Connacht	1,848	10.9	3,820	9.8	1,105	13.0	359	7.5	131	3.2	7,263	9.9
Total	16,941	100.0	38,930	100.0	8,531	100.0	4,802	100.0	4,054	100.0	73,258	100.0

Where did the free (that is, non-convict) migrants come from in the Irish homeland? As with every nation that received many migrants, the answer is, from all over Ireland, but with specific concentrations. It is technically accurate to say that between the 1840s and the 1880s the largest group (but not the majority of migrants) came from the province of Munster.[24] In a sense, however, this is misleading. The Irish migrants to Australia were not concentrated in Munster in the way that the Irish migrants to the USA were; they were concentrated in the "midland" regions of Tipperary, Limerick, Clare, and Kilkenny, and in the Ulster border counties of Fermanagh, Cavan, and Tyrone.[25] This pattern stayed remarkably stable until the 1890s. In that decade Leinster origins became proportionately stronger, and for a time after the turn of the century, they became prepotent. Just before World War I, Ulster became the chief source of migrants. The sharp drop in numbers of Irish migrants after 1890, however, means that, overall, the Irish midlands were the place of origin of most migrants to Australia in the last century.

As part of their policy of not only peopling Australia, but "civilizing" it, Australian authorities made strenuous efforts to recruit women (this policy was not exclusive to Australia, and is discussed in more detail in Chapter Seven which deals with women in the Irish diaspora). Historians of Australian immigration are agreed that by mid-nineteenth century the male-female ratio was approaching a rough balance as far as the Irish immigrants were concerned. One historian reports that the male-female ratio at mid-century was 109:100.[26] By 1870, the gender ratio was almost even for the Irish-born, with the exception of South Australia, which had an excess of Irish women.[27]

This gender parity is the normal situation among Irish immigrants throughout most of the diaspora, but here one should add three curious sidebars. The first of these is that at the tail-end of the nineteenth century — from the late 1880s onwards — until the mid-1930s, the number of Irish female migrants dropped sharply as compared to that of the men. The following figures are for Australia and New Zealand combined, the great majority representing migrants to Australia:[28]

Years	Women per 100 men
1877-80	83
1881-90	87
1891-1900	68
1901-07	54
1908-12	52
1912-13	60
1914-19	not available
1920-24	64
1925-29	61
1930-36	95

I suspect that what happened was, first, that after the mid-1870s, the Australian colonial governments stopped recruiting so hard for women, since there were by that time enough women in Australian society to establish a stable population base and, second, that as the generosity of governmental assistance schemes was reduced (very sharply after 1890), young Irish women chose to go elsewhere.

A second sidebar has to do with a curious anomaly that appears in the first census of the Commonwealth of Australia, 1911. At that time the male-female ratio for the Irish-born individuals (who in the median case had arrived in the 1870s), was almost perfectly equal, as indeed it had been in 1901. This was an "improvement" (from the official viewpoint) from 1891, when the number had been 96 Irish-born females to every 100 Irish-born males.[29] There are, therefore, two seemingly conflicting facts, namely that (a) from the 1870s onwards Ireland sent to Australia close to the same number of Irish men and women, but that (b) the gender ratio of Irish-born came closer to equality each year. The only way to reconcile these is to suggest that the Irish-born males re-emigrated from Australia in higher proportions than did the females. In other words, Irish women migrants were more apt to stay permanently in Australia than were male migrants.

And a third curious fact: that although the Irish-born in 1911 had an almost perfectly equal gender ratio, this masked a very striking difference according to religious denomination. (This census was for 1911, but it should be understood that most of the persons it enumerated as Irish-born had arrived well before the end of the century, most before 1890). The Anglicans who had been born in Ireland showed a very slight excess of females over males (100.4/100.0) and the Catholics born in Ireland had a slightly greater excess of females (101.0/100.0). But among Irish-born Presbyterians, there was a very noteworthy excess of males over females (116 males to each 100 females).[30] For the Ulster-Scots, apparently, emigration to Australia was somewhat more likely to be a male-thing than for either the Anglo-Irish or the Catholics. Ironically, if the wild colonial boys were mostly surplus males, then there was a fair whack of allegedly-stolid Ulster Presbyterians among the hell raisers.

The religious affiliations of Irish migrants to Australia generally mirrored those of Irish society. The following figures deal with Irish-born persons living in Australia in 1911, most of them being migrants from the 1880s or earlier:[31]

Denomination	Percent of Irish-born
Catholic	71.3%
Anglican	14.1
Presbyterian	8.7
Other Protestant	5.3
Other	0.6

Earlier in the century, the figures had moved around somewhat. A tally of assisted migrants to New South Wales in 1844-45 found that the Catholic-Protestant breakdown was 54.5/45.5. The proportion for 1848-50 for New South Wales was 70/30 and that for Port Phillip (Victoria) was 65/35. Thereafter, the Catholic proportion rose, being 80.5 percent for Victoria for 1852-59 and 81.4 percent for New South Wales for 1866-69.[32] These figures were for assisted immigrants; probably Protestants were a somewhat larger proportion of immigrants who came by their own means.

Among the Protestants, a point worth observing is that Anglicans predominated more among the Irish migrants to Australia than they did in the Irish homeland. This is largely because the Ulster counties from which Australia drew most heavily (Tyrone, Fermanagh, and Armagh)[33] were those in which the Protestant population was mostly of Anglo-Irish, rather than of Ulster-Scots origin. (This is yet another illustration of the fact that it is erroneous to equate a body of migrants having Ulster origins with their being Ulster Presbyterians).

Crucially, a quantitative study of the Irish migration to New South Wales in the heavy years of 1848-70 reveals that although among assisted migrants Protestants were more apt than Catholics to be literate (63 percent as opposed to 42 percent), their occupational backgrounds in Ireland were virtually identical. The men, Protestant and Catholic alike, were mostly farm labourers or general unskilled labourers and the women were either farm or domestic servants.[34] Indeed, the entire Irish migrant group was similar to the base population in the old homeland: mostly unskilled labourers, but with an infusion of small farmers and a few gentry and capitalists. (Of course, I am here excluding the early convict population, which by definition was a deviant group). Of the assisted migrants to New South Wales and to Port Phillip district in the years 1837-50, 79 percent of those who hailed from Ulster, and 77 percent of those from Leinster, Munster, and Connacht combined, had been either agricultural labourers or unskilled labourers in the homeland.[35] (Because of the nature of nineteenth-century record keeping, these data are for males only.) In 1857, 79.7 percent of all Irish male migrants to Australia and New Zealand combined were labourers and in 1867 the proportion was 72.3 percent.[36] In 1912-13, the skill profile of Irish migrants to Australia and New Zealand combined was as follows:[37]

Commerce and professional	17.3%
Skilled Trades	14.2
Agriculture (mostly unskilled)	24.0
Other unskilled labourer	44.5
	100.0

What really stands out about the Irish migrants to Australia is seemingly a contradiction in terms: once the convict period was over, the Irish migrants were distinguished by their very ordinariness. They were good solid representatives of Irish migrants throughout the diaspora: neither overly skilled, nor overly proletarian, balanced in their gender ratio, and representative of the Protestant-Catholic proportions of the homeland. Good Irish people.

(II)

The triumph of those good ordinary Irish migrants was that they became good ordinary Australians. In a lapidary phrase, David Fitzpatrick has noted that the "Irish-Australians were unique in their ordinariness."[38]

One aspect of their ordinariness in Australia is that they headed for the countryside. That is what most European peasants in the nineteenth century did when they encountered a New World. Having been land-starved in Ireland, it is hardly surprising that, as Patrick O'Farrell observes, "from the beginning of Australian settlement the Irish exhibited a veritable obsession with the acquisition of land and livestock."[39] Thus, the settlement pattern of the Irish migrants in nineteenth- and early twentieth-century Australia "reflected the Irish gravitation towards rural areas and pursuits.[40]

This does not mean that they all went out to far frontiers (although many did). Rather, most settled in rural areas where the bush had already been beaten back and in which a rural market economy was developing.[41] The 1856 census of New South Wales showed that only 29 percent of the colony's Irish immigrants were living in Sydney or its suburbs. Twenty percent lived in country towns and 51 percent in rural or pastoral parts.[42] This predominantly rural pattern for New South Wales was replicated in Victoria, where the highest ratios of the Irish-born and of Roman Catholics were found in areas that were rural and agricultural.[43] This pattern held for a long time, well into the twentieth century.

The 1911 census, the first conducted for the Commonwealth of Australia as a federal unit, is particularly interesting on this point. In 1911, there were 139,434 Irish-born persons in the country. Of these, almost 80 percent had been in Australia for at least twenty years,[44] which means that they had come as part of the great nineteenth-century Irish diaspora. In 1911, the census authorities tallied each person's place of residence and noted whether or not they lived in one of the six main cities or their suburbs: Sydney,

Melbourne, Brisbane, Adelaide, Perth, and Hobart. By including in the tally the vast suburbs (parts of which still were bush), the authorities erred in the direction of classifying some predominantly rural areas as cities. Even so, only 41.6 percent of the Irish immigrants lived in metropolitan areas.[45] The smallest of these areas — Hobart and its suburbs — in 1911 had a population of only 18,487, so even these city dwellers were not living in great urban concentrations.

In order to keep this in context, note that despite the legend of the pervasive Australian bush, the population of Australia at the turn of the last century was one of the most urbanized in the New World[46] — yet, even so, the Irish-born did not have strong urban proclivities. In comparison to the general run of immigrants, the Irish-born in 1911 were less urban:[47]

Group	Percentage living in metropolitan areas and suburbs
All immigrants	44.4%
Irish-born immigrants	41.6
Entire population	38.0
Native-born Australians	36.7

Viewing the settlement pattern of the Irish immigrants to Australia, David Fitzpatrick has remarked on "the particular readiness" with which the Irish settlers grasped the opportunities open to them, "as shown by their comparative concentration in agricultural districts." This propensity to settle in agricultural areas, he suggests, was in part the result of there being plenty of marriageable Irish women among the Irish immigrants; and "still more influential, perhaps, was their predominantly rural background, which gave most Irish settlers knowledge of how to work the land not shared by their urban counterparts from England."[48]

Notice that last phrase. It suggests a very important fact: the Irish immigrants, by virtue of their rural experience, had an advantage in societies that were predominantly rural. This is not to say that the bulk of the Irish migrants, who had been for the most part rural labourers (in the case of the males) or farm or house servants (in the case of females) were sophisticated in the sense of having knowledge of the commercial agriculture of the time. What they had, however, were eyes that were used to watching crops and livestock, hands accustomed to hard agricultural work, and a sense of comfort and security in living in a rural environment. They knew how to barter, buy, and sell in small town markets, how to sign on as hired labourers, and how rural credit networks operated.

Neither in the countryside nor in the cities were the Irish migrants to Australia ghettoized:

> In Australia, the diffusion of Irish expatriates throughout the population was remarkable. Those districts which gained local reputations as Irish enclaves, such as Shepparton or Belfast in Victoria and the Darling Downs in Queensland, were far less aberrant in terms of their proportions of Irish-born than were more "Irish" localities of Britain or America. Within the major Australian cities, also, the Irish were far more evenly distributed than folklore would suggest.[49]

A study of residential patterns of Melbourne and Sydney for 1861-91 revealed that at no time did either Irish migrants or the Roman Catholics as a group approach the threshold of significant residential segregation.[50]

Of course there were concentrations of the Irish-born and of their descendants: in particular in southwest New South Wales there was an "Irish" area centred on the counties of Bligh, Westmoreland, and King.[51] However, this portion of New South Wales was the only markedly "Irish" area in Australia and it was hardly a ghetto.

(III)

When we turn to the occupational mobility of the Irish migrants in Australia, the picture is similar. Just as the Irish migrants were not forced into residential ghettos, neither did they spend their lives in occupational ghettos. The census of New South Wales of 1901 is the first for any Australian state to provide cross-tabulations of occupation, place of birth and religious persuasion. It provides a valuable picture of the economic profile of the group of Irish migrants who, in the average case, had come to Australia in the 1860s and now were at their economic maturity. The single most important point is that among Irish immigrants and among Catholics generally (most, but not all of whom were Irish), agriculture was far-and-away the most popular occupation. Further, not only was it the most common choice of occupation in absolute terms, it was relatively more popular among Irish immigrants than it was among those from other countries.[52]

Group	Percentage of males in agriculture
Entire population	37.3%
Born in Australia or New Zealand	38.2
Foreign-born:	
England and Wales	25.6
Scotland	28.9
Ireland	33.0

These data make waste of the argument that Irish immigrants were too technologically backward to farm, or too given to communal living to stand pioneering loneliness.

Of course, the higher propensity of Irish immigrants to enter agriculture may have been chiefly a function of their having been in Australia longer in the usual case than had the English and the Scots immigrants, but if that is so, then it is hard to see how the following tally of farmers and ranchers by religious persuasion (a multigenerational set of categories) could have emerged:[53]

Religious denomination	Percentage in agriculture
Entire population	37.3%
Anglican	33.9
Methodist	40.1
Presbyterian	36.8
Catholic	37.7

The comments of Eric Richards are helpful in putting things in perspective:

> The Irish arrived later, in fewer numbers, and with smaller resources than much of the rest of the population: nevertheless there is little hint that they were systematically reduced to the margins of this society. They may have overcome their initial

disadvantages by their greater mobility...This does not of course trench upon other less mundane and measurable qualities — it is not to deny the peculiarities in the cultural baggage with which such groups as the Irish travelled. It may be argued, however that on many criteria the Irish were not greatly different from other groups in the colony and that their main importance was as exemplars of the broad mechanisms of international migration in that great age of mobility.[54]

Wonderfully ordinary indeed.

(IV)

Ethnicity: statistically, there are two ways to measure the number of persons in any given ethnic group. The first of these — sometimes called the "subjective" method — is to ask people what their ethnicity is and to take each subject's answer at face value. This is what has been done in Canadian censuses since 1870 and has also been done in random surveys of ethnicity of the U.S. population conducted in the 1970s and 1980s. The other approach — the so-called "objective" method — is to gather information on each person's place of birth or on that of his or her ancestors and then to assign to each person an ethnicity based upon this information.

If both methods are available, usually the subjective method is the more accurate, for who better knows a person's ethnicity than that person? (The chief exception to the superiority of self-definition occurs in the case of persecuted populations, wherein it is in the individual's self interest to lie). Unfortunately, very rarely in the past did governments inquire into the ethnicity of their populations, so one frequently has to fall back on extrapolations involving the "objective" method (as was done in the case of New Zealand in the preceding chapter.)

Were it not for the work of Charles A. Price, we would not know very much about the ethnic patterns of Australian society, save for the character of the first generation and (after 1907) of the first and second generations. Price's work (presented in Table 25) provides an overview of the magnitude of the Irish as an ethnic group, and these numbers are sensibly compared to those for other groups from the British Isles.[55] Seemingly, throughout the history of Australia, the Irish have been the second largest group and that is the position they hold at the present time. Even if one splits from each other the Irish Catholics and Irish Protestants, the Irish Catholics on their own have been the second largest ethnic group.

TABLE 25

Notional Ethnic Origins of Australian Population
1861-1988
as percentage of total Australian population
(excluding aboriginals)

	1861	1891	1947	1978	1988
Irish	25.5	25.7	23.0	17.9	17.2
English	49.0	48.8	51.3	45.8	43.9
Scottish	14.3	14.0	14.8	2.4	11.9
Welsh	1.5	1.5	1.6	1.4	1.4
Channel Isles, Manx	0.2	0.3	0.2	0.2	0.1
Total British Isles	90.5	90.3	90.9	77.7	74.5

Sources: Compiled from Charles A. Price, "Ethnic Composition and Origins," *Australian Immigration, A Biography and digest,* Number 4, Supplement (1981), Table 5:1, p. 46, and Charles A. Price, "The Ethnic Character of the Australian Population," in James Jupp (ed.) *The Australian People* (North Ryde, NSW: Angus and Robertson, 1988), Table 2, p. 124.

Hence, although the Irish unquestionably experienced discrimination, they were too large a group to push around for very long, a fact that is made clear in the occupational data shown earlier.

One of the more appealing theories about the Irish in Australia is Patrick O'Farrell's view that the Catholic Irish were the key creative element in Australia in the nineteenth century and the first half of the twentieth. He argues that the Irish Catholics operated like a loyal opposition. They acted as a constructive irritant in the general polity, questioning the consensus on values that he believes characterized the other (Protestant) groups from the British Isles. He argues that the dialectic of Irish Catholic minority versus "English" majority was, until roughly the middle of the twentieth century, the main unifying principle in Australian history. This dialectic occurred within the context of the Irish Catholics — in the sense of their accepting existing political conventions, as well as the British-derived constitution, and by their being committed to changing things by democratic means.[56]

This viewpoint, that the Irish were a distinct and dynamic element in Australian society, has to be juxtaposed to the undeniable statistical evidence that the Irish fit into Australian society like a hand into a glove. They were totally ordinary in most ways. Despite surface problems, O'Farrell's theory well may be correct. There is no logical contradiction between the Irish Catholics being identical with other Australians on most major social indices and still, in the mind of Australian society, being a distinct, active, and dynamic element.

The distinction thus drawn — between the structural and the qualitative characteristics of the Irish Catholics in Australian history — serves as a good entry point into a reflection on the nature of Irish ethnicity, and much of what we learn in Australia may be transferable to other places.

The Irish sense of ethnicity (that is, of a shared sense of national origin, however vague), potentially had a wide range of impacts, but the two most important are as follows. First, ethnic affiliation could have affected the Irish-born and their descendants by eliciting from the larger society prejudice and discrimination. Secondly, through stereotyping, the larger society could have made it clear to the Irish migrants and their descendants that they were expected to adopt certain postures and masks when dealing with the general society. (An example of this in another culture is the Step-and-Fetchit posture demanded for a long time of African-Americans when they were dealing with white society). Notice that these items make ethnicity an effect: in those instances, an individual's social position is determined largely by the degree of prejudice with which the larger society acts, or by forcing the Irish person to act in a certain stereotyped way in order to get along. Neither of these impacts has anything to do with the "Irishness" that a migrant and his or her descendants evinced in Australia (or in the USA or in Great Britain), but are meanings and status that a given society imputes to Irishness.

On the other hand, Irish ethnicity could be a causal factor. Attitudes toward work, family, and religion could directly help to determine the way the large group of persons of Irish ethnicity chose to think and to behave.

Let us consider chiefly the matter of ethnicity-as-cause. There is a wide spectrum of cultural practices and attitudes that the Irish migrants could have brought with them to their new homeland and could have passed on to their children. At one end of the spectrum are what we can label *instrumental* attitudes and beliefs, things that have a direct and quantum impact upon "big" matters, such as how hard people work, what occupations they choose, and where they live. At the other end of the spectrum, no less real, but much more subtle, are beliefs and attitudes that might form part of an Irish ethnic cosmology, a world-view, a *mentalité*. In the usual instance such things had little direct impact on the "big" matters of everyday life, but were extremely important to an individual's internal state, especially on how he or she interpreted economic and social realities encountered. In this spectrum, between the instrumental and *mentalité*, where any particular item of ethnicity-as-cause might fit is a matter of judgement to be made by the historian and the reader. However, whenever one operates on this spectrum, one must insist that evidence be produced. Mere assertion will not do. Inevitably this evidence must be a documented pattern of human behaviour. The only way we know how people feel inside themselves is through observing behaviour, such as that they write letters home expressing loneliness, or that they join a local Irish club. And, inevitably, any analysis of this behaviour has to be comparative. The Irish-born and the entire Irish ethnic group need to be compared in their behaviour to other groups. And, within the Irish ethnic group, it is important to know how widespread any given behaviour was, so that one can compare those who exhibit the particular behaviour with those who do not.[57]

Now, we have already established that in Australian society the purely instrumental effects of Irish ethnicity-as-cause were virtually zero, and this is true whether one talks about the Irish-born or the multigenerational ethnic group, and whether one discusses persons of Catholic background separately or as part of the cohort that includes both Protestants and Catholics. The Irish simply settled into Australian society and acted on the "big" matters of occupation, settlement and social mobility in essentially the same way as did the Scots, English and Welsh. The context within which this occurred is crucial. The Irish in Australia were a founding people, the second largest ethnic group, and they did not face structural discrimination (such as penal laws or slavery). The Australian case confirms for a society whose origins were pre-Famine what the New Zealand case taught for a post-Famine society: that being either Irish Protestant or Irish Catholic was no inherent handicap.

Establishing that there were no significant instrumental drawbacks to being Irish Catholic or Irish Protestant is a social scientific way of approaching a fact that is crucial, and less ponderously stated. This is that almost every ethnic group that settled in the English-speaking world in the nineteenth and early twentieth centuries exhibited fundamentally the same set of attitudes toward big issues. Almost everyone accepted the rules and principles of the modernizing capitalist world. They adopted the principle of private property (as distinct from collective ownership), embraced the market mechanism as the mode whereby scarce resources are allocated, and bought into liberal democracy, either in its parliamentary or its presidential variations. Almost everyone adopted the so-called "European family pattern," which implies a stem family system (rather than a joint family), and in comparison to the society from which the emigrants came, involved a lower death rate for children and a lower birth rate. And, whether they liked it or not, almost every group in the nineteenth and early twentieth centuries accepted the hegemony of English-language culture, even while, in many instances, trying to preserve what they could of their own distinct heritage. Granted, there have been exceptional groups, but they are unusual: the Amish who refused to accept modernizing technology and the French Canadians who resisted successfully the encircling Anglophone world. Still, those are exceptions. The Irish migrants (like the Irish in the homeland) embraced the modernizing, capitalistic Anglophone world, and being Irish made no difference on big instrumental issues.

Does that mean that the Irish sense of ethnicity is historically inconsequential? No. One of the few attempts at dealing with the *mentalité* end of the spectrum is here germane. This is David Fitzpatrick's analysis of letters by Irish migrants to Australia.[58] In its rigor this is a pioneering work. Doubtlessly it will be modified by further research, but even in its present form it is the best summary of what was inside the heads of average Irish migrants, and their immediate offspring. The study covers the years 1841 to 1915, and from it one can pull out a decade of salient observations. First, Fitzpatrick's study of emigrant letters indicates that on most matters there was scant difference between the *mentalité* of Irish Protestants and of Irish Catholics. Both groups felt themselves to be Irish. Yet, second, in neither group was there much indication of real enthusiasm for Irish nationalism. Third, even among those migrants who came from Ulster, there was no sense of Ulster's having a separate identity, and this held for Catholics and Protestants alike. Fourth, there was no indication of enthusiasm for, or attachment to, the indigenous Gaelic culture of Catholic Ireland. Fifth, the letters indicate a recognition of familial obligations, ones that frequently spanned thousands of miles. (Of course, this characteristic may be unrepresentative of the entire range of Irish-Australian attitudes; after all, these were letters home). Sixth, the literature indicates a continuing embrace of Irish "moral" values, even though the constraints of Irish society were now far behind the migrants. In Irish vocabulary, "moral" relates to sexual behaviour and to marriage. The emigrant letters show no sense of liberation from Irish restraints, but rather a continuing respect for the Old World moral values. Seventh, Fitzgerald's analysis indicates that religion continued to be extremely important in the life of the migrants, both Protestant and Catholic. Eighth, the economic attitudes of the migrants were "in sync" with those of the modernizing capitalist world. It was generally accepted that only hard work would bring true independence and that this, inevitably, had to be accomplished according to the rules of the new society. Ninth, there was an almost universal longing for good talk — for "crack" in the Ulster phrase. That is; for convivial unhurried conversation. And, tenth, this should not be confused with any desire to maintain a traditional Irish worldview and, much less, to indicate the existence of an Irish "exile mentality." The *mentalité* of the migrants to Australia as shown in their letters was of persons proudly Irish, but quick, adventuresome and willing to deal with a New World on its own terms.

Between *mentalité* at one end of the ethnicity-as-cause spectrum, and instrumentalism at the other, there is a big range, and it is a very ill-lit region indeed. In the data on the Irish in Australia (and in several countries to which Irish migrants went in significant numbers) there are two matters that are extremely confusing: those of crime and of mental ill-health. It is possible to argue that (a) although there were no instrumental effects of Irish ethnicity on big issues, (b) the intersection of the Irish ethnic *mentalité* with the larger society in the New World produced friction, and that this became noticeable in behavioral dysfunctions.

Take crime. There is a theme that runs throughout the literature on the Irish diaspora, namely that during the nineteenth and early twentieth centuries the Irish-born were disproportionately represented in criminal statistics. In the case of Australia, one finds that whereas in 1861, 15.6 percent of the population of New South Wales was Irish-born, more than one-third of the convictions at circuit courts and more than one-quarter at quarter sessions, were of Irish-born persons.[59] In 1889, a relatively late date in the Irish migration to Australia, almost 25 percent of all arrests in New South Wales were Irish.[60] To assay this phenomenon, one notes, first, that historically almost all immigrant groups in the English-speaking world found themselves in jail in numbers disproportionate to their portion of the population.

Being locked up relatively often is one of the prices a group pays for moving to a new country, one in which the newcomers are strangers and someone else enforces the rules. Further, any group containing a large proportion of single males, such as was the case with the Irish, will have inevitable troubles with crimes of exuberance: offenses relating to drinking, fighting, and general hell-raising. This has nothing to do with being Irish and a lot to do with being a twenty-year old male with money in pocket and Saturday night to burn. Moreover, it is probable that in most places the justice system was loaded against the Irish immigrants, and that therefore, they were more often charged than were established residents and more often convicted.[61] All that being granted, there probably was something real here, and not just in Australia.

Similarly, there was something real in the matter of mental ill-health. Immigration is hard on everyone, and all immigrant groups to Australia (to take the case at hand) had higher insanity rates in the later nineteenth century than did the Australian-born: roughly five times as high. And of these immigrant groups, the Irish-born had the worst rate. In 1881, the Irish-born in New South Wales had almost double the insanity rate of the English-born and of the Scottish-born, and this held for both men and women.[62] In the years 1900-01, nearly one-fifth of the inmates of insane asylums in Victoria and New South Wales were Irish-born, and this at a time when Irish immigrants were less than 5 percent of the national population.[63] This confirms American studies, conducted in New York state. In the year 1911, and again in 1949-51, persons of Irish birth were found to have much the highest rate of mental hospitalization of any immigrant group.[64] One can make all sorts of qualifications, ones which properly reduce somewhat the apparent magnitude of the phenomenon, but, like crime rates, mental ill-health rates among the Irish immigrants were not mere illusions. They indicated real pain.

The aetiology, however, escapes us. One argument, put forward by Nancy Scheper-Hughes, points out that the Irish homeland has been a fountainhead of mental illness. Scheper-Hughes notes that in the mid-1950s the Republic of Ireland had the highest psychiatric hospitalization rate in the world, despite its having a very backward national health service by European standards. As of 1971, the Irish Republic had double the schizophrenia rate normal for western societies.[65] The explanation that Scheper-Hughes puts forward for this high rate of mental ill-health has to do with the nature of the Irish rural family.[66] The details of the explanation are not here germane, but obviously if the Irish family structure was the cause of mental ill-health in Ireland, then it is possible that what was occurring in Australia and the USA and the other diaspora nations was that the Irish

Figure 3

Place of Birth and Child-bearing, Australia, 1911

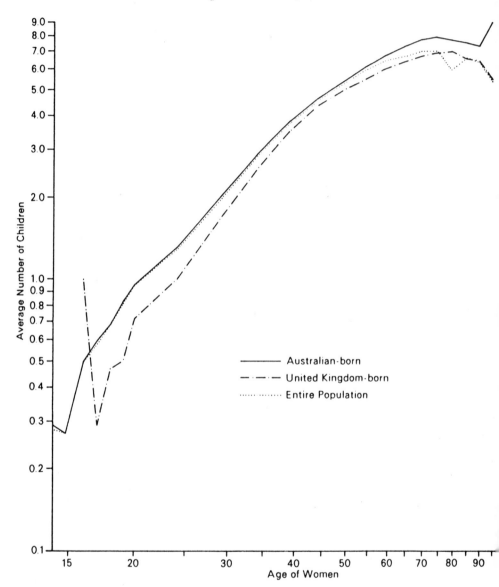

Source: Census of the Commonwealth of Australia, 1911, I:284.

Figure 4

eligious Persuasion and Child-bearing, Australia, 1911

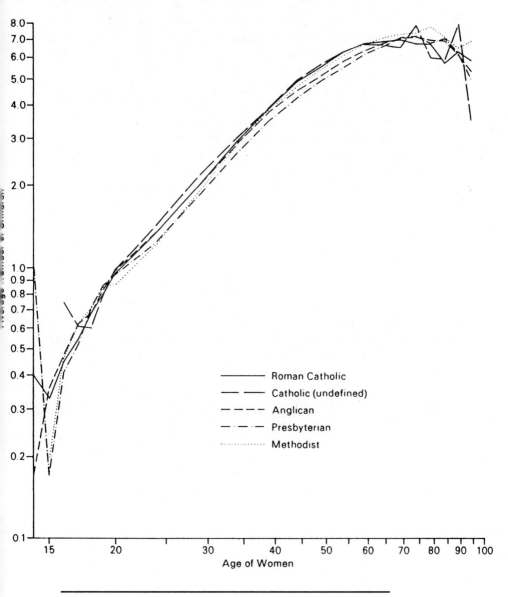

Age of Women

Roman Catholic
Catholic (undefined)
Anglican
Presbyterian
Methodist

Source: Compiled from *Census of the Commonwealth of Autralia, 1911*, I:282.

migrants brought with them a propensity to mental ill-health, a result of the family structure that they imported.

This does not work. Recall that one of the basic doctrines of historical explanation is that like-causes cannot be used to explain different-effects. Then, note that on major empirical indices, the structure of the Irish-born family in Australia in 1911 was not much different than that of other ethnic groups and that the basic structure of the Catholic family was very close to that of other religious groups, at least on the pivotal matters of age of child-bearing and the number of children. Thus, it is very difficult to suggest that it was the Irish family structure that produced the marked difference in mental ill-health rates. Of course, one could always argue that there was something internal to the Irish family (worldwide) that endangered mental health, but unless one has empirical evidence of this and on a wide scale, such speculations border on bigotry.

That brings us back to where we began when considering dysfunctions. We must accept the reality of their existence, at least in the immigrant generation, without having any convincing idea of what caused them. This is not very satisfying, but in a field such as ethnic history, where facile generalizations too often turn into ethnic stereotypes (even while wrapped in respectable pseudo-scientific language), it is better to admit real puzzlement than to propagate unreal answers.

Chapter 5

South Africa: A Small, Elite Band

(I)

Within the context of the entire Irish diaspora, the position of the Irish in South Africa is strange, and so too is the nature of their historical literature. That, though, is what one would expect, for South Africa sits at the far end of the spectrum as far as its migrants from Ireland were concerned. The great value of the South African case is that it defines one end of the range of possible patterns that Irish emigration could take.

In every major characteristic, the South African migration was usual. It was almost entirely a late-Victorian and twentieth century migration, later in its development than even the Irish migration to New Zealand. Until the eve of World War I, the migration was strongly loaded towards males.[1]

Year	Females per Male
1877-1880	.276
1881-1890	.378
1891-1900	.339
1901-1907	.490
1908-1912	.746
1912-1913	.925
1920-1924	.971
1925-1929	.830
1930-1936	.958

This preponderantly male group was anything but typical of the Irish migrants in other ways. For instance, migrants to South Africa in the twentieth century (and probably throughout the nineteenth, but especially from the 1880s onward) contained a much higher proportion of persons of high technical and professional skills, or persons in possession of significant amounts of capital, than those who went any place else. This is clearly indicated in Table 26, which shows that in 1912-13 the proportion of professional and commercial persons in the Irish male migrant stream was six times as great as in the flow to the United States and roughly three times as great as in the flow to Australia and to Canada. Conversely, the proportion of unskilled labourers was only $1/22$nd as high as among Irish migrants to the U.S. and $1/20$th of the proportion among migrants to Canada.

TABLE 26

Occupational Distribution of Irish Male Migrants, 1912-1913, to Various Locations from all United Kingdom Ports ("No information" excluded)

Occupation	To South Africa	To U.S.A.	To Canada	To Australia & New Zealand
Commerce, finance, professions	48.7	8.3	17.3	16.1
Skilled trades	32.1	9.9	14.2	15.3
Agriculture	17.0	33.6	24.0	54.5
Labourer (including agriculture & transport)	2.2	48.2	44.5	14.1
Total	100.0	100.0	100.0	100.0

Source: Derived from Carrier and Jeffery, pp. 116-23.

Simply put, in terms of the skills and the financial resources that they brought with them, the cream of the Irish diaspora went to South Africa. The officials of the General

Register Office of the United Kingdom commented:

> As South Africa has a high proportion of native population, it
> has no need to introduce white labourers, with the result that
> British [Isles] emigrants travelling there are of a higher class
> than those to any other country. The numbers of migrant
> labourers are negligible and since the end of the First World
> War nearly nineteen per cent of the emigrants to British South
> Africa [read: Union of South Africa] have followed commercial,
> professional or skilled occupations. It is for this reason that the
> effect of the Depression on the class of migrants going to South
> Africa was far less marked — the sudden increase in proportion
> of the higher class occupations which has been noted as a
> feature of every other country in the 1930s does not appear to
> considerable extent in the South African experience. *Even
> Ireland, whose migrants to other countries before the
> Depression contained such high proportions of labouring and
> agricultural workers, supplied eighty percent of her South
> African migrants from the higher classes.* (Emphasis added).
> The movement back provides a similar picture.[2]

If one compares the collective occupational structure
of the Irish immigrants to South Africa to that of the
Scottish and the English and Welsh, as is done in Table 27, it
is clear that the Irish males as a group had as elite a
background as did the English-Welsh contingent, and a
markedly higher profile than did the Scottish.

This high occupational profile and, therefore, elevated
social status of Irish migrants to South Africa may be related
to a collective characteristic unique in the Irish diaspora:
proportionately, the out-migration from South Africa of the
Irish-born was higher than from any place that the Irish went
in significant numbers.[3] One can speculate (and in the state
of the available data it is no more than a speculation) that we
have here two related phenomena. One of these is that part
of this "return migration" was real, consisting of middle and
upper-middle class migrants who went to South Africa as
young persons, did well, and after twenty or thirty years
returned to Ireland to buy a small estate and to live gentry
lives.

Map 4

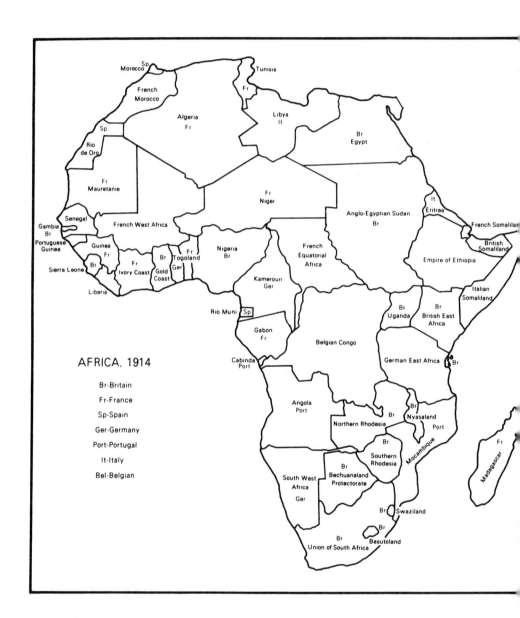

AFRICA, 1914

Br-Britain
Fr-France
Sp-Spain
Ger-Germany
Port-Portugal
It-Italy
Bel-Belgian

TABLE 27

**Occupational Distribution of Male Migrants to South Africa
from United Kingdom 1912-1949, Selected Years
("No information" excluded)**

1912-13

Occupation	Irish	English & Welsh	Scottish
Commerce, finance, professions	48.7	48.0	34.2
Skilled trades	32.1	43.8	60.1
Agriculture	17.0	7.4	5.5
Labourers (including agriculture & transport)	2.2	0.8	0.2
Total	100.0	100.0	100.0

1921-24

Occupation	Irish	English & Welsh	Scottish
Commerce, finance, professions	53.0	46.8	34.4
Skilled trades	29.3	37.1	53.4
Transport & communications	2.2	3.3	3.3
Agriculture	13.1	11.6	8.2
Labourers (excluding agriculture & transport)	2.4	1.2	0.7
Total	100.0	100.0	100.0

1925-30

Occupation	Irish	English & Welsh	Scottish
Commerce, finance, professions	39.8	48.8	35.7
Skilled trades	41.5	34.5	50.5
Transport & communications	2.3	3.5	3.2
Agriculture	12.7	12.4	9.8
Labourers (excluding agricluture & transport)	3.7	0.8	0.8
Total	100.0	100.0	100.0

Source: Derived from Carrier and Jeffery, pp. 122-23.

I suspect, however, that the return migration often
was more apparent than real. That is, among the Irish
migrants to South Africa one is seeing an early form of what

eventually was to become an international pattern: from the last quarter of the nineteenth century onwards, well-trained "technocrats" came to South Africa with education, skills, and resources in hand. They stayed five, ten years, and in many cases moved on. Sometimes they went back to Ireland for a time, but even then it was not necessarily to settle permanently, but to stop for a time before going off to Canada, or to the USA, or to the Antipodes or to Great Britain to practice their profession or trade.

Notice that in talking about the singularly high skills pattern among the Irish migrants, I have been discussing males. One of the everyday frustrations of historians of migration and of ethnicity is that occupational data on women are rarely as revealing as those for men. This is because the occupational categories traditionally employed usually are narrowly economic, and most women are listed as housewives or as dependents and, therefore, as unconnected with the economy. However, something interesting emerges from an examination of the data on the occupations of Irish female migrants. Throughout most of the diaspora the pattern is very clear: women migrants overwhelmingly had occupations as wives, as domestic servants, and as unskilled manual labourers. Given below is the percentage of women migrants who were either "wife or housewife" or who did not state any occupation (the U.K. authorities lumped these individuals together in one group) for the year 1912-13:[4]

Country to which Irish women migrated	% "wife or housewife" or not stating any occupation
USA	36.2
Canada	42.3
Australia & New Zealand	44.4
South Africa	66.8

This is a very marked difference and it suggests that Irish women who came to South Africa were much more likely either to be married or to be well-off dependents (such as sisters who accompanied brothers in the professions and ran their homes). Probably, as a group the South Africa female migrants were older than those who went elsewhere; almost certainly most were coming as part of family units headed by males who had a comparatively high degree of professional or commercial skill. Undoubtedly, as a group these women were of a higher social class than those who went to other destinations.

But even the single women who migrated to South Africa were sharply different as a group from those who went elsewhere. Here the litmus test is the proportion of migrant women who were in service, either domestic or in hotels, or the licensed trade. In 1912-13 the situation was as follows:[5]

Country to which Irish women migrated	Percentage in service
USA	87.1
Canada	80.2
Australia & New Zealand	72.7
South Africa	31.1

The majority of Irish female migrants to South Africa for whom occupations were reported, was from the commercial, financial, or professional sectors (52.2 percent of those employed). The next largest segment (31.1 percent) was in service and a sizable proportion (16.7 percent) was in the needle trade. The conclusion dictated by their overall occupational profile is similar to that inferred from the profile of the Irish males: the most qualified women migrants in the Irish diaspora went to South Africa.

If, from the end of the second Anglo-Boer War (1899-1902) onwards, South Africa received the best set of Irish migrants in terms of their skills, capital, and social cohesion (the latter as indicated by their marital pattern), how far back in time does this generalization hold? I do not know. One thing that is clear, however, is that a quantum shift occurred in female migration patterns among the Irish after the end of the Second Anglo-Boer War. This is seen in a sharp shift in the female-male ratio among Irish migrants. (A parallel shift occurred among migrants from Scotland and England and Wales). Whereas in the late 1870s almost three out of every four Irish migrants to South Africa were male, after 1910 in most years nearly half were women. This shift was so sharp that one is forced to conclude that it is inappropriate to project back into the nineteenth century our conclusion about the high quality of female migrants that was so marked in the early twentieth century. For men, there was no such discontinuity.

Associated with the unusually high skill level among the Irish migrants to South Africa was a geographic singularity. Their origins were overwhelmingly in the most economically advanced parts of Ireland, the provinces of Leinster and Ulster. Belfast, Dublin and their environs provided more than half the migrants. This is unique in the Irish diaspora, and is all the more notable because Munster, the leading source of migrants to most destinations, sent only a tiny proportion to South Africa. And in one final way, the migrants to South Africa and their descendants were atypical (although, in this regard not unique). Most of them were Protestants. It is safe to state that this held from the middle 1870s onward (what the situation was before then is unknown). And that proportion was approximately 57 percent Protestant to 43 percent Catholic. This proportion held both for the migrant generation and for the entire multigenerational ethnic group as of 1926, the one census which permits us to examine the religion question.[6]

(II)

Thus, the Irish in South Africa were notable for their being a striking departure from all of the norms of the Irish diaspora. There is more to their singularity than that, however. Their historiography is bizarre.

"Historiography." That is one of the abused words of the history profession. What it refers to is simply "historical writing," or "historical literature," and it is a convenient term to refer to what historians have done on any given topic. The word should frighten no one, but it frequently does, as when it is turned into a term of mystification in graduate-student seminars, where phrases such as "historiographical perspective," and "parameters of historiography" bounce around like a tether ball on a playground. That is codswallop and is not what is here intended.

The historiography of the Irish in South Africa is bizarre because until very recently there was almost none. This would be unusual in most countries, but considering that we are here dealing with South Africa — the single most racially conscious modernized society in the world —

TABLE 28

Geographic Origin of Natives of Ireland who Emigrated to South Africa from Irish Ports, Inclusive, 1905-1920

	05	06	07	08	09	10	11	12	13	14	15	16	17	18	19	20	Total
Province of Leinster																	
Carlow	10	11	10	4	5	2	1	3	4	1	0	1	0	0	0	0	52
Dublin	75	84	73	28	36	50	19	30	26	16	19	3	3	0	0	0	462
Kildare	42	24	16	13	15	15	12	19	31	16	15	0	0	0	0	0	218
Kilkenny	2	4	1	2	4	2	2	0	1	0	0	0	0	0	0	0	18
King's	7	1	4	1	0	0	1	1	1	1	0	1	0	0	0	0	18
Longford	5	11	10	6	3	2	1	0	1	0	0	0	0	0	0	0	39
Louth	23	16	9	6	4	6	3	6	13	0	1	0	1	0	0	0	88
Meath	10	9	5	1	3	3	3	5	2	2	2	1	0	0	0	0	46
Queen's	2	6	1	1	1	5	0	0	1	0	2	1	0	0	0	0	17
Westmeath	2	4	5	0	5	0	0	0	3	1	0	0	0	0	0	0	21
Wexford	3	1	2	3	1	5	2	4	0	0	1	0	0	0	0	0	23
Wicklow	17	12	10	4	4	6	0	6	4	4	2	0	0	0	0	0	68
Sub-total: Leinster	198	183	146	69	81	96	44	74	87	41	41	6	4	0	0	0	1,070
Province of Munster																	
Clare	2	1	0	0	3	1	5	0	2	2	6	0	0	0	0	0	22
Cork	3	2	0	9	8	6	10	3	1	3	1	2	0	0	0	0	48
Kerry	0	0	0	10	0	4	1	1	1	0	0	2	0	0	3	0	22
Limerick	4	5	1	0	5	2	1	0	1	2	0	0	0	0	0	0	21
Tipperary	3	12	9	5	1	3	7	1	0	3	1	1	0	0	0	0	46
Waterford	7	7	1	1	2	0	1	1	0	0	0	0	0	0	0	0	20
Sub-total: Munster	19	27	11	25	19	16	25	6	5	10	8	5	0	0	3	0	179

TABLE 28 (Continued)

	05	06	07	08	09	10	11	12	13	14	15	16	17	18	19	20	Total
Province of Ulster																	
Antrim	31	30	38	26	26	40	22	28	32	26	14	0	4	0	4	41	362
Armagh	8	8	4	4	1	1	1	3	9	3	1	0	0	0	0	0	43
Cavan	11	8	11	5	3	2	3	5	4	6	0	2	0	0	0	0	60
Donegal	1	0	0	2	0	0	1	0	0	0	0	0	0	1	0	0	4
Down	40	23	11	4	10	7	8	14	45	22	0	0	4	1	4	10	203
Fermanagh	1	0	2	2	0	1	0	3	5	3	0	1	0	0	0	0	18
Londonderry	5	3	0	0	0	0	5	4	8	1	0	0	0	0	0	0	26
Monaghan	0	3	0	5	3	0	1	3	3	2	0	0	1	0	0	1	23
Tyrone	10	2	0	1	2	0	0	6	13	1	0	0	0	0	0	4	39
Sub-total: Ulster	107	77	66	49	45	52	41	66	119	64	15	3	9	1	8	56	778
Province of Connacht																	
Galway	0	4	1	0	1	0	0	0	1	2	1	1	0	0	0	1	12
Leitrim	0	1	0	0	0	0	0	0	1	0	2	0	0	0	0	0	5
Mayo	0	1	0	0	1	0	1	0	0	0	1	2	0	0	0	0	6
Roscommon	0	1	1	0	0	0	1	0	0	0	0	0	0	0	0	0	3
Sligo	0	1	1	5	1	1	1	1	0	1	0	2	0	0	0	0	14
Sub-total: Connacht	0	8	3	5	3	1	3	1	3	3	4	5	0	0	0	1	40
Total:	324	295	226	148	148	165	113	147	214	118	68	19	13	1	8	60	2,067

Sources: Compiled from *Emigration statistics of Ireland for the year 1905*, p. 13 [Cd2868], HC 1906, p. 13, [Cd3376], HC 1907, xcvii. 1907, p. 13, [Cd3987], HC 1908, cxxii. 1908, p. 13, [Cd4550], HC 1909, ciii, 169. 1909, p. 15, [Cd5088], HC 1910, cix, 479. 1910, p. 15, [Cd5607], HC 1911, lx. 1911, p. 15, [Cd6131], HC 1912-13, cv. 1912, p. 15, [Cd6727], HC 1913, lv. 1913, p. 15, [Cd7313], HC 1914, lxix. 1914, p. 15, [Cd7883], HC 1914-16, lxxx. 1915, p. 15, [Cd8230], HC 1916, xxxii. 1916, p. 13, [Cd8520], HC 1917-18, xxxvii. 1917, p. 10, [Cd9013], HC 1918, xxv. 1918, p. 10, [Cmd77], HC 1919, ii. 1919, p. 5, [Cmd721], HC 1920, l. 1920, p. 5, [Cmd1414], HC 1921, xlii.

the omission is extraordinary. Beginning in the 1980s Professor Donal McCracken has organized ex nihilo Irish studies in South Africa, producing two excellent studies and one solid academic journal.[7] These heroic efforts, though, are very recent and mark a turning point in the self-consciousness of the Irish in South Africa. Before that point there was only one item in print (other than in fugitive form) that dealt directly with the Irish as a group: Graham B. Dickason's *Irish Settlers to the Cape. A History of the Clanwilliam 1820 Settlers from Cork* (Cape Town: A.A. Balkema, 1973). This is a fascinating piece of amateur history, informed by a deep respect for the people being chronicled as well as by solid archival research. There are useful references to the Irish in E. Morse Jones' volume on British Settlers in South Africa up to 1826,[8] and the Irish feature as occasional sidelights in Harold Hockly's chronicle of the 1820 settlement.[9] Irish mentions occur in John Clark's biography of the Natal settler-agent John Moreland.[10] R.H. Henderson's autobiography, *An Ulsterman in Africa* (Cape Town: Uni-Volkspers, 1944) is well-known and has some amusing anecdotes. Of course there are fleeting biographies of Irish-born notables in the *Dictionary of South African Biography* and occasional entire biographies of South Africans of Irish extraction.[11] But, essentially, one is dealing with a scholarly vacuum.[12]

Perhaps there was virtually no written history of the Irish in South Africa because the Irish had no real history. That idea, though, is given the lie by Donal McCracken's recent organization of a large-scale collective project on the Irish in South Africa, as well as by his own recent scholarly work. The Irish do indeed have a history. That granted, it is true that in absolute terms the Irish immigrants in South Africa were never very large in number — always under 20,000 in the twentieth century. The Irish multigenerational ethnic was an estimated 3.8 percent of the white population of the Cape Colony in 1891. Nationally, in the Union of South Africa in 1926, the Irish as an ethnic group were 3.5 percent of the total white population. (See Tables 30 and 31). Those are not large proportions, but the ethnic group certainly was large enough to support some degree of historical writing, had it desired — witness the vigorous historical literature produced by the smaller Jewish community in South Africa.[13]

TABLE 29

Irish-born Population in Union of South Africa
(and its constituent predecessors)

Year	Cape Colony No.	%	Natal No.	%	Transvaal No.	%	Orange Free State No.	%	Total Irish-born	% of white pop.
1875	3,759	1.6								
1891	4,184	1.1	1,060	2.3						
1904	8,601	1.5	2,229	2.3	5,362	1.8	1,703	1.2	17,895	1.6
1911	5,290	0.9	1,775	1.8	6,531	1.6	976	0.6	14,572	1.1
1918	4,418	0.7	1,906	1.6	4,953	1.0	545	0.6	11,822	0.8
1921	4,439	0.7	2,098	1.5	5,232	1.0	520	0.3	12,289	0.8
1926	4,481	0.6	2,239	1.4	5,126	0.8	490	0.2	12,336	0.7
1936	3,827	0.5	2,007	1.1	4,484	0.5	304	0.2	10,622	0.5
1946	3,171	0.4	1,847	0.8	3,664	0.3	221	0.1	8,903	0.4
1951	3,433	0.4	1,988	0.7	3,948	0.3	251	0.1	9,620	0.4

Note: 1. The 1891 Cape figures includes the Cape Colonies, then-dependencies. 2. From 1921 onwards "Ireland" includes both Northern and southern Ireland.

Sources: Derived from *Results of a Census of the Colony of the Cape of Good Hope ... 1875*, pp. 4-5, 156; *Results of a Census of the Colony of the Cape of Good Hope, 1891*, pp. xii, xxxii; *Census of the Colony of the Cape of Good Hope, 1904 General Report ...* , pp. ii, xlvii-xlviii; *Results of a Census of the Transvaal Colony ...1904*, pp. vi, 142; *Census of the Union of the Union of South Africa, 1911*, pp. x, xii, 988-97; *Census of the European or White Races of the Union of South Africa, 1918. Final Report ...* , p. 18 and Part VII, *Birthplaces*, p. 4; *Third Census of the Population of the Union of South Africa ... 1921. Report*, p. 27 and Part VI, *Birthplaces*, pp. 4-8; *Fourth Census of the Population of the Union of South Africa ... 1926, Report*, p. 7 and Part VII, *Birthplaces*, pp. 10-13; *Sixth Census of the Population of the Union of South Africa ... 1936*, vol. I, *Population*, p. xvii and vol. V, *Birthplaces ...* , pp. 1-5; *Union of South Africa ... Population Census ...1946*, vol. I, p. 1; *Union of South Africa. Population Census ... 1951*, vol. I, *Population*, p. 2 and vol. IV, *Birthplaces*, pp. 1-5; *Uniestatistieke oor Vyftig Jaar* (Pretoria: Bureau of Census), p. A-23.

% = % of white population

TABLE 30

Notional Ethnic Composition of the Cape Colony, 1891

Origin	Immigrants	Second & subsequent generations in South Africa	Total ethnic cohort	Percentage
Dutch & French			230,000	61.2
English & Welsh	27,689	65,763	93,452	24.8
Scottish	6,644	15,781	22,425	6.0
Irish	4,184	9,939	14,123	3.8
Other European			16,000	4.2
Total white population			376,000	100.0

Sources: Derived from *Results of the Census of the Colony of the Cape of Good Hope ... 1891*, pp. xvii, 120. For methods, see Akenson, *Occasional papers on the Irish in South Africa* (Grahamstown: Rhodes University, 1991), pp. 66-67.

TABLE 31

Revised Estimates, Ethnic Composition of the Union of South Africa, 1926

Ethnicity	Numbers	% of the white population
Dutch South Africa	954,400	56.9
English	356,681	21.3
Irish	59,196	3.5
Scottish	125,965	7.5
Welsh	13,573	0.8
"Other British groups"	9,211	0.6
Other white groups	157,321	9.4
Unspecified	313	0.0
Total	1,676,660	100.0

Sources: South Africa, *Fourth Census . . . 1926, Report*, p. 27. On methods, see Akenson, *Occasional papers on the Irish in South Africa*, pp. 67-69.

So, a reasonable start at explaining why there was so little written about the Irish is to suggest that we should recognize that what people say often says a lot about them, and what people don't say frequently says a good deal more. That holds for individuals, cultures, and nations.

Next, note that the Irish were not alone. There was not (indeed, still is not) a significant historical literature on ethnicity among any of the Anglo-Celtics — Scots, Welsh, English or Irish. There is, however a major body of historical literature, written in English and in Afrikaans, that deals with the topics of Afrikaner identity, nationalism, and folk culture. The English-language and the Afrikaans-language writings on these matters tend to be in opposition to each other (although this is not a universal situation), but they share a fundamental agreement: that the Afrikaners bear analysis as a cultural entity, and that they comprise what in most western historiographies would be denominated as an ethnic group. Significantly, however, this discussion is conducted not in the vocabulary of ethnicity, but as a footnote to what is usually called "Afrikaner nationalism." The subject, therefore, is viewed almost entirely within political rubrics.

Within the white population, the great rivals of the Anglo-Celts, of course, were the Afrikaaners, and, indeed, from 1948 until the late 1980s, Afrikaner hegemony over the Anglo-Celts was quite unremitting. In that political context, anything that showed a division within the ranks of the Anglo-Celtic phalanx (as between English, Scots, Welsh, Irish Protestants and Irish Catholics) had the potential political impact of weakening that group's political hand against the Afrikaners. Unconscious though this motivation may have been, one almost feels that historians of South Africa had taken a vow not to raise the matter of ethnicity as it affected the Anglo-Celtic population. Indeed, even in the 1970s and 1980s, the historical literature gave evidence of rather strenuous efforts to subordinate ethnicity as a phenomenon to gender,[14] to race[15] and to the economic substructure of class.[16] Anything, in other words, to avoid facing ethnicity as a phenomenon amongst whites of non-Afrikaner background.

In the case of the English and the Scots, there exists a great deal of history-of-imperialism literature and it is valuable in its way. However, from the viewpoint of the history of ethnicity, its collective defect is that in the usual case the individual settlers and their communities are treated as subcategories of an overarching theme, the development of the British Empire in South Africa and its conflict with the Afrikaners. Only two collectivities have a substantial scholarly literature, the 1820 settlers and the Natal settlers. In addition to the works of Jones and of Hockly mentioned earlier, for the 1820 group one must note significant studies by Jeeves,[17] Keppel-Jones,[18] Rivett-Carnac,[19] and Edwards,[20] among others. And for Natal, A.F. Hattersley's older work stands out.[21] But the curious thing about all of these works is that although they are valuable pieces of local and of regional history, none of them pays attention to the definition of and the maintenance (or the dilution) of the cultural characteristics that defined these groups of settlers. The apperceptions of the *folkliv* school and the methods employed by professional historians elsewhere in ethnic and local studies are missing. The way in which the scholarly literature in these instances is tilted is culturally diagnostic. Effectively, a "Mayflower mentality" reigns, whereby the Charter Group significance of any group is taken to be its most important characteristic. This Mayflower mindset means that the first generation receives all of the attention. Then their descendants are quietly forgotten.

This ties into a larger matter, namely that successive governments of what is now the Republic of South Africa, and its pre-Union constituents, collected very little information on ethnicity among white groups. Only in 1891 and 1926 were direct investigations of ethnicity attempted, and these were bungled. Yet, at the same time, the various governments were collecting information on non-white groups that was broken down into ethnic and racial categories that were very narrow indeed. The reason for collecting information on ethnic differentiation among the non-whites was that these data facilitated white control of those groups. The reason for not collecting demographic information on continuing ethnic differentiation among the white minority is that to do so would reveal fissures and fractures and thus would imply weakness. Successive white minority governments (whether headed by Anglophones or by Afrikaans speakers) were terrified of having their weakness become known.

All that is changing very rapidly.

Anyone who reads the newspapers or watches television news knows that South Africa in the late 1980s went over a vast moral and intellectual watershed, a transition that in the 1990s will be the remaking of its political and social geography. This transition will have by-products that are well beyond anyone's ability to predict. However, within the context of the Irish diaspora, I believe that a set of related mental empowerments have occurred and that one result will be a blossoming of historical literature concerning ethnicity of all sorts, and that the leading sector will be the Irish.

Consider a salient fact: that the concept of ethnicity necessarily implies a pluralistic way of thinking if the concept is applied evenly across a society. This clashes with the dichotomous mindset that dominated South African political life from the 1820s onward and which, quite unconsciously, set a very narrow pair of blinders upon the vision of South African social historians. The habit of thinking in terms of pairs was deeply ingrained: black versus white was the fundamental dialectic, and the main secondary ones were Afrikaner versus Anglophone, imperial versus local, and capital versus labour. It is very difficult to break this mindset and to introduce pluralistic thinking, for the emphasis upon shading, texture, and variation requires an abandonment of some old and fundamental assumptions about the nature of the national history. Yet, a radically transformed view of the national history is an absolute prerequisite for the white minority's survival in the new South Africa. If the politicians can embrace major mental shifts, surely social historians can do the same.

Chapter 6

The Irish and Empire

(I)

Here is another story concerning the great John Kelleher.

He had a habit of taking his students for walks along the Charles River, and of exhausting them by walking much too fast. The cunning ones among his students found that by feigning interest in the ducks, coots, and mud-hens that paddled among the debris in the Charles, they could get John to sit down on a bench for a while. The trick was to pretend fascination with the marking of some ugly little paddling bird and John would talk. One time we were so engaged when he asked, "Has it ever struck you that whatever a culture thinks of itself, the opposite usually is true."

It had not.

"I mean: for example, that the English who think of themselves as being very stiff-upper-lip are the most stickily sentimental and romantic people on earth. Every time Vera Lynn sang something during World War II, proved it."

I had to agree.

"And the Irish. They like to think that they are charming and unpredictable in a winsome way. And very happy-go-lucky."

A greasy mud hen joined us — this was before the Charles was cleaned up — perhaps in search of a detergent.

"In actual fact, the Irish are by nature a nation of bank clerks. Penny-pinching, gimlet-eyed, risk-avoiding, and always looking for that little edge." He concluded, "Our Lord genetically predisposed the English to become a nation of lachrymose bartenders. And the Irish are his chosen bank managers, civil servants, and small-time politicians."

Neither the mud-hen nor I said anything.

Professor Kelleher's point, though, is not to be left in silence. It leads to the theme — indeed, almost a theory — that I wish to sketch here, namely this: that despite their image of being democratic, rebellious and (among the nationalist majority in Ireland) anti-imperialist in general and anti-British Empire in particular, the Irish have actually been among the greatest supporters of the second British Empire and the Commonwealth.

That is something about which most historians of the Irish diaspora are silent. But we can learn a lot from historians of empire. In a seminal essay on the non-European foundations of European imperialism, Ronald Robinson outlined a theory of "collaboration."[1] In it, he hypothesized the existence of a "collaborative mechanism" between the imperialist powers and certain members of the indigenous populations that they governed. Collaborators from among the indigene were necessary as a synapse of social and economic control. Had not some such mechanism been in existence, it would be impossible to explain how so few Europeans were able to manage such large groups of indigene over vast territories. Although Robinson's idea excites a good deal of nervousness — no one wants to be labelled a collaborator — the concept helps to explain a number of things about imperialism that merely mechanical models cannot handle.

As a sidelight to his main argument, Robinson pointed to what he called "*the ideal prefabricated collaborator*" — the white colonist.[2]

Among the potential prefabricated collaborators, the Irish were perfect. As early as the 1830s, they had a well-established tradition of emigration to every corner of the British Empire as well as to the United States. Because the Irish had a higher emigration rate than any other major European nation, from their early days Irish children learned of the possibility that their adult years would be spent in some other land, and thus an Irish childhood was a preparation for emigration (whether or not the individual actually left). More than that, during the eighteenth and the first half of the nineteenth centuries, Ireland underwent two processes that were central to the establishment of British imperial control over any territory: by 1850, all of Ireland, even the most backward area, was part of the market economy, and by the same date cultural Anglicization had gained a permanent hegemony. The subsistence economy and the Gaelic world were mostly matters of memory, a few shards of which were preserved with reverent awe, but the children of Ireland did their calculations in sterling and their thinking in English.

There were four major types of collaborators with empire: soldiers, administrators (including police), clergy (of all faiths) and ordinary settlers. Each played his or her part.

The ubiquity of the Irish soldier in the British army and in the armies of the various British colonies is well known. Recent studies have shown that a surprisingly high proportion of mid-Victorian enlistments by the Irish-born — 40 percent — came from Irish-born persons living in England and Scotland.[3] This is significant because it indicates that army service for many young men was part of the experience of being an Irish emigrant. They left Ireland and worked for a while; then in hard times they joined the army and ultimately were discharged, some to settle back in Ireland, but often to take their pensions in some corner of the British empire. In this life cycle, collaboration was an integral part of being a member of the Irish diaspora.

H.J. Hanham has tabulated the percentages of the Irish-born in the British army during the nineteenth century:[4]

Irish population as % of U.K. population		Irish-born % of British Army
1831	32.3%	42.2%
1841	30.6	37.2
1861	20.0	28.4
1871	17.5	24.5
1881	14.8	20.9
1891	12.5	18.4

These were overwhelmingly Catholic young men; also, in the 1880s and 1890s, Hanham suggests, English-born children of Irish Catholic background were prone to enlist.

During World War I, over 140,000 Irish young men volunteered for the British forces, of whom approximately 65,000 were Catholics.[5]

To some observers of the Irish diaspora, the widespread Irish engagement in military support for the British empire has not been entirely palatable, and as a result, two sorts of special pleading have been pressed forward in the hope of making this phenomenon go away. The first of these is to agree that, yes, the Irish soldiers were a great support to the empire, but to point out that at the same time other Irish young men cancelled this out by fighting against the empire. A case in point is the Anglo-Boer war of 1899-1902, when a highly publicized Irish brigade fought on the side of the Afrikaners, who were trying to regain the freedom of their republics from United Kingdom domination. When one examines the actual situation, however, one finds that there were 28,000 Irish troops in the United Kingdom army during this war, and only about 150 men in the Irish brigade in South Africa.[6] Indeed, at any moment in the nineteenth and early twentieth centuries, the number of Irish soldiers fighting for the empire of the United Kingdom was hundreds of times greater than those fighting against it.

A second sort of special pleading tries to make the effects of this military collaboration go away by arguing that the motivations of the young men were not imperial. It is frequently suggested (these days more in romantic fiction and in journalism than in serious historical work) that many of the lads in the United Kingdom military were there to gain experience so that they could one day use their military knowledge to free Ireland. Perhaps, but if so, where were they when Ireland needed them? An additional argument is that most of the young men joined up because of the lack of alternative employment. Given their lack of skills and their consequent marginal position in the economy of the British Isles, this suggestion is undoubtedly true. But to suggest that because their motives were not imperialistic, the Irish young men were not imperialists, is to confuse cause and effect. The effect was real, whatever the cause of their having joined up. These Irish young men helped to carve up Africa; they manned the forts in British North America; they fought the Maori in New Zealand; and, in short, served imperial interests all over the globe. In fact, we should not automatically assume that the Irish young men did not believe in the empire. Many of them must have done so. But even those who served empire only for monetary reasons were prosecuting not only their own self interest but, inevitably, those of the empire.

The second sort of "ideal prefabricated collaborator" was the Irish-born colonial administrator. The empire was full of them. For example, one-third of the United Kingdom governors of South Africa were Irish, as was a similar proportion of judges and middle-level bureaucrats. When the Anglo-Irish Sir Lowry Cole arrived at the Cape, people at the dockside were heard to complain that yet another Irish governor had been sent to rule them.[7] The Irish were especially prevalent in colonial police forces, acting as the strong arm of empire. In New South Wales, for example, 67 percent of the police force in 1865 had been born in Ireland. In Victoria, in 1874, 82 percent of the police were Irish-born.[8] If the second generation of Irish ethnicity had been counted the proportion would have been even higher.

Probably the most revealing case study of the Irish as administrators in empire is that of India, the empire's crown jewel. There the Irish were pivotal. Scott B. Cook has done a valuable study of Irish persons in the management grades of the Indian civil service during the second half of the nineteenth and early twentieth centuries. Cook's research makes it clear that the famous 1855 reforms of the Indian service, which made entry competitive, were a boon to the Irish. Whereas between 1809 and 1850 only 5 percent of the recruits had been born in Ireland, between 1855 and 1863, inclusive, 24 percent were Irish. This was at a time when the Irish proportion of the British Isles' population was a bit above 20 percent. The Irish numbers began to drop in the late 1860s when the English horror at having so many Irish university graduates in the Indian service led to the entry process being rigged against the Irish, and eventually the Irish entry settled down to between 5 and 10 percent in most of the late Victorian years. Less severe discrimination existed in the Indian medical service: one finds that the Irish were 38 percent of the recruits in the 1870s and 10 to 19 percent in the decades thereafter.[9]

The most interesting trend among the recruits to the administrative grades of the Indian civil service was that the proportion of Roman Catholics continually grew. In the years 1855-64, inclusive, only 8 percent of Irish recruits to the service were Catholics, but this increased steadily, reaching a high in 1905-14 of 29 percent.[10] Had not World War I and the Irish war of independence intervened, the trend would probably have continued upwards. That there ever would have been an "Irish Raj" — a term Scott used in the title of his study — is doubtful, but certainly Scott is correct in inferring that one has to view the reactions of Irish society to British imperialism in a much less simplistic fashion than usually is the case. Instead of postulating that resistance to imperialism was the natural Irish response, one should accept the view that there was a great variety of responses and that one of these was wholehearted participation in the imperialist enterprise. "Of the various Irish responses," Scott argues, "the one most common, contrary to what most of the historical literature has stressed, was that of support: a broad category encompassing conscious and active collaboration as well as acquiescence in laws, values, and social structures that were partly shaped by British hegemony."[11]

Actually, the Irish tradition of imperial administration began at home. From Catholic Emancipation onwards, department after department of the Irish civil service from bottom to almost (but not quite) the top came under the purview of persons born in Ireland. Increasingly after the Famine, and even more so after the establishment of the Intermediate Education System in 1878, these posts were taken by Catholics. By 1911, Catholics held nearly 60 percent of all of the Irish civil service posts,[12] and had the Irish war of independence not intervened, it is probable that by the early 1920s the religious composition of the Irish civil service would have mirrored that of the Irish population in general.

A third sort of collaborator was the religious professional, clergy of all faiths, missionaries, priests, nuns, and pastors. For the most part, these clerical persons viewed themselves as servants of their particular faith and not directly as servants of empire, but, whatever their motivations, their actions effectively aided empire. Here the most important point is the most obvious: that the expansion of Christianity that occurred after 1815 as western European cultures swept through several New Worlds, was the single greatest expansion in Christian history. For the Christian churches in the British Isles, the United Kingdom's empire presented both a great challenge and an unprecedented opportunity.

Again, to remind ourselves of the obvious: the British empire at its height was the largest that the world has ever seen. At its zenith, approximately one-quarter of the land surface of the earth was either part of the empire or associated with it as self-governing dominions. The churches, if they took seriously the Great Commission to go forth throughout the world and preach the Gospel, had to follow the emigrants throughout the empire. Of course, the churches' expansion within the United Kingdom's empire was conditional upon the clergy not undercutting the empire but implicitly supporting it.

The Irish Catholic church was especially active in the empire. From the 1860s onward, it was successful in gaining control over the Catholic churches in Australia, New Zealand, South Africa, English-speaking Canada, and the United States of America. Irish-trained clerics were sent all over the English-speaking world, just as young subalterns were sent all over the secular empire. As with their secular counterparts, the clerics' job was to manage the colonial enterprises and to keep the locals up to standard.

In practical terms, the Irish clergy had two tasks. The more important of these was to minister to the Irish migrants and to their descendants, as well as to other Catholics. In so doing, the clergy helped to maintain the cohesiveness and the morale of the Irish settlers all over the British empire. In addition, the clergy sometimes tried to convert the indigene. These efforts were very much secondary in the nineteenth century to the churches' serving the settlers, but they were not insignificant. Whatever the motives of the clergy in converting various aboriginal communities to Christianity, the ultimate effect was to convince the indigene to abandon their own cultural systems and to embrace those of the conquering peoples. Thus, by accident, but with remorseless effectiveness, the missionaries aided the spread of empire.

Although we know much less about the Irish Protestant clergy than about the Catholic during this rapid expansion of Christianity, one theme that is becoming clear in several countries is that among the Anglicans, clergy trained at Trinity College, Dublin, had a major impact upon what is usually (and mistakenly) thought of as the Church of England. In Canada and in New Zealand, for example, the general "low church" tone that emerged — evangelically oriented, liturgically sombre, "Protestant" in theology — is in large part ascribable to the Irish clergy and to their influence upon succeeding generations of locally-trained churchmen.

(II)

Ireland's greatest boon to the United Kingdom empire, however, was through the massive numbers of everyday settlers that it provided. One of the most striking things about the overseas settlement pattern of the Irish has been how non-ideological that pattern has been. From 1815 until the Great Famine, the first overseas choice of Irish migrants (excluding for the moment Great Britain) was British North America (modern day Canada). This was a set of British colonies most of which had been founded by people opposed to the principles of the American revolution and extremely loyal (among English-speakers) to the Crown. Then, from the Famine until roughly World War I, the great republican nation, the United States of America, became the first choice, and, after the war the old enemy, Great Britain, became the preferred new home of Irish emigrants.

This is all very confusing, the more so because the most intriguing part of the Irish out-migration, that to Great Britain, is especially blurred for most of the nineteenth century. In 1841, there were reported to be 415,725 Irish-born persons living in Great Britain,[13] which means almost certainly that more Irish emigrants had chosen England and Scotland between 1815 and 1841 than had chosen either Canada or the United States. It is easily forgotten, also, that Great Britain was the second most important recipient of Famine emigrants: in 1851 there were over 727,000 Irish-born persons living in Britain,[14] making it second among diaspora lands, exceeded only by the United States, which had approximately 962,000 Irish-born.[15]

The problem with the nineteenth-century figures is that it is uncertain how many of the Irish-born living in Great Britain were transient labourers who eventually returned to Ireland. And even if we did know that, the distinction probably was too fine for reality: labourers who arrived as transients one year, turned into permanent residents of Great Britain in another.[16] In any case, "after 1914 there were radical changes in the direction, rate, volume, and composition of emigration," Sean Glynn notes. "America was gradually replaced by Britain and increasingly by England as the main destination. In the years 1946-51, over eighty percent of Irish emigrants went to the U.K."[17] Thus, by 1951, more Irish-born emigrants were living in Great Britain than any place in the world, including the United States.[18] When, in 1978, *The Tablet* issued a special supplement on the Irish diaspora, Donald MacAmhlaigh provided a reminiscence in which he said:

> Britain was a revelation to the work-eager Irish who flocked here during the great post-war boom, and I often wish that Englishmen, who persist in the notion that the Irish dislike them and their country could only have heard the remarks which were commonplace when the Irish workers spoke among themselves. I say among themselves for with a stubborn loyalty the Irish never admitted to an outsider what they were forever saying to each other - that there was nothing "back yonder," that the crowd in Dublin couldn't run a booze-up in a brewery, that Britain was the best bleddy country in the world, better even than the States where, for all the blow and big money, a man couldn't afford to fall sick.[19]

The point to be taken is that as regards the British Empire (and its centre, Great Britain) the Irish emigrants could take it or leave it. Evidentiary problems prevent our knowing where from 1815 to the present day most Irish emigrants chose to go, at least with any degree of precision, but for the purposes of the present discussion it is enough to be able to assert that the hundreds of thousands — indeed millions — of "ballots" cast by the migrants in making their life choices showed clearly that there was no general anti-empire phobia among them. They were willing to settle all over the world under the Union Jack, quite happily if economic and social conditions suited them, and they found

Scotland, Wales and especially England to their liking. Whatever anti-empire valence there was in the value structure of the Irish in the homeland, this was much less important for the migrants as a whole than were other factors. Indeed, it is presumptuous for us to assume automatically that the empire was a negative factor in any individual decision. It is entirely conceivable that a large segment of the Irish population, and not just Protestant loyalists, viewed the empire as a good thing.

All of this involves the United Kingdom empire. In the nineteenth century, another was rising, one that would succeed the British Empire, namely the American. The American empire was (and is) a rather more subtle beast than was either the first British empire (that is, the empire up to the American Revolution) or the second (the nineteenth- and twentieth-century empire that eventually phased itself out of existence as the Commonwealth of Nations). In its overseas aspects, the American empire depended less upon actual conquest of territory (although, as in the case of the Philippines and of Cuba, that sometimes occurred), but more upon commercial conquest. United States hegemony in Latin America, for example, was marvellously efficient, for most of the surplus wealth of those nations was drained off without the necessity of the American government paying for a colonial administrative service.

What is too easily forgotten, however, is that like the British, the Americans had two successive empires. In the American case, the informal hegemony of the second empire over the entire western hemisphere was based on a prior piece of imperialism, namely the physical conquest and occupation of the most fertile and productive portions of the North American continent. The Protestant Irish migrants and their descendants were particularly important in the conquest of the territory just west of the Appalachian mountains and of much of the American south. But it is well to remember that even as late as the mid-nineteenth century, most of what is now the United States was not yet effectively colonized, and that the post-Famine Irish immigrants in the U.S. were part of the colonization process. Whether or not the Irish immigrants or their descendants ever went to the American frontier, they became part of the social and economic machinery that ineluctably ate up most of the continent. It is true that in journeying to the U.S., Irish migrants were joining a nation that had no monarch and that ascribed allegiance to democratic republicanism (except for blacks and for native Americans, who were effectively excluded). It is true also that many individual Irish persons subscribed to organizations that supported the cause of Irish independence from Great Britain, and that sometimes they sent money to buy arms and explosives for that cause.

Yet, these facts should not blind anyone to the overall pattern of the Irish diaspora: that whether they settled in the British or the American empire, the members of the Irish diaspora were an integral part of the nineteenth- and twentieth-century tidal waves of European imperialism. In the empires-of-settlement (which includes the English-speaking world), the success of imperialism was contingent upon the displacement of indigenous populations, upon the legalized theft or confiscation of land previously held by the native inhabitants, and upon the breaking of aboriginal cultures. The Irish participated energetically, efficiently, and enthusiastically in all of these processes and they were very well rewarded for doing so.

Irish Diaspora

Intermezzo

Upon leaving Part I, the area of Clear Themes, it is well to review what we now know, for in Part II we enter a region of considerable historical uncertainty.

From our survey of the Irish homeland, we acquired the necessary points of reference to define the characteristics of the Irish emigrant group in terms of age, gender, religion, and occupational background. Employing New Zealand as a case study of the post-Famine diaspora, we noted two major points: that behind the aggregate numbers of Irish migrants were four fundamentally different migration strategies, those for single women, single men, married couples with children, and married couples without children; and the New Zealand data made it clear that Catholicism and the cultural practices associated with it were not hindrances to adaptation in a modernized, mostly agricultural New World.

The fact that Irish Catholicism was not an impediment to adaptation and success was confirmed in the second case, Australia, and this time in a society whose Irish community was founded in the late eighteenth century and which already had a strong ethnic base before the Great Famine. That in the Australian case, as in the New Zealand one, Irish ethnicity had no demonstrable "big" effects does not mean that it could not have other, less measurable ones.

The case of South Africa was employed to give us a clear picture of one end of the spectrum of possibility, namely of a society wherein Irish migrants arrived late in the diaspora and came with a high level of skills, immediately joining a ruling elite.

Finally, in our discussion of the Irish and empires, it

became clear that the Irish migrants and their descendants implicitly supported the two major empires of the nineteenth and twentieth centuries, the British and the American. Indeed, the very existence of the Irish diaspora (which is overwhelmingly a phenomenon of the English-speaking world) was contingent upon that support.

Those themes are clear. We must now turn to historical areas that are anything but clear:

Part II

Considerable Mysteries

Chapter 7

Women and the Irish Diaspora: The Great Unknown

(I)

The single most severe limitation on our knowledge of the Irish diaspora is this: we know surprisingly little about Irish women in the nineteenth and early twentieth centuries, either in the homeland or in their New Worlds. With any ethnic group this sort of deficit would be a serious problem, but with the Irish it is especially debilitating, because females were half of the diaspora.

Still, there is an analogy that provides grounds for optimism: the history of women in Ireland and in the Irish diaspora is in a position similar to that which prevailed in the field of working class history in, roughly, 1960. A field of research had been defined, able scholars were assaying it, and they were beginning to winnow out useful methods of research from those that were bogus or merely trendy. In the three decades after 1960, a formidable body of scholarship on the working class emerged throughout the English-speaking world. I believe that the next three decades will see a similar development in Irish women's history, worldwide.

The analogy to working class history is apposite because many of the problems that historians of the working class were encountering in 1960 are similar to those at present facing historians of Irish women. As with society's working- and under-classes, women have left behind many fewer records than have privileged males and therefore it demands a lot more effort and ingenuity to do good women's history than it does to engage in more traditional historical work. It requires greater assiduousness in finding and more subtlety in interpreting obscure sources.

The historical study of Irish women in the homeland and abroad faces the same three dangers that bedeviled the development of working class history in the early 1960s. The first is the simple human temptation for the historian, when faced with the requirement of extra work and ingenuity to take the easy path and to write history from pieces of evidence that are colourful, anecdotal, and ultimately unrepresentative. The history of Irish women worldwide involves millions of human beings and the only sort of evidence that will do justice to their stories is systematic data, garnered as much as possible from the whole group, not just from a relatively few interesting cases. The second shortcut that seemingly obviates the need to work patiently through evidence and to operate by tight logical design is "theory." By that one means not genuine theory in the sense of a network of interrelated concepts and constructs that can be used to draw testable hypotheses, but theories in the sense of ideology. Ideology is very useful in forming daily political agenda, but when used as a source for conclusions that are accepted prior to the collection of evidence and before the interrogation of that evidence, then ideology precludes real historical understanding.

The third temptation is to engage in "presentism." One form of presentism is to note (correctly, let us assume) that a certain condition or a certain cause-effect relationship exists in the present and automatically to believe that it held in the past. A common form of presentism is to focus one's research on a period in the near past and then to project it backwards. This is an especial danger in women's history, because it is relatively easy to do "oral history" — that is, to talk to living persons and from such interviews gain a sense of the texture of individual lives that would not be possible from dead pieces of paper. These data, while excellent, usually are only valid for a quite recent period. There is no woman living today in Ireland or any place in the Irish diaspora who can have direct memory of what life was like before the year 1900, let alone in the third quarter of the last century, when the diaspora was at its height.

Everything that we know about the history of Irish women in the diaspora revolves around one central set of facts. One-half of the great Irish diaspora was female. Between the Act of Union of 1800 and the independence of southern Ireland in 1922, about four million Irish females left the homeland. Those who were not minor children, not merely left, but chose to leave. That is crucial. Each made a conscious decision as a result of weighing alternative futures. Those who, after assessing the alternatives, chose to stay in Ireland were just as much involved in choosing their own futures as were those who left. The reader will recall that in Chapter Two I emphasized that it was historically inaccurate and unintentionally demeaning to see Irish emigrants as merely passive in the emigration process, as being unwilling exiles rather than as having been actively engaged in charting their own futures. That point must be re-emphasized here, because the view of the Irish as forced emigrants, passive before the fates, is doubly demeaning to women.

I repeat: women in the Irish diaspora made a conscious decision to emigrate, a volitional choice. That so many left is a clear indication that these women perceived a better future for themselves outside of Ireland, but this does not necessarily mean that they were right. Nor does the massive female outflow necessarily imply that things were bad in absolute terms for Irish women, but only that they believed things would be better for them elsewhere, a relative judgement.

The most intriguing attempt to relate the position of Irish women to the flow pattern of the Irish diaspora is Robert E. Kennedy Jr.'s *The Irish. Emigration, Marriage and Fertility* (1973).[1] Although I am skeptical of some of his arguments, the book should be required reading for any student of the Irish diaspora or of Irish women's history.

As a starting point, Kennedy notes that in western society women live longer than do men. He believes this is primarily the result of biological factors, but the exact cause is irrelevant to his argument. The central point is that this is a dominant western pattern and thus can be used as a cross-cultural point of comparison. As measured by this norm, Irish women in the nineteenth and early twentieth centuries did not live very much longer than did Irish men and in some parts of Ireland actually had shorter life spans. Hence, the Irish pattern resembled more closely that of Bulgaria or of India than it did the United States or Great Britain in the same era.

What caused this? Kennedy suggests that Irish women were badly treated in comparison to the women in most western countries. The specific mechanism of this ill treatment, he suggests, was the result of a strong pattern of male dominance, one so strong that it resulted in relatively high female mortality. Kennedy cites the following specific practices: men and boys eating first in rural households and thereby getting the better and more nutritious food; men keeping the income from the sale of animals and of cash crops for their own use; men being required to look after the needs of wife and children only after taking care of their own needs; sons being given preferential treatment; women in rural areas being required to do heavy agricultural labour as well as housework.

Now whether or not Kennedy is right in suggesting the generality of these male-dominance practices will be a matter of long-term investigation (for example, it is now suggested that in the century after the Famine, wives and daughters were increasingly excluded from performing farm work).[2] However, his central logic train is not dependent upon such relatively minor details. His major observation about life expectation holds.

One possible alternative is that because Irish married women were near or at the top of the international marital fertility table, and because in the nineteenth and early twentieth centuries, childbirth was the single most common cause of adult female death, then this, and not the mistreatment of women, was the cause of lower life expectancy. This suggestion takes us into an area that is totally unknown. Granted, one could argue apodictically that the high marital fertility rate was merely another evidence of excessive male dominance, and another form of male mistreatment of females. The trouble is, we have no idea if it was or not. It is equally possible that women as much as men desired large families and that this degree of risk to female life expectancy was taken on quite willingly by most Irish wives. As one observer shrewdly notes, "Historians have scarcely begun to explore the emotional and sexual interaction of men and women in Irish history."[3]

Still, there is another reason to question Kennedy's formulation about Irish women being treated worse than those in other European countries, and this relates directly to the diaspora. Alone among major western countries, Ireland sent out approximately equal numbers of men and women. This out-migration was a filter as far as women were concerned. The least healthy, most disadvantaged, did not gather enough momentum even to try to leave; further, from roughly the mid-nineteenth century onwards, most recipient nations had health screening procedures to keep out sickly migrants. Thus, the relatively high outflow of Irish women as compared to other European countries included a higher proportion of the nation's healthy women than was the case for other European countries. Therefore the seemingly-real statistical phenomenon of the relatively shorter life span of women in Ireland (as compared to males, using European norms) was a chimera. It was a reflection not of excessive ill treatment by Irish men, but of the strongest, healthiest, toughest Irish women leaving for more promising shores. The high degree of female outflow explains why the life-expectancy figures were skewed and thus destroys the main evidence for male dominance in Ireland being more marked or more cruel than elsewhere in Europe.

One of the hardest things to do in assaying the position of Irish women in their homeland and in the diaspora is to find an appropriate temporal base line, a place to put the measuring stick. A recent book by Janet A. Nolan illustrates just how misleading a false base line can be. In her study, *Ourselves Alone. Women's Emigration from Ireland, 1885-1920* (1989) she attempts to deal with a real historical question: why in the years 1885-1920 did female emigration from Ireland (via Irish ports) exceed that of males (by 2.7 percent)? Her answer is as follows. Prior to roughly 1830, the Irish family "was based on the free attachment of romantic love; it was more democratic than authoritarian."[4] That era, the early 1830s, is her base line. Although there was some sexual segregation in this period in Ireland, Nolan believes that male and female roles were more fluid than they would become later in the century. Here is her description of a fair in those happy days before the Great Famine:

Women in universally tight, low-necked bodices and red flannel skirts extending only halfway down their shins (for freedom of movement) mingled unchaperoned in the holiday crowds. They also took part in faction fights, often putting rocks in their stockings for use as weapons. They provided food and drink for the assembled celebrant — themselves included.[5]

But this happy period came to an end and was replaced by fifty years of steady decline in the status of women, Nolan believes. She suggests that this is the result of "economic recovery [after the Famine] and the introduction of materialistic and individualistic values..."[6] These fifty years of materialistic and individualistic values are said to have created their own backlash, an awareness in women of what they had lost so that more and more women took to seeking a new control over their lives by emigrating.

Now, aside from the fact that no reputable social historian of Ireland accepts the notion that Ireland on the eve of the Famine was a happy period for women (or for almost anyone else for that matter), notice what the use as a base line of a situation that is alleged to have existed in 1830 does when it is used to help assay a situation that began in 1885: it occludes from the explanatory system the period 1830-85, and those were the very years in which most Irish female emigration took place.

Still, Nolan is correct in believing that in the present state of knowledge, the most productive context in which to place the discussion of women's emigration is the history and structure of the Irish family.[7] This holds (for reasons that will be explained in a moment) even for the post-Famine years when, in fact, most Irish female migrants were unmarried. Until roughly the middle of the twentieth century, the economic base of Irish society, as well as the chief social unit, was not a factory, not a multi-owned corporation, but the family-operated farm. This congruence of the main social unit and the main economic unit of society meant that all of the important decisions of a woman's life — whether or not to marry, whether to take a job as a domestic servant, whether to accept employ as a farm worker, whether or not to emigrate — were made with the family as the backdrop of the decision.

A shorthand term used to summarize the Irish marriage system as it developed after the Great Famine is "the match." In necessarily simplified terms, the main components of the match were: (1) a male farmer, wishing to keep his farm intact (instead of subdividing it as had usually occurred early in the nineteenth century); (2) chose one of his sons to receive the farm when it came time for him to retire; and (3) arranged a "match" for that son through another male farmer, one who had a marriageable daughter and would provide that daughter with a sufficient dowry; then, assuming that the two young people assented to the match and that it went ahead, (4) the girl's dowry was used to help the other adult children of the farm family to leave the holding to get a start in life elsewhere.[8]

It has been aptly remarked that one of the great paradoxes of post-Famine Ireland is that while the commercial and cultural systems were being modernized, the fundamental familial-economic structure was becoming increasingly archaic.[9] Facing this set of contradictory forces, a woman's options were limited, but she had more choices open to her than might at first appear. For most women, the most advantageous position was to enter a rural marriage. A woman thus became a junior partner in an enterprise whose two primary goals were production and reproduction. Each was important: a childless marriage was considered a failure. There were strong traditions (admittedly hard to document in detail) of childless women in pre-Famine Ireland being "sent back" to their fathers.

A woman who did not become part of a match could choose to emigrate from her home. For many, "emigration" was within Ireland, a move to Belfast or Dublin, where they might work as domestic servants or, if lucky, find places in the needle trades or in a textile factory.[10] (Many of the others who did not leave the home region found employment in service with doctors, lawyers, or better-off farm families). Emigration could be to Liverpool, Glasgow, or London; or to the far side of the world. One of the things that we do not know about Irish female migration to New Worlds is whether the journey was done in one big step or whether it was more common for Irish women to do it in stages, for example, first spending time in Dublin or Liverpool, saving money and making useful contacts, before then being off to Australia or Canada, or the USA.

These options were real, but were not all there was. Joanna Bourke recently has pointed out that to see emigration as the only alternative to marriage open to most young Irish women is much too stark. She argues, first, that those performing housework were far from powerless. Portraying female houseworkers as powerless may, in our own time, "serve an important ideological function, but it does not reflect the reality of the lives of those women choosing in this period [the later nineteenth and early twentieth centuries] to become houseworkers. For these women, patriarchy was not the problem and threats to the individual woman's power were liable to come from other sources."[11] Further, Bourke argues that many women chose to become full-time houseworkers without being married to the person for whom they maintained the house. Bourke is not here referring to everyday domestic servants, but to people who effectively ran a house. The position of houseworker in charge of her own turf most often was a situation with a relative, a widower, or a bachelor cousin who had a farm. Housekeeping for the parish priest was a prized post in any rural community. And, Bourke argues, in families where a widow was head of the farm operation, a younger daughter frequently stayed on and became the "head housekeeper." This occurred more often than one might think, because in the century after the Great Famine, it was the custom for men to marry women ten to twenty years their junior, and therefore widowhood was common. Thus, Bourke believes that between the extremes of marriage and of emigration there was a third, viable alternative for women in rural Ireland and that this was chosen by many as not only an acceptable position, but, indeed, as the best of all alternatives.[12]

That argument accepted, two points of clarification are necessary. The first of these is that Bourke's argument, compelling as it is, works only for the late Victorian era and for the first decades of the twentieth century. When one goes back to the pre-Famine era, the picture is much starker, the position of women more marginal and the options open to them much more limited. This was well documented by a remarkable investigation into the poor of Ireland conducted in the 1830s. This was the first social survey in the British Isles set up by methods that would be recognizable to present day social scientists. Inevitably, it produced a large mass of material, and this material documented that among the very poor of Ireland, women were the very worst off. The secretary of the commission, John Revans, wrote and published his own observations and conclusions separately from the official governmental report. He was probably better informed on the state of the Irish poor than anyone in the country, so his conclusion is important: "[It] cannot be a matter of astonishment, when it is considered that *females cannot maintain themselves by honest industry, however well inclined.*"[13]

Revans was not a person given to overstatement. What he meant was terrifyingly simple: in those years, before the Famine, an unmarried woman, or a widow who did not own land, could not support herself in Irish society. A woman either had to leave Ireland, or become part of a family unit (either as a wife or as a clinging-on spinster daughter) — or she had to live in abject poverty. This confirms the earlier point: that anyone who sees the "freedom" of this pre-Famine era as being a Golden Age for Irish women is being irresponsible.[14]

The other qualification to Bourke's important work is that although being a "head houseworker" was a desirable position in later Victorian Ireland, the proportion of unmarried women in Irish society was increasing faster than was the number of desirable posts. Given below is the percentage of Irishwomen aged 25-34 who were unmarried:[15]

Year	Percentage unmarried
1841	28
1851	39
1861	39
1871	38
1881	41
1891	48
1901	53

Now, if one compares those percentages to the female portion of emigration from what is now the Republic of Ireland (that is, the twenty-six counties, which excludes Northern Ireland), one has a fascinating parallel:[16]

Year	Percentage female
1852-60	49.8
1861-70	45.6
1871-80	47.1
1881-90	49.4
1891-1900	54.1
1901-10	52.2
1911-20	52.6
1852-1920	50.1

Female emigration only came to exceed male emigration in the 1890s, just when, for the first time, it became obvious that about half the women in the most marriageable age group were not finding a match. Emigration for tens of thousands of women was not a terrible fate, but a safety net, for "even the humblest husband or job abroad was better than no husband and no job at home."[17]

(II)

There are five main periods of female emigration from Ireland but, unhappily, only on one of them do we have much information. The first period is from the end of the Napoleonic War until the Famine, spanning 1815-45. The data for that era are fragmentary, but it is clear that the bulk of the long distance migration (that is, excluding Great Britain), was in the form of family groups or childless married couples. A reasonable estimate (really, an educated guess) is that unmarried women of adult age comprised somewhat less than one-half of the outflow of Irish females before the Famine.[18] The second period, 1846-51, encompasses the Famine and is a time of great confusion. The exodus swamped the record-keeping system. Not until 1 May 1851 was a reasonable system of counting emigrants developed, and then it had to be recalibrated, in 1853. The great historical loss is that we really know very little of what happened in the years 1846-51. Women left in the hundreds of thousands, but whether they were married or single, young or old, is unknown. A third period, 1851-76, was the classical era of Irish emigration. Unlike the years of the Famine exodus, when everything was whirl and there was no obvious continuity with anything that either had come before or would come after, the period 1851-75 blended into the fourth era, 1876-1920. The chief difference between the two is that in the earlier period males almost always outnumbered females in the emigrant flow, whereas in the late Victorian era and in the early twentieth century, females were apt to be the majority. Finally, after 1920, the character of female emigration changed considerably, most of it now being to Great Britain rather than to distant locations. Only from the last quarter of the nineteenth century to 1920 do we have good information on the basic matters of Irish female migration: good record keeping on most matters started in 1876 but, after the partition of Ireland in 1920, the quality of emigration records declined to pre-1875 levels.

Using the period of good data, 1876-1920, as a window on the entire history of female emigration from Ireland, it appears that there were six distinct sorts of emigrants, and that each of these categories represents a quite distinct strategy of migration. Each strategy uses emigration as a part of the life cycle, but in ways very different from each of the others.

The most important matter in approaching all of these various categories is to ask whether an individual female was married or single. Given below are data (excluding migration to Britain) for 1883 to 1920.[19]

Year	Percentage of female emigrants married or widowed
1883-1890	17.7
1891-1900	13.1
1901-1910	12.8
1911-1920	13.2

Notice here that an implied time-gradient exists. This suggests that earlier in the century (the 1850-70s) the proportion of unmarried women, though still dominant, was somewhat smaller.

Particularly noteworthy is that the married/unmarried breakdown was radically different according to the destinations of the female emigrants. Given below are the data for the earliest period on which we have this information, the years 1877-80.[20]

Destination	Percentage married
USA	16.9
Australia and New Zealand	16.3
Canada	30.7
South Africa	61.6

These data exclude permanent emigrants to Great Britain. Although precise information on that matter is not available, the leading demographic authorities of intra-U.K. migration suggest that in the 1880s the traffic to England, in contrast to that to most overseas destinations, was mostly the migration of entire families.[21] Thus, one could set 20 percent as a rough indicator of the proportion of all Irish female overseas emigrants in the middle and late 1870s who were either married or widowed.

With that as background, let us define the six basic categories of Irish female emigrants, and, at the same time, draw some heuristic estimates of what proportion each group was of the overall female outflow in the mid to late 1870s.

Group 1, the smallest, consisted of widows who had dependent children accompanying them. This was not an insignificant group because, as was pointed out earlier, post-Famine marriages involved a considerable age gap between men and women so that widowhood was a common experience. In the cases of women emigrating with children, it was not their widowhood that was unusual, but that it had come to them sooner than expected, while their children were still dependents. A very rough estimate (based on the Vogel sample for New Zealand for 1876, the only full sample we have)[22] is that widows with dependent children made up slightly more than 1.5 percent of Irish female emigrants. In most cases these were women above thirty years of age.

Group 2 consisted of married women who had a husband and children accompanying them. If the Vogel sample is at all representative, these were mature women, on average in their early thirties. We can estimate such women as being between 11 and 12 percent of total female emigration.[23] These women were individuals who had begun

marriage in the dominant marital pattern of the time —
engaging in a match, creating a family economic unit, and
having children — but for whom life for some reason
became less satisfactory than they thought it would be
elsewhere. These people were not necessarily the failures of
Irish society. Some failures, yes, but, this group must also
have included the persons whose lives were going well but
who had bigger ambitions than Ireland could satisfy.

Group 3, although also consisting of married women,
was very different. It comprised women who were
accompanied on their journey by their spouses, but who had
no dependent children. Again, using the Vogel sample as our
guide, we see that they made up perhaps 7 percent of the
Irish female emigrants. In the usual case they were younger
than married women who emigrated with children. Probably
most were still in their twenties.[24] The key thing here is that
these women, although married, cannot be automatically
assumed to have been part of the full-blown traditional Irish
family pattern. Some may have been so, having contracted
traditional matches, and then, with husbands, deciding to
emigrate. But for others, marriage and then emigration soon
after being married, represented an alternative to the
traditional match. Young persons with minimal resources
were free to marry, so long as they then quickly escaped
Ireland. But whatever the individual background, these
women who emigrated with spouses, but without children,
were adopting what was perhaps the most effective
emigration strategy. They left home accompanied by an
insurance policy. Unlike single migrants, and unlike couples
with dependent children, women (and men) in childless
marriages usually had someone in employment to fall back
on when themselves sick or unemployed. Crucially, in such a
marriage, each partner usually was able to work. A childless
couple was highly mobile geographically, and was eagerly
sought by farm managers, hotel keepers, and a range of
employers who needed both female and male skills in their
businesses. As long as the couple postponed pregnancy,
women who emigrated in this fashion were the most
advantaged among female emigrants.

Group 4 was made up of dependent unmarried
females — most of these were below the marriageable age.
These mostly were girls who travelled to a New World with

their mothers and fathers, or with at least one parent. In a small, but still noticeable minority of cases, young dependent girls emigrated with older brothers and sisters. A few of young age (as young as age seven, in records that I have seen) emigrated alone, being in essence shipped overseas to family or relatives who had emigrated earlier.

Our historical problem is that we lack direct data on female dependents. The problem becomes more complicated when one realizes that although most dependent single females were young girls, there were significant numbers of mature women who emigrated in family groups as dependents. One finds "spinsters" in their thirties and forties being carried as family dependents, and on occasion I have encountered an old aunt in her seventies being brought along. The best way to estimate this large, but disparate, group of female single dependents is to use age categories. We can assume as a base for our estimate that virtually all girls under fifteen were dependents. They comprised 15.6 percent of all female emigrants from Ireland in the decade 1871-80.[25] The problem is that the official categories, covering ages fifteen through nineteen, include two sorts of females: mostly eighteen- and nineteen-year old girls emigrating on their own, but also a large number of younger teenage girls emigrating *en famille*. My own guess is that roughly 5.2 percent of the 15-19 age group were single dependent girls.[26] Finally, one must make a small addition, say, one-fifth of 1 percent, to account for the number of older dependent females found in the total numbers of single women over age twenty. In total, a very rough estimate is that 21 percent of the Irish female migrants in the later 1870s were unmarried, but were dependent upon families for their support. These individuals would not have to encounter the fundamental, and fundamentally traumatic, foundation of the Irish social system, the match, but they were hardly free spirits: they were emigrating as dependents upon other family members, persons whose own values and behaviour had been formed in the Old Country.

Group 5 in many ways is the most interesting. It consisted of non-dependent females who were of marriageable age, but who emigrated as unmarried women. These women should have found emigration emancipating, for they were leaving behind the archaism of the Irish countryside and were not doing so in the company of their parents. On the other hand, they were taking greater risks than married women or single women who emigrated as family dependents. The key here is that they were of marriageable age and could look forward in the usual instance to forming a family in the new land, and (perhaps) under new rules. If one sets for statistical purposes the end of the marriageable age bracket as thirty-five years, then it appears that slightly over half (50.5 percent) of the Irish female migrants in the 1870s were unmarried, non-dependent, and marriageable.

Group 6 is numerically much smaller and represents an entirely different life course. These were women who had not married in Ireland and who for the most part were now past the age at which marriage was likely: over thirty-five. They had either been family dependents at home or had been employed as domestics, farm servants, or in the needle trades, and now for whatever reasons were seeking a better life. Some few of them might marry in the New World, but most would not. Moreover (given nineteenth-century dietary conditions), they were in, or at least approaching, an age when child bearing was unlikely. This group, comprising about 8.5 percent of female emigrants in the 1870s, probably faced the most uncertain future of any group. Unskilled, single, most of them could look forward to supporting themselves for the rest of their lives by hard labour in a strange land.[27]

Let us sum up this picture and the heuristic estimates that accompany it. By "heuristic" I mean that this accounting is intended more to produce research questions than to answer them. The assumptions that were involved in drawing up the figures were reasonable, but guesses, are guesses no matter how well informed they may be. One of the first tasks of women's historians as they study the Irish diaspora should be to do a direct and accurate account of the various strands of Irish female emigration from the earliest days (at least from 1825) onwards. The Irish outflow in the 1870s can be conceptualized as follows:

1. Widows with children	1.5 %
2. Married women with husbands and children	11.5
3. Married women, with husbands but without children	7.0
Sub-Total Married Women and Widows with Dependent Children	20.0%
4. Dependents (mostly juveniles)	21.0
5. Non-dependent women of marriageable age	50.5
6. Non-dependent women, past marriageable age	8.5
Sub-Total Unmarried Girls and Women	80.0%
	100.0

Although the accounting here employed is heuristic, I must emphasize that the categories of female emigrants are not. Nor are the categories merely a case of drawing fine academic distinctions. The six categories of female migrants are rooted in the experiences of real people. The categories represent the six most fundamental ways in which emigration fit into the life cycle of Irish women. Each category is a product of a specific major sort of female past spent in Ireland, and each, equally, implies a set of personal strategies for the future. Anchored as they are in reality, these categories are an elementary step in coming to terms with the full complexity of the Irish diaspora.

Just how rich, complex, and pleasing the tapestry of Irish women's history in the Irish diaspora will eventually become after a generation or two of serious scholars will have worked in the field is indicated by bringing together the three primary variables that I have suggested we need to employ as a first step in understanding the female diaspora. The first of these is time, five distinct periods of clearly separable emigration history. The second is the demographic character of the female emigrant group. We have seen that six major sorts of emigrants were found in the female outflow. And third, the variable of destination is important, there being six major destinations (the USA, Great Britain, Canada, Australia, New Zealand, and South Africa), and at various times specialization in the sort of women who went to each place. For example, the reader will remember that women who migrated to South Africa were more apt to be married and, if unmarried, more apt to be skilled, than females who went to any other destination.

As far as female emigration was concerned, the USA represents the other end of the spectrum: in the later Victorian era it tended to receive female migrants who mostly were young, unmarried, and unskilled. In 1881-90, for example, 75 percent of female migrants to the USA were under twenty-five years of age, and about 60 percent of them were in the fifteen to twenty-four age group.[28] Nor is it inconsequential that in the late Victorian era not only were most Irish women who moved to the USA young, but they were mostly from the poorest, least economically and socially modernized parts of Ireland. Nor that from these most-backward areas, more women than men went to the USA. To take County Mayo as a case: in the period 1876-85, the female/male emigration ratio by way of Irish ports to the USA was 120/100, and in the years 1886-1905 it reached a high of 175/100.[29] This means that what really gave the Irish-born in America their unique character were not such things as Tammany Hall or riotous male behaviour, but rather the presence of large numbers of women who emigrated, young and single, from the embracing poverty and social constrictions of the least advanced parts of Ireland.

Five distinct time periods. Six distinct groups of women. Six major destinations. This divides Irish female emigrants, four million or more of them, into 180 separate cells, each representing a distinct form of female experience within the Irish diaspora. And that is just the beginning.

(III)

Was emigration an emancipating experience? An answer to this query must necessarily focus primarily (although not entirely) upon the unmarried, non-dependent women. Presumably, women who migrated with their spouses or even as widows with children, were continuing a familial pattern that had begun in Ireland and would not be fundamentally altered in their own lifetimes. Dependent female children were by definition carried along by the force of their parents' emigration, hardly a liberating situation. But for the unmarried and non-dependent female majority, the possibility of emancipation (however one wishes to define the concept) was there. Two polar views of this possibility exist. Some writers, such as Ide O'Carroll, see emigration in general as freeing Irish women from family constraints and thus ensuring that they took over the direction of their own lives.[30] Other scholars, such as Brenda Collins, believe that "it is a late twentieth century viewpoint to see migration as an event freeing the actor from traditional constraints... Irish immigrant women carried their cultural baggage with them."[31]

Whatever the Irish women leaving the old homeland wanted in their New World, various governments all over the English-speaking world wanted them for purposes of their own. Central among these were production and reproduction — the very functions that had been ascribed to women in the traditional Irish marriage. (In addition, many governments had a secondary use for Irish women, namely that they were supposed to civilize the male population, or at least quiet it down).

There was nothing charitable or disinterested about the way the British colonies and the USA facilitated Irish female immigration. All of the nations to which the Irish migrated (with the exception of Great Britain itself) were in the midst of seizing large tracts of land and resources from native peoples, and they needed increased population, agricultural and industrial growth and, if possible, civil order. That various governments actively wanted Irish women is clear from a whole range of governmental policies. These ranged from the active importation of women (Australia, New Zealand and South Africa) to the facilitation of banks and telegraph companies in transmitting "remittances" home and in the forwarding of pre-paid tickets from migrants in Canada and the USA to potential migrants in the Irish homeland. As remarked earlier (in Chapter Three), later in the 1870s and in the early 1880s, the New Zealand government wished to restrict Irish immigration, but decided not to do so because most of the Irish immigrants were single women, and as an official noted, "the Government have not deemed it desirable to exclude any of these..."[32] In 1832, authorities in New South Wales voted £10,000 to bring in the two sorts of persons they wanted most: one-third of the sum went for mechanics, two-thirds for single women.[33] In 1848 and again in 1855 South Australia imported bunches of single girls, 5,000 in all, mostly Irish. Most of these were juveniles, with little education or training in anything like housecraft. The first group, more than 600 orphans and former Irish poorhouse residents, were brought in during 1848 and did quite well. Though they were generally a "rough lot," in the contemporary view, and did not know either how to milk cows or how to wash clothes efficiently, they learned fast; and in any case by 1852 most of them were married. And (here the self-reinforcing nature of Irish female migration becomes apparent) they soon were employing their own servants and thus implicitly encouraging further female in-migration. The second group, that of 1855, numbered more than 4,000, too large a group to fit in so easily. Many of these girls had been abandoned by their families and they were an even rougher bunch than those brought in 1848. Traumatized already, many of them had agreed to the long voyage in expectation of going to Sydney or Melbourne, but they landed in Adelaide. They settled in badly. Many left South Australia the moment they could. Others, sent into the outback as agricultural labourers, barely survived.[34]

These two groups of single female Irish juveniles, shipped around the world, were different in one way from most Irish unmarried women immigrants in the nineteenth century: they had no friends or relatives where they settled. That is important. As I will argue in a moment, despite how the emigration data looks on the surface — being comprised of roughly six-tenths unmarried non-dependent adult women — the overwhelming majority of these women were actually going someplace where they had immediate family, close relatives, or, at minimum, friends from their neighbourhood in Ireland.

The synergistic energy of Irish female migration and governmental policies is remarkable. In some places for some time periods (Australia and New Zealand in particular, places for which travel costs were very high), governments had to pay to import women, but for the most part governments did not have to do so, despite needing women badly: Irish family ties led the Irish to pay for the importation out of their own resources.

Take a simple example, the case of two Irish brothers
each of whom needed a woman to complete the basic
economic unit for settlement on a frontier in a fast
modernizing society. One observes the first brother,
Alexander Gordon McClure, writing in a thoroughly
pragmatic tone to his sisters in Belfast. In a letter from
Invercargill on the South Island of New Zealand, he says
that he would like to come home to Ireland to fetch a wife.
This idea he presents in the same tone of everyday
calculation as if he were considering coming home to
acquire a really good iron plow or a team of draft horses.[35]
Alexander had not planned quite far enough ahead. When
one of his brothers — James — decided to emigrate, he
planned better. He first collected information on various
possible places to settle (other relatives were in Australia
and the United States, so his sources of information were
good). Then, having decided to join Alexander in New
Zealand, James kitted himself out for the journey. That
included acquiring and moving a wife with him. He did this
with great calculation and without making a family matter of
it. Just on the verge of sailing from London to New Zealand
in June 1860, James wrote to his sisters in Belfast:

> We are all about to start for New Zealand in a few days ... I
> think it is as well to take a wife with me. Her name is Emily
> Humphreys, the orphan daughter of a solicitor. She is in her
> 25th year [he was 35] so not too young. I am to be married next
> Tuesday at Kensington church from her Uncle who is pretty
> high up in the Board of Trade.[36]

When, from New Zealand, James McClure reported back to
his family in Ireland, his letters had a factual tone, but not
the unnerving flatness that had characterized the
announcement of his impending marriage. He wrote the
following to one of his sisters in 1865:

> Now to relieve your mind regarding us we are getting on slowly
> but *steadily* thank God. The changes in this Colony are very
> sudden; men one year apparently realising fortunes and the next
> losing everything.
> **
> We thank goodness through all have continued to hold our own
> and advance as well, not so fast as we should wish, but still
> improve. Our house is comfortable and is the best in the
> neighbourhood.

176

Then he refers to his wife, whom the family at home have never met, with a mixture of warmth and of defensiveness:

> My wife is all I could wish but do not run away with the idea that she is a humdrum commonplace woman; she is a gentle woman in every sense of the word and respected and esteemed by all who know her; she is very handsome and only now twenty-nine.[37]

Clearly, James McClure had imported the right sort of wife as part of his travelling gear.

Of course it is offensive to modern ears to encounter concepts such as importing women, or as taking them as part of some male's emigration gear, but, in hundreds of thousands of instances that was the historical reality. All historical realities have more than one side, however, and what from one perspective was simply good governmental policy (encouraging Irish men to import their own wives) from another perspective was family loyalty and continuity. Thus, it was reported to be common practice in the pre-Famine years for husbands to migrate first with the hope of saving enough money in the New Land to bring out their wives;[38] and, indeed the pattern has not disappeared at the present day.

But this financing of female emigration by private means was not limited to men who supported their spouses. Brothers frequently financed their sisters' migration. Just how extensive Irish self-financing of emigration is indicated by the magnitude of remittances sent from North America to Ireland. Studies done for the years 1848 and 1868 indicate that enough prepaid passages were sent back to the British Isles from United Kingdom emigrants to bring out three-quarters of all British and Irish emigrants to North America.[39] The proportion sent by Irish persons must have been at least as large, for studies elsewhere (in Australia and New Zealand, for example) indicate that the Irish over-participated in such arrangements.

What this implies as far as the single non-dependent female migrants to North America are concerned is that in the usual instance they were being sponsored on their journey out of Ireland by members of their immediate family, by relatives or by close friends (the same held for the "nomination" schemes to Australia and New Zealand). Chris

McConville has conducted a valuable examination of assisted migrants to Victoria, Australia, in 1861. This is a well-documented group and can be taken as a cognate of the much larger, but ill-documented group of persons in Ireland assisted by those in Canada and the United States who already had emigrated. Under the Australian nomination scheme, a person (by paying a portion of the costs) could obtain a passage for someone at home, so the effect was much the same as when someone in Boston or Toronto sent a pre-paid emigration ticket to Ireland. This is the breakdown of the sorts of persons who were sponsored by nominators resident in Victoria.[40]

Relationship of Sponsored Person to the Nominator	Percentage
husband	3.2
wife	4.8
child under twelve years	9.1
mother	3.2
son over twelve	2.3
daughter over twelve	2.9
brother	21.8
sister	29.6
cousin	19.7
friend	3.3
	99.9

These percentages imply two interesting points. One of these is a minor, but intriguing sidebar: namely that 3.2 percent of the sponsored migrants were men being assisted by their wives. This is a sharp break from the stereotyped pattern and implies that in a significant minority of cases, the woman went first, made a start in the new land, and then brought over her spouse. Second, and of much more importance, is that 71.1 percent of the sponsored migrants were being brought over not by parents, but by brothers, sisters and cousins.

What this says about most of the single, adult non-dependent female emigrants is that although they may have gotten on the boat alone, in fact there was an entire familially-derived support network for most of them on the other side. Fascinatingly, this network was familial, but without the traditional heads of the family — mother and father — being involved. (Had they been present in the new land, they, rather than brothers and sisters and cousins, would have been the official sponsors.) This confirms something that I observed when taking apart and reconstructing one full year's shipping registers to New Zealand: that official records — both in the Irish homeland and in the receiving countries — understate family ties. Brothers and sisters travelling on the same emigrant ship were tallied as single individuals, and if one did not do a family-reconstruction of that ship's passengers, one would miss the fact that this actually was a family migration, but with parents absent. Sometimes the young people of entire extended families — cousins, brothers and sisters — travelled together. Yet, the records make it appear as if they had no connection with each other.

Now, in neither case — the huge number of single, non-dependent women who were sponsored by previously-emigrated family members, or those who actually travelled with cousins or siblings — do we have any systematic record of the familial aspect of the relationship, aside from the general statistics of massive numbers of pre-paid tickets and assisted passages. Nor do we have any indication of what clearly must have been the case: that, having been sponsored by some family member to travel to a new land, most of the single women used these same family members, cousins, and friends, as a support network. I think that what we had all over the world among Irish emigrants was a transitional phenomenon, congeries of non-patriarchal families. These were the networks of sisters, brothers, cousins, and friends who lived near to each other and acted as families (indeed, they were families) until individual members married and established their own nuclear families.

In pointing out this phenomenon, one that is hidden behind the opaque numbers of the official records, I am implicitly explaining why it is better to talk of the great majority of females being non-dependent, meaning that they made their own living, rather than independent, implying that they had broken free of the old family networks and their derivatives. Most had not broken free, but that is no failing on the part of the emigrants. By not abrogating family ties, but instead using them to help themselves to slide into a new life in a new land, the hundreds of thousands of unmarried Irish emigrant women were being shrewd and self-preserving, and that is no weakness.

(IV)

How well did Irish women perform the two functions that the several governments of the New World assigned to them: production and reproduction?

Generally, they seem to have done just what the governments wanted but, perversely, official records of this are thin, and that holds worldwide. The reason that things are so fuzzy is that (1) in all probability most single Irish women eventually married in the New World and (2) when they became pregnant, they usually left the work force and became full time mothers and houseworkers.[41] However, (3) until very recently, government statisticians all over the English-speaking world have treated women who work in the home or farm either as "dependents," or, at best, as "housewives" as if work within the family were a single undifferentiated activity. This is misleading for urban societies, but even worse for countries such as Canada, Australia and New Zealand, where many (probably most) women settled in rural areas and frequently became full-time partners in farms or ranches. Further, one loses in the available data any real indication of the productivity of married women through part-time work done in the home. Taking in laundry and taking in boarders were two common activities of Irish housewives. All of which is to say that one has to assume (but cannot directly prove) the continued economic production of Irish women migrants after they began to raise children.

Before they married, what did the Irish emigrant women do in their new homeland? In every country and (one strongly suspects) in every period of diaspora history from 1815 to 1920, the most common occupation of single Irish women was domestic service, either in a city or on a farmstead. This pattern reached its peak in the USA where the Irish-born female population was the most urban of any in the world. There a majority of Irish women who were in full-time employment were in service. In 1900, the

employment profile of Irish-born women in the USA was as
follows:[42]

Occupation	Percentage of employed Irish-born women engaged therein
Professional	3.3
Service	70.4
Manufacturing	20.1
Agriculture	<u>2.8</u>
	96.6

In the USA, the predilection of Irish immigrant women for
domestic service as an occupation, combined with the large
absolute size of the group, meant that for a time they
dominated that field. A study conducted in 1920 estimated
that 43 percent of the domestic female servants in the USA
were women born in Ireland.[43] In the other countries of the
Irish diaspora, domestic service was the most common
occupation of Irish migrant women in the nineteenth and
early twentieth centuries, but it did not engage the majority:
agricultural, industrial and commercial occupations,
combined, exceeded domestic service.

Generally, Irish women migrants were successfully
integrated into the economies of their new homelands.
However, long distance migration is an unsettling process.
No matter how helpful the family-derived social network
was to these women, there always were some failures. As
discussed in Chapter Four, the Irish as a migrant group had a
high degree of mental illness compared to groups from other
countries, and the women's mental hospitalization rate was
as high as was the men's. That was human wastage, and so
too was the proportion of single Irish women who turned to
crime, an activity that not only is not economically
productive, but often reduces the sum total of society's
economic resources. In her study of women in Port Phillip
and Victoria, Australia, 1840-60, Sharon Morgan found that
Irish-born women constituted almost half of the female
prison population at the end of the 1850s; this was at a time
when the Irish-born were roughly 15 percent of the total
population and about one-quarter of the foreign-born. Public

drunkenness was the most common offense committed by Irish immigrant women and vagrancy the second. The former offense was not totally incompatible with economic productivity, but the latter is an indication of economic failure. Petty crimes such as minor thefts and prostitution were the other most common offenses. Heavy crime was not frequent.[44] Even when one makes compensation for the loading of the justice system against immigrants, it is clear that a real problem existed in Australia. This suggests a matter that should be researched in all societies that received single Irish women in significant numbers: what happened to those who neither married nor found a decent job?

(V)

When we turn to examine the second "official" duty of Irish migrant women — reproduction — the state of knowledge is even more discouraging.

We should reasonably expect to find, as a basis for any discussion of the history of Irish migrant women, three things for each major destination and for each time period except the pre-Famine era (for which demographic records are so sketchy as to make it unreasonable to ask too much): (1) an indication of the total percentage of Irish migrant women who never married, (2) some rough, but systematic, data on the average age of marriage of those who did marry, and (3) an indication of the average *completed* family size of those who did. Crucially, this is very different from information on the average size of the Irish immigrant family at any given time. Average family size data is a false indication of fecundity. *Completed* family size (the total number of children born to the average marriage) is much more accurate a guage of a culture's fecundity.

Three very simple items, one would think. One cannot carry out even the most basic discussion of the collective history of Irish migrant women without knowing them. Knowledge of such items is especially important because there is a debate among women's historians concerning the degree to which in diaspora lands, Irish women and men replicated the familial patterns of the old homeland. Thus, Janet Nolan believes that Irish immigrants in the USA engaged in "the practice of early and universal marriage."[45]

Hsia Diner, on the other hand, suggests that "the rate of marriage among the Irish in the United States did outpace that in Ireland, since people no longer were bound to the single-inheritance system," but argues for the "continuity of peculiarly Irish family patterns," involving low rates of marriage and high ages of marriage for those who did marry.[46] What Nolan and Diner have in common is that neither scholar has any systematic demographic evidence to support her position, only anecdotal material and small-set community studies.

Indeed, for no nation of the Irish diaspora do we possess a full set of data, covering most time periods, and for no single time period do we have cross-national comparative data.

The best hints at historical reality come from Australia. Chris McConville conducted the only available longitudinal study of whether or not Irish immigrant women married in their new homeland. Among Irish-born women who in the early 1890s died in Victoria, 90 percent had been married at some time.[47] This fits well with data collected in 1911 on all Irish-born women and men over age fifteen throughout Australia. In that group (many of the women were below the typical marriage age), 52.6 percent were married.[48] Using Roman Catholicism as a surrogate for the multigenerational Irish ethnic group, one finds that in 1911, 66.3 percent of women of Irish ethnic background aged twenty or above were married, widowed, or divorced.[49] These data, which are systematic and cover an entire nation, are far superior to anything that we yet have for the USA. They tend to support Janet Nolan's theory that Irish-born women took marriage as being a normal part of the life cycle and they tend to invalidate Diner's idea of the reluctance of the Irish to marry.

Given that most Irish women (both immigrants and second and subsequent generations) married, and given the attitude towards birth control that ran through all religious denominations until at least the 1920s, it was inevitable that the great majority of Irish women procreated. In what degree (what was the average completed family size?) remains to be discovered, but there is no doubt that generations of Irish migrant women did what nineteenth- and early twentieth-century governments wanted them to do: helped to breed an indigenous white population.

A very touchy problem for contemporary Irish men and women (as well as for some modern historians) is the matter of endogamy — meaning, "Did the Irish immigrants marry their own kind?" and "Did Catholics marry Catholics, or did they step outside of the faith?" This latter possibility worried everyone, Catholics and Protestants alike. As David Fitzpatrick has shown in his study of emigrant letters, the greatest challenge to trans-oceanic cultural unity and family ties was when a marriage was contracted in the new homeland. Migrants were frequently at great pains to assure family at home that the new spouse was acceptable, and this was especially true when they married, as the Irish migrants frequently did, outside of their own group.[50] Out-marriage, or to use the term that the migrants themselves used, "mixed marriages" in the religious sense of the term, had long been condemned in the Irish homeland by both Catholics and Protestants.[51] This carried over to the several new homelands. In Australia, for example, one finds at mid-nineteenth century, a strong newspaper campaign which argued that the central purpose of Irish female migration was to subvert the Protestant family through mixed marriages. Protestant men would be seduced by the young Irish girls and, after marriage, their children would be raised Roman Catholic.[52] On the other side of the religious divide, the bishops of the province of Australia in 1869 issued a pastoral letter that declared "the frequency of mixed marriages is a terrible blot upon the character of our Catholic community. It is sad to think with what facility Catholic parents consent to such irreligious connections .... The sad truth is, dearly beloved, that the indifferentism, which we have already stigmatised as the mother heresy and pestilence of our day, has reached us ...."[53]

A study of the Catholic community in Victoria showed that in the decade after 1851, between 33 percent and 50 percent of Catholic women married in Protestant churches, a sure sign of a religiously mixed marriage. In Catholic churches in the same period, one out of three Catholic women married non-Catholic men.[54] For the year 1911, we have information on all marriages existing in Australia (not merely those contracted in that year: existing). These data indicate that 26.10 percent of Catholic women had married outside of their faith, and 17.73 percent of Catholic men.[55]

There is a second, less emotionally-sensitive form of "mixed marriage," namely a union in which an Irish person married a non-Irish one (this would not necessarily mean that they were of different religious faiths, just different ethnic groups). In Victoria in 1870-72, 52.3 percent of Irish immigrant brides were joined with a spouse who was also an Irish immigrant. (In the same time period 65.5 percent of Irish-born bridegrooms married Irish-born women)[56] Matters changed somewhat as the century progressed. If one surveys all extant marriages in Australia in 1911, one finds that among Irish-born women, less than half (47.52 percent had married Irish-born husbands, and even fewer Irish immigrant males (43.57 percent) had married Irish-born spouses.[57] Of course this means of calibrating an ethnically mixed marriage exaggerates the degree of out-marriage, because when an Irish-born woman married a second or third generation man of Irish ethnicity, the alliance was tabulated as being mixed. Nevertheless, the important point is that there undeniably was a good deal of leakage in the Irish community, by intermarriage with persons of various other ethnic groups. This implies, among other things, that Irish-born women were not totally restricted by their ethnic or religious group. A very large minority of Irish women must have stepped outside of either their ethnic or their religious groups, or both, when selecting a husband.

Are there systematically-collected data from other countries that confirm this picture? To move to another continent and another era, in 1970 the demographic authorities of England and Wales for the first time collected data on ethnically mixed marriages among immigrants. Of the 11,783 Irish women from the Republic of Ireland who contracted a marriage in England or Wales in 1970, 54 percent married men who had been born in the Republic of Ireland.[58] Given that the Republic of Ireland (that is, the twenty-six counties) is overwhelmingly Roman Catholic (94 percent in 1971), this implies that over half of the women who migrated to England and Wales kept within both their national and religious heritages when marrying. On the other hand, it is also true that 48 percent of the Irish migrant women married persons whose own origins were outside of the Republic of Ireland. Of course, some of these marriage partners were second generation British, of Irish extraction, but many of them would not have been. As in the case of the Australian data, the most reasonable interpretation is that Irish-born women married mostly within their own religious and ethnic group, but that a large minority of them did not do so. One interpretation of these data for England and Wales is that, as far as the Irish migrants were concerned, "theories of the social and cultural ghettos were largely myths."[59]

Unfortunately, there are no systematic historical data about inter-marriage of either the religious or the ethnic sort for the USA, the greatest recipient of Irish single women from 1850 to 1920. At present there is in progress a major study of the "Public Use Sample" of the manuscript census data for 1900, a recalibration of the original census material to provide cross-tabulations not done in the original census reports. Hence, in a few years time we may learn what proportion of Irish single women in America married either first- or second-generation Irish men. However, we will never systematically know what the degree of religious inter-marriage was, because the U.S. constitution has been interpreted as forbidding the collection of information on the religious preferences of individuals.[60]

(VI)

Thus, whether or not emigration was a big step towards emancipation for most Irish migrant women, or merely the method by which they obtained in a New World what they could not have in the old — a husband and family — is something we cannot know. The great danger for us as modern observers is to draw simple correlations based on modern assumptions — such as the idea that the unmarried non-dependent women were emancipated from their Irish past, but that the ones who married and had children were not. We have already seen that most of the seemingly-independent single female migrants were helped by family members and that there were non-patriarchal family networks made up of brothers, sisters, cousins, within which it was possible for many of them to spend their entire lives. Economic independence and the abandonment of social and cultural networks derived from the Old World were not at all the same thing.

Conversely, many of the Irish migrant women who married actually lived very independent lives, quite emancipated from the restrictive aspects of Irish culture, while enjoying its considerable good points.

I should like to close this survey of Irish female emigrants with the story of a woman whose life embodied this fact, Ann McCleland of Dunronan County, Londonderry. As a young woman, Ann had taken herself off to New Zealand. This was in the 1840s, very early in the history of the colony. Her emigration was a trial to her mother, especially because she had learned from a local clergyman that New Zealand "is a wicked place, and little or no clergy or public worship."[61] Wicked or not, Wellington of that era was a place of opportunity for any unmarried woman and Ann soon met and later married Johan Augustus Heldt, a native of Hanover, Germany. They married in July 1843 in the Presbyterian Church, Wellington. Ann's new husband was a skilled cabinet maker, but instead of following that line, he and Ann booked passage to Chile where Johan (now "John") had previously done some gold mining. There she bore him two children. Mining must have been at least moderately rewarding, for in March 1847, the family booked passage for Liverpool. This they paid for with 8 and ³/₄ ounces of gold. The irony of their movement is obvious: thousands of famine-starved Irish were flooding into Liverpool, trying to catch a passage to a New World, and Ann and her family were coming back to Ireland on the Liverpool boat. They travelled in comfort, in a private cabin with its own water closet. Presumably they had a reasonable amount of money with which to take up life in Ireland. They settled in Moneymore, County Londonderry, and there Ann bore seven more children. Somehow, Ann and John still had the energy to search for yet-better fortune: in 1859 they boarded the *Mermaid* in Liverpool and shipped to Auckland. Ann set up in a millinery shop and John followed his trade until the late 1860s, when gold fever struck them again and John went mining. In this he was modestly successful, and in the early 1870s they sold out their claim and returned to Auckland. For Ann McCleland, and for persons like her, emigration was not a passive experience to be borne stoically, but an active and energetic strategy for getting on in the world.[62]

Chapter 8

Great Britain: The Place Nearest Home

(I)

Professor Liam Ryan of St. Patrick's College, Maynooth, introduces a major essay on post-war emigration from Ireland to Great Britain as follows:

> The past one hundred and fifty years have witnessed the greatest mass migration of human beings in world history. By the late twentieth century, however, in most western nations this process has come to an end. In Ireland alone does emigration persist with a nineteenth-century intensity. In Ireland alone, in 1988, probably uniquely among the nations of the earth, did the number leaving the state... come close to the annual number being born.[1]

He continues:

> Certainly for all our assertions of patriotic love of country, we have repeatedly proven that, given free access to any country with a standard of living higher than our own, we will readily relocate. While mass migration of the nineteenth century was largely to America, that of the twentieth century was largely to Britain.[2]

Great Britain, being close by, was well known to potential migrants, its temptations seemingly within easy grasp. Transportation to Scotland and to England and Wales always has been cheap. Before the Famine one could at slack times cross the Irish sea for as little as ten pence in steerage, and three pence on deck, less than the daily wage of an unskilled labourer.[3] The same relative cost holds today. If a person is willing to travel rough, the cost of a journey to the "mainland" is less than a day's wage.

Considering Irish migration as a whole from the beginning of the nineteenth century to the present day, Great Britain has received the second-largest number of Irish migrants, second only to the United States of America. In all probability, Britain was the number two choice of Irish migrants from 1801 to 1914; from World War I onwards it became the first choice, a position that it holds to the present day. This realignment of migrant choices has not simply been a matter of the United States's having laid down tight quotas after World War I, for, in fact, during the inter-war years the Irish did not fill their quota.[4] Something real, but as yet unexplored, occurred in the attitudes of Irish migrants which led them to decide that the benefits of a move to Britain, as compared to the costs, were much better value than the move to the USA with its attendant costs.

Here then, is a paradox. Given that Great Britain numerically has been the second most important reception area for Irish migrants, nevertheless it is the place for which we have the least and lowest quality of information on the migrants, particularly systematic data. In the face of this situation, scholars have worked heroically and, in the case of local community studies, to great effect. Nevertheless, there are very few candles in what is a very large and unlighted cavern. One can point to no more than a dozen published books and monographs that deal with the social history of the Irish in Great Britain at a level of scholarly quality that is quite easily reached in places where reliable data are easy to find.[5]

The nature of the evidentiary chasm that confronts historians of the Irish in Great Britain will become increasingly clear as this chapter progresses. However, two central matters should be clearly recognized. The first of these is that there are *no* systematic data on the Irish in Great Britain as a multigenerational ethnic group. None. The first census to record Irish migrants (the "Irish-born" of the census categories) was that of 1841. This is a valuable enumeration, because it provides for Scotland and for England and Wales the numbers of Irish-born persons before the Great Famine. Subsequent censuses have tallied parallel information. But that is all there is. Never have British census authorities asked an ethnicity (or "national background") question, nor has any private survey filled this void. Since most persons of Irish background in Great Britain are now of third or subsequent generations, they are excluded from the data pool, which only identifies the first generation.[6] This means that we have no information whatsoever on the great majority of the Irish in Britain as an ethnic group.

Second, *never* have the British authorities collected information on the religious affiliations of individual members of the population. The famous 1851 census provided data on the general pattern of religious adhesions. These data, however, were not compiled from individual census forms, but were collected by denominational authorities. And even this rudimentary enumeration was not repeated. What this means for historians of the Irish is that we have no idea what the religious persuasion of the Irish migrant to Britain actually was. Faced with this difficulty, most historians of the Irish in Britain have slipped into an easily understandable, but methodologically slack, posture and simply assumed that the Irish migrants to Britain were Catholic. In fact, as I will argue later, there is every reason to believe that the non-Catholic proportion of the migrant flow was between 20 and 30 percent, depending upon the time period involved. Further, because of intermarriage with non-Irish persons, it is probable that in the second, third, and subsequent generations, the non-Catholic proportion grew considerably.

(II)

In terms of their ultimate travel destinations, the migrants from Ireland to Britain were of three sorts: (1) individuals who used Great Britain as a launching platform in the process of what is known as "stepwise migration." They stayed in Britain for weeks, months, perhaps years, before embarking on a transoceanic voyage that they hoped would provide them with a permanent home in North America, Australasia, South Africa, or elsewhere. (2) Transient labourers who worked for some months each year in Britain, but who made their permanent home in Ireland, to which they returned each year, usually for several months at a stretch. (3) Permanent emigrants who remained for the rest of their lives residents of Scotland, England or Wales.

Even the simple listing of these three sorts of migrants makes it obvious that the migration to Britain was unique within the Irish diaspora. Britain was a matrix point for the whole Irish diaspora. Its great ports — Liverpool, Glasgow, Plymouth — were nodes through which the lines of communication of the worldwide diaspora flowed. Moreover, because of its closeness to Ireland, Britain did not have to be a final destination, even for those who had no intention of going far overseas: going home was easy. So different was the nature of Irish migration to Britain, therefore, that one can readily suggest that a basic analytic distinction be made in Irish diaspora studies between migration to Great Britain and that to every other place in the English-speaking world. Britain comprises a very large, very special case.

Only when individuals have come near the end of their lives can one tell whether they were involved in stepwise, transient, or permanent migration. What they thought they were doing before they left Ireland is not relevant: so easy was it within British society to move from intending to be a permanent resident to returning to Ireland or migrating overseas, that intentions were plastic. And self-deception was always present. "The ability to delude oneself that emigration was temporary has been one of the persistent features of Irish migration to Britain among all social classes."[7]

As yet, historians have not even crudely sorted out the relative magnitude of these three types of migration. In particular, because of limited embarkation information, the size of the stepwise component is unknown.[8] However, for the pre-Famine period, Ruth-Ann Harris has produced a pioneering study which establishes a baseline for distinguishing between transient and permanent migration to Britain.[9] Harris suggests that the typical seasonal (or "transient") labourer was an unmarried male who worked primarily in harvesting in Britain. Most of these labourers in the pre-Famine period were recruited under the "padrone system" (to use the Italian term): that is, an experienced harvester acted as gang leader. He assembled a team of veteran workers, recruited new ones and, when in England and Scotland, negotiated wages with employers on behalf of his entire work gang. Some workers went to Britain on their own, but most as part of these organized groups. Usually the workers put in two months of heavy harvest labour. Harris's study indicates that only one in six of the seasonal workers stayed longer than three months in Britain. In the pre-Famine years, the source of migrant labourers was sharply defined. Most came from the far west of Ireland and from County Donegal. Significantly, the province of Munster provided very few transient labourers in the pre-Famine years, a point that is notable in view of Munster's being so strongly represented in overseas migration, especially to North America. It well may be that in the pre-Famine era, working in Britain was an alternative to long-distance migration, and that the people of the far west and northwest preferred (for whatever reasons) working in Britain, while those of the south and southwest preferred overseas emigration.

Although the details of Irish migration to Britain are complex, the basic reasons for much of it are obvious: Ireland was one of Europe's poorest nations, and it was located close to what, at mid-nineteenth century, was the world's richest. The only thing required to connect the two nations was for the potential migrants from Ireland to wish to improve their lot in life. Stereotypes of Irish commercial fecklessness aside (they are completely inaccurate), the Irish had a great ability to sniff out jobs. Harris points to one case during the construction of the Caledonian Canal. Most of the construction jobs were intended to serve as aid for economically distressed Scottish Highlanders. Before the Highlanders could arrive, however, the Irish appeared and built huts and announced their intention of staying. The only way to cope with these work-hungry Irishmen was to denominate them "exotic crofters" and give them a share of the jobs.

Harris employs the 1841 census (the first information of a systematic character that we have on Irish seasonal workers) to yield the following estimate: that in the pre-Famine era, for each male migrating permanently to Britain from Ireland, there was a cognate female, and between five and six men who were transient labourers and who would return home within a year, usually much sooner.

That was before the Famine. The picture afterwards is very cloudy indeed. One view is that the seasonal migration pattern increasingly was "rationalized," with the "padrones" becoming stronger and the system settling into an annual pattern in which there was a regular routine of migration with employment on the same farms year after year.[10] It is clear that although the system of harvest labour migrations continued, they declined. Reports made by the Royal Irish Constabulary indicate that in 1880 about 21,000 seasonal workers went to Britain, but that this number had diminished to about 8,000 in 1915 — and that, despite wartime demand for labour.[11] In the years 1888-1915, well over 90 percent of the seasonal farm workers hailed from Mayo, Donegal, Galway, Roscommon, Sligo, Leitrim, and Armagh.[12]

The number of seasonal labourers, with their short enlistment period (one to three months) continually declined, and in the twentieth century a new form of transient labourer came to the fore, consisting of young women who took jobs on a short term basis in hotels and bars and in domestic service, and male construction workers. Unlike the farm labourers, these workers did not follow a customal calendar. They tended to stay longer in Britain and to come home at odd times. Yet even when they worked for two or three years before coming home, they were transients. Others came home to Ireland for a month or two every year and finally retired there at seventy, the age of the old age pension. Construction workers among the men and service workers among the women dominated the scene until the 1960s, when yet another type of Irish short-time worker began appearing in British labour markets: skilled technicians, white collar workers and nurses (a particularly strong tradition of Irish nursing developed after World War II). These supplemented, but did not replace, the traditional construction and service trades.

(III)

The most surprising hole in our knowledge is that we do not have accurate yearly figures on the out-migration of Irish persons to Great Britain. Although in 1852, the United Kingdom government began to keep useful (if not completely accurate) statistics on emigrants to most destinations (earlier records are highly problematic), they made no distinct tally of migrants to Britain. Only in 1876 did such record keeping begin and these data were maintained only until 1920, and the Partition of Ireland. Table 32 includes this information, but it should be used only with great caution, because of massive undercounting that stemmed from basic incompetence. In the port of Dublin (which had more than 7,500 ship crossings to Britain in the year 1900, to take a typical year), two elderly ex-policemen were hired to keep track of all passengers leaving the port, a task completely beyond their ability. Then, at Rosslare, the two enumerators assigned to the job simply did not count any passengers who left Ireland by boat train, since the boat left port only half an hour after the train arrived in the station, too short a time to do the tally.[13]

TABLE 32

Migration of Persons "Natives of Ireland" to Great Britain
1876-1920

Year	To England and Wales	%	To Scotland	%	Total
1876-1880	47,366	55.9	37,387	44.1	84,753
1881-1890	43,341	61.2	27,445	38.8	70,786
1891-1900	17,518	62.7	10,443	37.3	27,961
1901-1910	22,612	60.9	14,532	39.1	37,144
1911-1920	11,441	72.1	4,423	27.9	15,864
Total 1876-1920	142,278	60.2	94,230	39.8	236,508

Sources: same as for Table 20.

The extraordinary magnitude of the undercounting is indicated by the fact that according to the figures produced by these methods gross migration to Britain for the years 1876-1920 totalled 236,508. Yet competent calculations of net migration (not gross, net) in the same period indicate that it was potentially as high as 300,000 persons[14] — and certainly 200,000.

Cormac Ó Gráda has made heroic efforts at finding bedrock beneath these spongey official numbers, and in so doing has provided useful estimates of Irish migration to Britain from 1852 onwards. He suggests that between 1852 and 1875, inclusive, the total net movement from Ireland to Great Britain was between 730,000 and 810,000 persons, and that from 1875 to 1910, inclusive, net migration was nearly 185,000. In making these estimates, Ó Gráda came to the conclusions that for the years 1852-1910, Irish outmigration to all countries was not the roughly 4 million that previously was believed, but rather nearly five million, and that most of the missing one million migrants were migrants to Great Britain whose movement had been unrecorded. Thus, he believes migration from Ireland to Britain from the immediate post-Famine years until World War I can be taken as comprising between one-fifth and one-quarter of total Irish emigration in that period.[15]

Now, if we do not have accurate official figures on gross out-migration to Britain before Partition, we have even less after that. All that was collected was information on how many passengers got on ships (which means virtually nothing) and information on annual net migration. The trouble is, net migration data hide the flow pattern: an outflow of one million persons, when combined with an inflow of one million persons, yields a figure of nil net migration. So too does an outflow of ten persons and a return flow of ten, but the historical realities these two cases represent are entirely different. There have been ingenious attempts at circumventing the refusal of both southern and northern governments in Ireland to collect data on gross permanent out-migration. For instance, immediately after World War II, travel permits were required for southern Irish persons going to employment in Great Britain, so for a brief time these were an accurate barometer of gross permanent out-migration.[16] Rather more ingenious have been the efforts of the Northern Ireland authorities who, after the creation of the National Health Service in the 1940s, began to measure out-migration by the number of health service cards transferred from Northern Ireland to doctors' offices on the mainland. Such transfers almost always involved a time lag (perhaps as many as several years) before the migrant registered with a new British doctor, but the information was better than none at all.[17]

Accepting then, that the actual migrant flow to Britain is something that we cannot know, we have ways to take us partially around this roadblock. A reasonably simple method is to look at the pictures taken at ten-yearly intervals by the British census authorities. From 1841 onwards they reveal the number of Irish-born persons (that is, the number of Irish immigrants) in Britain. That provides a very rough indication of what the flow pattern from Ireland must have been and, more important, is a first step towards dealing with the Irish migrants in their new homeland. These basic data are found in Table 33.

Where did the Irish live in Great Britain?[18] The easy answer is "in cities," but in which cities is something that changed over time. If one takes the 1850s and 1860s, there were three main areas. Of the 601,634 Irish immigrants living in England and Wales in 1861, 245,833 (40.1 percent) were in the "northwestern counties" of Lancaster and Chester. The second area was London, in which 106,877 lived (17.8 percent of Irish immigrants in England and Wales).[19] A third concentration, in Scotland, centred on Glasgow. In 1851, of the 207,367 Irish immigrants in Scotland, 59,801 (28.8 percent) lived in the city of Glasgow proper, and many others in contiguous areas.[20]

Some local studies have shown that in specific locales — Manchester, York, and parts of London — especially grisly instances of residential segregation and impoverishment of Irish immigrants occurred. However, David Fitzpatrick has argued that though the Irish were prone to clustering, there never was an Irish ghetto in the original sense of that word: "ghettos" referring to enclaves in Europe in which settlement was restricted to a single group.[21] Colin G. Pooley in an essay on segregation-vs.-integration in the Irish migrant experience in Great Britain argues that "the stereotypical view of the poor, segregated and outcast Irish migrant is a partial picture based mainly on the experience of some poor Catholic migrants in large industrial towns. As other studies have hinted, but rarely developed, Irish migrants to Britain were a diverse group."[22] Both Fitzpatrick and Pooley point to the undeniable fact that the Irish immigrants in Britain diffused quickly and did not stay huddled in their major reception areas. For instance, an examination of the 1871 census reveals that of the 556,540

TABLE 33

Irish-Born Persons Living in Great Britain
1841-1971 (32 Counties)

Year	England & Wales		Scotland		Total
	Number	% of Gr. Britain total	Number	% of Gr. Britain total	
1841	289,404	69.6	126,321	30.4	415,725
1851	519,959	71.5	207,367	28.5	727,326
1861	601,634	74.7	204,083	25.3	805,717
1871	566,540	73.2	207,770	26.8	774,310
1881	562,374	72.0	218,745	28.0	781,119
1891	458,315	70.2	194,807	29.8	653,122
1901	426,565	67.5	205,064	32.5	631,629
1911	375,325	68.2	174,715	31.8	550,040
1921	364,747	69.6	159,020	30.4	523,767
1931	381,089	75.4	124,296	24.6	505,385
1951	627,021	87.6	89,007	12.4	716,028
1961	870,445	91.5	80,533	8.5	950,978
1971	891,670	93.1	66,155	6.9	957,825

Sources: *Census 1961. England and Wales. Birth Place and Nationality Tables*, p. 70; *Census 1961 Scotland*, vol. 5, *Birthplace and Nationality*, pp. xviii, and 39; *Census 1971. Great Britain. Country of Birth Tables*, pp. 26-28; John A. Jackson, *The Irish in Britain* (London: Routledge and Kegan Paul, 1963), p. 11.

Irish immigrants living in England and Wales, 91,171 (16.1 percent) were living in London, but that the next *sixty-two* largest cities in England and Wales were home for 229,689 (40.5 percent). Some of these "cities" were smallish towns, such as King's Lynn, at 16,000 population. At minimum, what these 1871 figures means is that 245,680 Irish migrants (43.4 percent of those living in England and Wales) were living outside of the sixty-three largest cities and towns, which is to say that they were spread outside of anything that even remotely approached large urban concentration.[23] As Colin Pooley argues, any assertion that the Irish migrants as a group were ghettoized is a matter of the manipulation of demographic method rather than of the evidence itself, for "it is possible to manipulate spatial boundaries and definitions of clustering to produce any outcome."[24]

Since the beginning of the twentieth century, the Irish migrants have conformed to (and, indeed, have exaggerated) the two main trends in British population development. They have turned their faces away from Scotland — the proportion of the Irish-born who lived in Scotland dropped from 32.5 percent in 1901 to less than 7 percent in 1971. And, within England and Wales, they have been part of the shift of population to the south, particularly to the huge London conurbation.

If the Irish immigrants were not for the most part caught in residential ghettos, they nevertheless could have been ghettoized in their occupations. This probably was the case during the twenty years before and after the Great Famine. In that era, most Irish migrants to Britain were desperately poor and few had the sort of skills that an industrializing economy would most reward. Ruth-Ann Harris estimates that from 50 to 75 percent of all Irish-born persons in Britain in the years just before the Famine supported themselves by casual labour.[25] The Scottish census authorities' survey of the results of the 1871 enumeration concluded that the large number "of the Irish race in Scotland has undoubtedly produced deleterious results, lowered greatly the moral tone of the lower classes, and greatly increased the necessity for the enactment of sanitary and police precautions wherever they have settled in numbers."[26] (So much for the brotherhood of the Celts.) As late as 1960, the sterotypical emigrant was "single, young, unskilled, and with just primary education, arriving off the boat-train to English cities with little money, no job, and nowhere to live."[27] The great nineteenth-century social investigators found plenty of evidence of Irish poverty and also of their commercial acuteness. The following is Henry Mayhew's picture of mid-Victorian London street sellers:

> It is curious to observe that the most assiduous and hitherto the most successful of street traders, [the Jews], were supplanted not by a more persevering or more skilful body of street-sellers, but simply by a more starving body .... An Irish boy of fourteen, having to support himself by street-trade, as was often the case, owing to the death of parents and to diverse casualties, would undersell the Jew boy similarly circumstanced. The Irish boy could live *harder* than the Jew .... Thus he could sell at a smaller profit, and did so sell, until gradually the Hebrew youths were displaced by the Irish in the street orange trade."[28]

Undoubtedly, most Irish persons in Britain found jobs in the twenty years before and after the Famine in casual labouring, agricultural labour, textiles, and street selling.

Yet, even in the 1850s and 1960s there were skilled workers among the Irish migrants, and their numbers grew. "Although the majority of Irish in most towns were poor," wrote Colin Pooley, "a substantial minority of Irish-born migrants were in skilled and white-collar employment and lived in widely scattered middle class residential suburbs."[29] Pooley is correct in asking that we pay attention to the full range of occupational experience of the Irish migrants, but the problems are considerable. We face the "melt away" phenomenon: the skilled, the educated, the commercially acute, just melted away from the Irish immigrant settlements, and they went largely unobserved by contemporaries. We have no solid data on the occupational profile of the Irish-born in Britain until the mid-twentieth century. Moreover, because of the great physical mobility of the Irish migrants, studies of individual towns and cities which purport to show that in various occupations the Irish-born had little upward occupational mobility, actually do nothing of the sort. The people who lived in Manchester in 1851, would have moved away and been replaced by, say, 1871 with brand new migrants. Of course this replacement came at the bottom of the occupational ladder: new migrants always start at the bottom. The real, unknown issue, is whether those who moved away also moved up the occupational scale.

Now it is clear that gradually the Irish migrants who entered England brought an improved level of education and greater skills. Middle class elements became significant links in the migration chain. However else, for example, can one explain a notice in the London *Observer* in 1928, proposing to establish in London a dining club for graduates of the National University of Ireland?[30]

Tables 34 and 35 provide an accurate indication of the employment pattern of the entire Irish-born adult group in 1961. (The census of occupations employed twenty-seven separate categories; only the main ones are included in the table.) For men it is clear that the building industry (which included virtually all of the construction labourers, most of the unskilled labourers and a fair proportion of the engineering trades) remained the great redoubt of Irish immigrant employment, taking up about one-third of the employed immigrants. This was an industry of mostly hard physical work, but relatively good wages. If one-third of the Irishmen were in the construction area, the rest were scattered throughout the remaining forms of work in so diffuse a pattern as to defy generalization.

"For Irish girls, the problems were never as acute as for men," a well-informed present-day observer has noted. "Irish girls never had quite the same working-class image in Britain as their men-folk acquired."[31] The good reputation of Irish-trained nurses accounts for the strong professional element in the female occupational profile. Service occupations (now more often in hotels and bars than in domestic service) were still in 1961 the leading occupation of employed Irish immigrant women, but they only comprised about one-eighth of the entire adult group. Actually, the most revealing occupational category in Table 35 is the one labelled "economically inactive." This somewhat insulting category includes the unemployed and the retired, but consists mostly of those housewives who did not work outside of the home. It indicates the continuance of a pattern that Lynn Lees presciently noted in her study of mid-nineteenth century London: "Most Irish married women, even the wives of unskilled workers, did not have regular paid employment..."[32] And it further confirms the earlier observation in

Chapter Seven (on women in the Irish diaspora) that once they had a family to raise, Irish immigrant women usually did not take employment outside of the home.

TABLE 34

Principal Occupations of Irish-Born Males in Great Britain, 1961

Occupation	From Republic of Ireland %	From Northern Ireland %	32 Counties total %
Economically inactive (age 15 and up)	7.4	11.7	8.6
Unskilled labourers	21.7	14.2	19.5
Engineering trades	12.8	14.5	13.3
Transport and communications	7.1	7.8	7.3
Construction workers	6.7	5.0	6.2
Professional, technical, artists	5.6	7.5	6.2
Service, sport, recreation	5.5	6.1	5.7
All other occupations (combined)	33.2	33.2	33.2

Sources: Derived from: *Census 1961. England and Wales. Occupation Tables*, Table 30; *Census 1961. Scotland.* vol. 6, *Occupation, Industry, and Workplace.* Part 1, *Occupation Tables*, Table 30.

TABLE 35

Principal Occupation of Irish-Born Females
in Great Britain, 1961

Occupation	From Republic of Ireland %	From Northern Ireland %	32 Counties total %
Economically inactive (age 15 and up)	50.0	60.1	52.9
Service, sport, recreation	13.5	11.1	12.9
Professional, technical, artists	9.7	6.2	8.6
Clerical	6.5	7.3	6.7
Engineering trades	2.4	1.8	2.3
All other occupations (combined)	17.9	13.5	16.6

Sources: same as for Table 34.

(IV)

Thus far I have not mentioned either the region in Ireland from which the migrants came or the ever-sensitive matter of their religious persuasion. As indicated earlier, there are no direct data whatsoever on where the Irish migrants (and their descendants) in Britain fell on the great Protestant-Catholic divide. However, by merging the discussion of regional origins of Irish migrants with the religious issue, there is some possibility that we may be able to draw indirect inferences. In any case, the method of data interpretation is illustrative of both the problems and the possibilities of place-of-origin material.

Our best chance of drawing solid inferences concerning the religious allegiance of the Irish migrants to Great Britain would seem to be focused on the years 1876-

TABLE 36

Geographic Origin of
"Natives of Ireland" who Emigrated to Great Britain
1876-1920, Inclusive

Province	1876-90		1891-1900		1901-10		1911-20		Total: 1876-1920	
	No.	%	No.	%	No.	%	No.	%	No.	%
Ulster	81,312	52.3	12,858	46.0	25,251	68.0	8,607	54.2	128,028	54.1
Leinster	17,044	11.0	2,661	9.5	3,680	9.9	5,196	32.8	28,581	12.1
Munster	50,303	32.3	10,640	38.1	7,234	19.5	1,072	6.8	69,249	29.3
Connacht	6,880	4.4	1,802	6.4	979	2.6	989	6.2	10,650	4.5
Total	155,539	100.0	27,961	100.0	37,144	100.0	15,864	100.0	236,508	100.0

Sources: Derived from the same sources as Table 20.

1920, when the United Kingdom authorities tried to obtain and process information on the matter. The results of their work are compiled in Table 36, which gives an indication of origin according to the four historical provinces. This material can be reworked to show the situation according to the modern boundaries of Northern and Southern Ireland:

	Twenty-Six Counties	Six Counties	Total
1876-1890	85,342	70,197	155,539
	54.9%	54.1%	100.0%
1891-1900	16,526	11,435	27,961
	59.1%	40.9%	100.0%
1901-1910	13,963	23,181	37,144
	37.6%	62.4%	100.0%
1911-1920	8,497	7,367	15,864
	53.6%	46.4%	100.0%
Total, 1876-1920	124,328	112,180	236,508
	52.8%	47.4%	100.0%

One could go farther, if one wished, and draw up county-by-county tabulations of emigration. Then one could relate the outflow to the religious composition of the individual counties and, potentially, have some idea of the religious adherence of the migrants to Britain. If, that is, one trusted these data.

Because this is a primer, this is a good opportunity to provide an example of basic data-testing. Data assessment in historical work is not a precise science: two equally good scholars can come to different conclusions about the same set of evidence.[33] However, there are some simple basic rules. One of these is that good pieces of evidence usually fit with other good pieces, and that if there are disagreements, then something is wrong.

With that in mind, compare the figures given in the text above with the information in Table 37. Compare particularly the proportion of persons coming from the six counties and from the twenty-six counties in the two sources. Something appears to be wrong, for the figures in the text indicate a much higher proportion of migrants from the six counties than Table 37, which deals with permanent residents (not migrants), suggests.

TABLE 37

Irish-Born Residents in Great Britain, 1911-1971
According to 26-County, 6-County Breakdown

	England and Wales	
Year	**26 counties %**	**6 counties %**
1911	80.5	19.5
1931	81.3	18.7
1951	77.8	22.2
1961	77.5	22.5
1971	73.0	27.0
	Scotland	
1931	55.0	45.0
1951	49.0	51.0
1961	48.5	51.5
1971	48.8	51.2
	Great Britain	
1931	74.7	25.3
1951	74.1	25.9
1961	75.0	25.0
1971	71.2	28.8

Note: 1. The census dates were generated on a 10 percent sample of the entire population. 2. In deriving the percentages, the "not known" category was excluded. This ranged well under 10 percent in most years, and, usually under 5 percent.

Sources: Derived from same sources as Table 33.

There are three possible explanations of this clash. First, it may be that there is no real clash. This would occur if the migrants from the north of Ireland (the six counties) were radically different in their use of their British experience. Specifically, if a considerably larger proportion of them used Britain as a platform for eventual migration overseas than did those from the south of Ireland, then the two data sets could both be accurate. Secondly, both data sets could be accurate if a considerably larger proportion of northern Irish persons came home than did those from the south; in other words, if migrants from the twenty-six counties had a stronger propensity to stay in Britain as their permanent residence.

The difficulty with both of these suggestions is that for neither one do we have any historical evidence and, indeed, neither suggestion is a part of the welter of anecdotal material that surrounds Irish migration. Moreover, each suggestion involves great complications because, to make it satisfying as an explanation, one would have to specify the precise social mechanisms that would lead to such sharply different behaviour between northern and southern Irish. A fundamental rule of explanation in the social sciences is that everything else being equal, one chooses the simplest, explanation.

And here is the third, and simplest explanation of the dissonance between the two data sets: the material on Irish migration to Britain collected for the years 1876-1920 is virtually useless. The retired policemen doing the tallies at Dublin and Rosslare harbours just lost too many bodies. The enumerators in Belfast and Larne harbours did a better job, with the result that the massive undercounts in the data were not spread evenly. The 1876-1920 data were tilted strongly towards northern migrants, but by an unknown degree. So they have to be abandoned.

Table 37, though, introduces us to a second sort of logic path. As a set of basic observations, compare the twenty-six county/six county breakdown of the population in the home country with the same breakdown as shown in Table 37 for Irish migrants living in Great Britain:

Year	% of 32-Counties Population Living in the 26-Counties in Ireland
1926	70.3%
1951	68.4
1971	66.0

Year	% of the Irish-born in Great Britain with Origins in the 26 Countries
1931	74.7%
1951	74.1
1971	71.2

One could argue that, given that the Irish in Britain tended more often to have come from the "Catholic South" than was the case in the Irish homeland, then it follows that the population of Irish immigrants in Great Britain had a somewhat higher proportion of Catholics than did the population of the thirty-two counties.

Actually, it does not follow, and that is the lesson. "Historians of the Irish in Britain have rightly stressed the predominance of Roman Catholics among the immigrants, but wrongly neglected the locally significant minorities of Protestants among Irish settlers... Even in the late 1850s, up to one-fifth of Irish paupers admitted to the Liverpool workhouse were Protestants, a fact that suggests a still higher Protestant proportion for the Liverpool Irish outside the work house. But *in the absence of a reliable religious census*, Ireland's elusive Protestant expatriates have been widely ignored..." Those are the words of David Fitzpatrick[34] (the emphasis is mine.) Despite strenuous efforts at calculating the religious persuasions of Great Britain in the later nineteenth century[35] we have to proceed inferentially, as above.

But one assumption in the logic train employed above misses something. This is the fact that from the "Catholic South," Protestant migrants have been *overrepresented*. If one takes just the twenty-six counties, it is clear that in the nineteenth century, Protestant and Catholic populations had roughly the same emigration rate. However, as Sean Glynn notes, from 1911 to 1926, the Protestant proportion of the twenty-six counties fell by one-third, while the Catholic population dropped by little more than 2 percent. Then, between 1926 and 1946, the Protestant population dropped 24 percent, while the Catholic population actually increased.[36] Several factors contributed to this sharp Protestant decline from 1911-46 (the Protestant birth rate was lower than the Catholic, for example), but none of them obviate the fact that Protestants were more likely to migrate out of the twenty-six counties than were Catholics.

Why the Protestants began to clear out after 1911 does not require any complex theory: many Protestants saw little future in an overwhelmingly-Catholic nation-state. Immediately after Southern Ireland became independent in 1922, British military and civil service personnel withdrew. This accounted for no more than one-quarter of the Protestant emigration in the 1920s, however. The real source of Protestant emigration was native-born Irish Protestants who cleared off in large numbers as they began to perceive job discrimination against them, and cultural intolerance. (Not all of their perceptions were accurate, but some certainly were). So up to the end of World War II, Protestants were strongly overrepresented in the migrant stream from the twenty-six counties. This changed after 1946, but even so it is clear that if one takes the twentieth century as a whole, Protestants are more apt to have migrated than Catholics.[37]

Almost a mirror-image of this situation prevailed in Northern Ireland. From the time of Partition, 1920, onwards, Catholics were more likely to migrate than were Protestants. That the reasons for this were similar to those that caused Protestant overrepresentation in out-migration from Southern Ireland is illustrated by a study in 1988 at the major exit points from Ulster — namely, Larne and Belfast harbours, Aldergrove and Belfast City airports. One thousand permanent migrants to Great Britain were interviewed. Most of these individuals were home on holiday from Britain. The majority (58 percent) had emigrated in the period 1980-87, the rest earlier. They had emigrated at a time when Catholics were a little more than one-third of the Northern Ireland population. Yet Catholics made up 39.6 percent of the emigrants in this fairly large sample. (51.6 percent of the emigrants were Protestants, and the rest claimed no religion or refused to give religious affiliation). Significantly, not only were the Catholics in this sample overrepresented in out-migration, but a lower percentage of them (57 percent as against 68 percent for the Protestants) had intentions of ever returning to Northern Ireland to live permanently.[38]

In sum, during the twentieth century, the situation in the two main Irish jurisdictions has been as follows: (a) from Southern Ireland the majority of emigrants to Britain have been Catholics, but Protestants have been overrepresented in the flow, and (b) from Northern Ireland, the majority of out-migrants have been Protestants, but Catholics have been overrepresented. This suggests that in the present century roughly 25 percent of the Irish emigrants to Great Britain have been Protestants. That is a rough figure, but a variation of 5 percent either way (making between 20 and 30 percent of the total) will certainly bracket the historical reality.

These large numbers of Irish Protestant emigrants need to be incorporated into the history of the Irish in Great Britain. As David Fitzpatrick suggests, we can no longer deal with Irish Protestants in Britain as some kind of minor, sectarian band. "The religious history of Irish settlement in Britain ought to be more than a catalogue of Catholic pietism, Protestant anti-popery and broken heads."[39] Thus, we require not only studies of places where Irish Protestants settled in compact communities (such as Paisley, Glasgow, Girvan, and parts of Liverpool), but also locales where they were "invisible immigrants" who dispersed quickly into the British mainstream.

(V)

Thus far we have been discussing only the first generation, the immigrants from Ireland to Great Britain. However full of holes that particular historical fabric is (and given that we have no direct religious data and no trustworthy direct information on flow patterns, it is a very tattered cloth indeed), compared to the matter of Irish multigenerational ethnicity it is a tapestry. Never have authorities in the United Kingdom collected systematic information on the ethnicity (that is, the "national origin" or whatever term one prefers) of the population in a way that would help to establish how many British residents are of Irish background. Nor has an adequate privately-funded survey been attempted that would define the basic outlines of Britain as a multicultural society. I have yet to find a single volume that deals with Irish ethnicity in Great Britain at anything other than a speculative level — and this despite the fact that Ireland is almost certainly the source of the largest non-British component of the present population of the mainland.

Writing in 1990 in a survey of the Irish in Britain since World War II, Liam Ryan stated:

> Irish assimilation into British society is among the fastest that occurs among immigrant groups anywhere in the world. Assimilation is practically complete in a single genera-tion. The children of Irish immigrants, sometimes to the distress of their parents, grow up seeing themselves as English or Scots; they may acknowledge their Irish ancestry and exhibit a few inherited traits, but for all practical purposes they are indistinguishable from their British peers whether in respect of dress or in social, cultural, or religious behaviour.[40]

Certainly for the 20-30 percent of the Irish ethnic group who are Protestant, this change into British-with-a-small-difference was quick and easy, but I suspect that Ryan is correct in suggesting that for the Catholic Irish assimilation also was quick, if not quite so easy.

Among historians of the Irish in Great Britain, there is a small controversy about how much stereotyping and prejudice the Irish faced in their new home.[41] Undoubtedly the situation varied greatly according to historical time period and undoubtedly matters were worse for the Irish in 1851, than, say, in 1951. Paradoxically, however, the level of prejudice and stereotyping probably did not greatly affect the rate of Irish assimilation. That is, if one grants that in Victorian England there were strong anti-Irish prejudices and stereotypes, than we have a direct motive for the Irish migrants and especially their children and grandchildren to make themselves as "British" as possible, so as to escape the effects of these negative views. If, on the other hand, one accepts the argument that much (but certainly, not all) of the stereotyping was benevolent and essentially good-natured, then one can suggest that this made it easier for the Irish migrants and especially the second and subsequent generations to assimilate to British society.

I suspect — and at this stage it can be no more than a speculation — that in the long-run, the greatest single agency of Irish assimilation into British society was intermarriage. In 1970, intermarriage data became available and they revealed that of the Irish-born men from the

Republic of Ireland who married in England and Wales, 48 percent did not marry women from the Republic of Ireland. The parallel figure for Irish-born women was 46 percent.[42] Of course much of this out-marrying was apparent, not real, in the sense that many of the men and women were taking spouses from Northern Ireland or spouses who were second or third generation of Irish background. However, it is inevitable that a significant proportion of the marriages were genuine out-marriages with English, Scots, or Welsh spouses, or with individuals who had migrated to Britain from either the "Old" or the "New" Commonwealth.

For the purposes of exposition, let us assume (1) that 25 percent of the marriages were to non-Irish persons, meaning individuals neither of Irish birth nor of Irish ancestry, and (2) that most persons of Irish ethnicity living in Great Britain in, say, 1971, were of third or subsequent generations in Britain (that this was indeed the case is clear from the figures of Irish migrants living in Britain in the Victorian period; they were the base of the multigenerational ethnic pool, and would have had great-grandchildren in Britain by the 1970s).

So, (a) one starts with roughly 75 percent of the Irish migrant group as one's base. (We assume that the 25 percent who were Protestants merged very quickly with the larger British society. The remaining 75 percent is made up of Catholic migrants.

(b) In Generation One, the immigrants rate of out-marriage (25 percent) reduces the "pure Irish" portion in Generation Two to 56.25 percent. (One assumes that half the children of intermarriages will follow the "Irish Catholic" side of the family and half will follow the "British side.")

(c) In Generation Two, the out-marriage rate (25 percent) will produce an "Irish Catholic" proportion in Generation Three of just over 42 percent.

(d) In Generation Three, the out-marriage rate (25 percent) will produce an "Irish Catholic" rate of under 32 percent.

And so on.

That, of course, is a schematic exposition, but it makes clear how easily a moderate rate of intermarriage (25 percent) over three or four generations could yield this clear result: that a majority of persons who had some Irish ancestry nevertheless were no longer culturally Irish except in some very flaccid nostalgic sense. And this degree of ethnic leaching would occur even without the phenomenon that Liam Ryan noted, namely that the Irish in general assimilated quickly in Great Britain.

The multigenerational ethnic history of the Irish in Great Britain, then, has been a process by which Irish men and women began families whose members (their children and grandchildren) quickly became British-with-a-very-slight-difference. This phenomenon is the chief reason that the Irish in Britain have had so little political clout. Their moments in the political sun have been limited to the election of a few home-rule MPs in the nineteenth century and to London councillors in the more recent past. The political influence of "the Irish" has been much less than their numbers, and political analysts do not even use "Irish" as a psephological category except in a few fringe ridings. Neither have the Irish as a multigenerational ethnic group created any major set of ethnic organizations in Great Britain. Most political and cultural clubs have served the first generation and, at most, their children. The rest of the ethnic group have found them embarrassing and have stayed away in droves.

The one institution that has most been associated with persons of Irish ethnicity has been the Roman Catholic church, but even here the picture is far from simple. It is true, as A.E.C.W. Spencer notes, that the force of Irish migration to Great Britain moved the centre point of Roman Catholic Christianity in the British Isles from Ireland to Great Britain. As late as 1911, more than half of the Roman Catholics in the British Isles lived in Ireland. By 1926, the scales had tipped and more than half were in Great Britain. By the end of World War II, more than half of the Catholics were in England and Wales (51.3 percent), with somewhat under four-tenths (38.2 percent) in Ireland, and the rest in Scotland.[43]

What is not true, however, is that the Irish migrants and their descendants were as keen on the church as is often believed (and this question arises independently of the issue of intermarriage with persons of non-Irish Catholic background). In a pioneering essay entitled "Irish and Catholic: Myth or Reality?" Gerard Connolly has demonstrated that when dealing with Victorian and Edwardian Britain one must not employ the traditional binary terms usually used in Irish religious history — namely "Catholic and "non-Catholic" — but must introduce a third term — "non-practising." Connolly cites a wide variety of studies of religious practice which indicate that in the nineteenth century, between 40 and 50 percent of Irish-born Catholics in Britain did not meet even the minimal religious obligation, their Easter duties.[44] That such a large proportion of the Irish-born Catholics in Britain chose to disregard the church's minimum standards for affiliation, Connolly argues, opens a serious reservation about the usual procedure of employing Catholicity as the major link in Irish cultural identity. Connolly suggests that, parallel to the non-observant Catholics there probably was a group of non-observant Protestants, both groups being of Irish background, but neither very keen on organized religion. This is a very interesting suggestion, for it opens the possibility that there is an Irish ethnic identity that is not tied to religion, but is something different, deeper.[45]

If Connolly's suggestions have considerable virtue in approaching that most religious of eras, the Victorian age, they have even greater appeal in helping us to come to terms with twentieth-century British culture, which has become, decade by decade, less religious, until at present the great bulk of the nation is vaguely Christian, but overwhelmingly non-observant.

(VI)

In part, the reason that Great Britain — despite its being the most important receptor of Irish migrants in the twentieth century, and the second most important in the nineteenth century — has been the focus of so little historical work on the Irish is that the official and systematic data sources are so weak. But there is more to it than that. As a culture, Great Britain has only in the last decade become aware that it is itself a multicultural society; and the old colonial mindset, which has only just faded, meant that one simply did not study the lesser breeds among the old quality, especially if their origins happened to be next door. On the other side of the coin, migration to Great Britain has been a source of embarrassment to the Irish establishment, an embarrassment both national and moral. It was a matter of public shame to successive governments of the Irish Free State, and of its successor the Republic of Ireland, that each year thousands of the brightest and most energetic of Ireland's young people left home for life with the Old Enemy.[46] Further, until quite recently, a simple moral dualism befogged the issue. Virtuous Ireland was contrasted to sinful Britain. Churchmen and politicians publicly and perpetually regretted the abandonment of life in virtuous Ireland, the land of saints and scholars, for the materialistic and secular life of Britain.[47]

Those days, although not long past, are gone. Irish migration and Irish ethnicity in Great Britain can be studied without apology. The workers in the field are few, but talented. One hopes that young historians will adopt the perception of the hundreds of thousands of young Irish migrants and recognize that in this scholarly matter, as in many other areas, Britain is indeed a land of challenge and of opportunity.

And, when writing the history of the Irish in Great Britain, an appropriate multicultural attitude will be important, not least when assessing the English. Thus, the wonderful autobiography of Nesca A. Robb, *An Ulsterwomen in England, 1924-1941* is a good place to start, and most especially her opening paragraph:

> Some years ago, in my native city of Belfast, I met a former schoolfellow whom I had not seen for a long time. During our conversation, I told her that I was now living in England.
> "And how do you like the English people?" she asked.
> I replied that since I had got used to them, I like them very well.
> "I can't stand them," said my friend, decidedly. "They're so gushing."[48]

Irish Diaspora

Chapter 9

North America: The Big Case
Part I: General Character

(I)

Now, finally, we are ready for the big case: North America. Behind all the data and all the details about the worldwide Irish diaspora, are two fundamental attitudes that should frame our thinking about the Irish migrants to North America and their descendants. The first of these is that stereotyping the Irish, even if it is done with the best of intentions and by persons who are themselves of Irish descent, is wrong, both historically and in terms of modern multicultural understanding. The Irish migrants to the various New Worlds were not all Catholic or Protestant, not all from Connaught or Munster or Ulster or Leinster, not all working class or rural labourers or domestic servants, or all single women or single men. The migrants were an amazingly variegated group and their descendants are equally multifaceted. Although one can generalize to some degree about the Irish migrants and their descendants, one has to do so with a clear emphasis upon the variety behind the norms.

Second, it should by now be clear that when a statement of fact is made, it requires proof. This might seem obvious, but studies of "the Irish," especially in diaspora lands, have frequently not been based upon evidence, but upon wishful thinking, prejudice, evidentiary bias, and downright silliness. So, always keep in mind the character of the available evidence. And when evidence is lacking, or wobbly, one admits the fact, rather than faking it.

One other point requires reassertion, for it is often ignored in studies of the Irish in North America: that the migrant generation and the entire ethnic group in any country are quite different entities. The migrants are sometimes referred to as the *Irish-born* or as the *first-generation*.[1] In contemporary historical accounts they are called "emigrants" or "immigrants." These terms apply to a single generation.

In contrast, the ethnic group is a *multi-generational* phenomenon: in historical discussions it includes not only the migrant generation but their direct offspring and, often, subsequent generations of descendants. Exactly what the borders of any ethnic group are is a matter of great argument (for how long does a sense of ethnicity last?), and certainly cannot be decided here. The effective point is that when an historian refers to "the Irish" in the USA or Canada (or in Great Britain, or in any new homeland), he or she should make it clear whether the reference is to the migrant generation or to the multi-generational ethnic group. Assertions that hold true for the migrant generation frequently are not true for the entire ethnic group; too often, conclusions about "the Irish" as a multi-generational group have been drawn from data that really concern only the Irish-born. Remember, "the Irish" means the entire ethnic group. When the migrant generation is meant, that should be clearly indicated by terms such as "Irish-born" or "migrant generation" or "first generation."

The USA and Canada are the big anomalies in the history of the Irish diaspora, although with characteristic North American arrogance we sometimes assert that it is the rest of the world that is out of step. Recall here that the "ideal type" of the Irish diaspora was an historical situation in which for any receptor-country: (1) the Irish migrants were mostly young, and (2) were made up of approximately equal numbers of men and women; (3) the age profiles of males and female migrants were nearly the same; (4) unskilled labourers dominated among the men and domestic servants among the women, but with an intermixing of other groups; (5) in the immigrant generation Roman Catholics predominated, but with a significant minority of Anglo-Irish and Ulster-Scots; and (6) the entire multigenerational group, when surveyed at any moment, had approximately the same religious make-up as did the immigrant generation: normally this would be between 70 and 80 percent Catholic.

As far as the available evidence allows us to draw conclusions, the USA and Canada were roughly (if not completely) typical in matters one, two, three, and four. But, as will become clear in this and in the succeeding chapter, in matters five and six strong deviations from the ideal type occurred.

The wonderful thing about the study of the Irish in North America is that it is full of surprises, massive departures from the conventional wisdom about who the Irish were, and are. The first of these is the almost universally ignored fact that *the bulk of the Irish ethnic group in the United States is at present, and probably always has been, Protestant*. This is in spite of the fact that the overwhelming bulk of the historical literature of the last fifty years deals almost entirely with Roman Catholics and, in many cases, states that the Irish in the United States were, and are, almost entirely Catholic.

The data which indicate that "the Irish" — that is, the entire multi-generational group — in the United States are predominantly Protestant come from three independent sources. The first of these is a set of studies done in the 1970s by the National Opinion Research Center of the University of Chicago[2] and the second in the 1980s by the Gallup polling organization.[3] These revealed that most Americans who said that their primary ethnic group was Irish, were Protestants — 56 percent in the NORC survey and 54 percent in the Gallup study. These were sophisticated and technically expert studies, but they have been dwarfed by the material that at present is being published as a result of "The National Survey of Religious Identification, 1989-90," being conducted under the directorship of Professor Barry A. Kosmin, by the Graduate Center of the City University of New York. This study involves the random survey of 113,000 American households (a massive number for a random survey) and deals with religion, ethnicity, race, and a number of demographic variables. The religious affiliations of persons who identified themselves as being of

Irish ethnic origin are as follows:[4]

Christians ("so stated")	3%
Roman Catholic	33
Jewish	0
Protestant	51
No religion, or non-Christian other than Jewish	<u>13</u>
	100%

Within Irish demographic studies a standard (if perhaps unintentionally sectarian) mode of expressing religious identity is as a ratio of Catholic to "non-Catholic." In the USA in 1989-90, the Catholic/non-Catholic ratio of persons of Irish ancestry was 33/67. I think, however, that this ratio over-emphasizes the degree of implied Protestantism, for it is only in the Irish homeland that a person who is non-Catholic can with reasonable accuracy be assumed to be a Protestant. I would suggest that the most accurate reading would be to lump only the "undefined Christian" category with the Protestants. This would yield the following conclusion: that the ratio of Protestants to Catholics among persons who professed a Christian religion was 54 to 33. That is to say that the Protestant proportion of Irish persons in the United States was 58.6 percent of those professing Christianity.

The import of these studies cannot be rationally denied: they were conducted independently of each other, at an acceptable level of professional competence, and they produced similar results. Yet, by taking them seriously (as obviously, one must) we are entering a mine field, one in which there are hidden explosive charges that arise from widespread, and only shallowly buried, prejudices. Some of the more politically "progressive" attacks on racism (as, for example, the Human Rights Code of Ontario) have defined racism as not merely appertaining to skin colour, but to ethnicity, religion, and national origin. Anything that demeans, derogates, or devalues an individual or group unjustly on any of these matters is seen as racism. And rightly so. With very rare exceptions, the history of the Irish in the United States and, especially, almost all of the general surveys, have been written either so as to make the Irish

Protestants in the U.S. non-existent, or to make them appear as historical anachronisms, odd groups that arrived before the 1840s and faded into inconsequence thereafter. This would be morally wrong (for racism is a moral, more than a merely intellectual, failing), even if the Protestants were merely a slim minority of the Irish ethnic group. Considering that they were the majority, one is encountering an historiographical omission of astounding proportions.

A variety of ingenious methods of excusing this racism have been (and I think will continue to be) employed. The crudest of these is simply to argue that no Protestant can be "truly" Irish. This viewpoint has a considerable resonance in Irish nationalist thought, and at present is used by extremists to justify acts of violence against Protestants within Ireland. There is little one can say in response to such a viewpoint, since it is based upon a faith equivalent to that of religious belief, and so is not capable of examination in the present world. Within the USA it has its counterparts in persons who say that Jews, Blacks, Buddhists, or Gays cannot be real Americans.

Sometimes it is suggested that the Protestants from Ireland were almost entirely Presbyterians (Ulster-Scots) and that they called themselves "Scotch-Irish" and refused to identify themselves as Irish in the USA, so they can therefore be ignored. There is just enough accuracy in these beliefs to be misleading. It is true that when the Famine floods arrived, the Irish Protestants in the inland rural areas were willing to escape nativist prejudice against the Irish Catholics. But, in fact, the adoption of a separate sobriquet was not so much something necessitated by American events, as a function of something that happened in the homeland in the first half of the nineteenth century. Daniel O'Connell, the Great Liberator, was not merely one of the greatest persons in modern Irish history, but one of the shrewdest. He understood that to be successful, he had to unite in one crucible, Irish nationalism, Irish cultural identity, and Roman Catholicism. In this he succeeded. As D.G. Boyce has pointed out, by 1840 when a person in Ireland talked of "Ireland for the Irish" everyone knew that he meant the Catholics; and when someone talked about the Irish people, he meant the Catholics; and when someone talked of the faith of the Irish people, he meant Roman Catholicism.[5] This nominalist by-play is a standard technique of the propagandist, but no less successful for being that. The result was that the Protestants of Ireland, while thinking of themselves as being "Irish and a bit more," were forced to make it clear when talking to a wider audience that they were not Irish in O'Connell's sense. In the USA, since the name that they had once used for themselves now was preempted by the Catholic migrants, they had to develop a new terminology. Among themselves they kept alive a sense of their Irish background (however else would they have been evident in the NORC, Gallup, and CUNY surveys?) but to uninformed outsiders who told them that they were not Irish, they merely shrugged and walked away: they knew they were Irish, whatever the stranger said.

In almost all of the instances when Protestants have been included in the historiography of the Irish in the USA, they have been mislabelled and chronologically segregated. Segregated? In the sense that it is held that there was no significant Irish Protestant migration after the Famine. This almost certainly is untrue, although it is difficult to ascertain directly. And mislabelled? This has occurred because of the assumption that the Irish Protestants were overwhelmingly Presbyterian — that is, Ulster-Scots — in background. Actually there is no solid proof that the Presbyterians predominated. It is probable that the other major Protestant group — the "Anglo-Irish," consisting of "Anglicans," (to use an anachronistic term, or, properly, adherents of the Church of Ireland) — sent nearly as many migrants.

Given that at present most persons of Irish ethnic background are Protestants, one naturally asks, by what migration patterns did the Protestant dominance occur, and how far back in the history of the United States does the predominantly Protestant character of the Irish as an ethnic group hold? For reasons that I will explain in section "2" of this chapter, one cannot cite any direct data in answer to that question, because the United States government never collected any information on the matter. It is theoretically possible that the Irish as a group in some period early in their history in the U.S. (in the colonial period or, in any case, prior to the Great Famine) were overwhelmingly Roman Catholic and that these numbers were later swamped by great hordes of migrating Irish-born Protestants.

However, the one thing that we know for certain from Irish demographic sources (see Chapter Two) is that most of the Irish post-Famine population loss came from the Catholic sector, and further, we know that most emigrants in the period 1850-1914 went to the USA. Therefore, it is mathematically impossible that Protestants prevailed in the post-Famine migration flow (indeed, I have never encountered such a suggestion any place in the historical literature). Therefore, this possibility is void.

Secondly, it is possible that most Irish migrants to the thirteen colonies and later to the USA were Roman Catholics, but that a major apostasy occurred whereby the predominantly Catholic group of Irish persons switched to Protestantism. As I will discuss in Chapter Ten, there is just a grain of truth in this idea. In fact, in the colonial period, there is an indication of a significant degree of conversion to Protestantism. However, the number of conversions that it would have taken to turn the ethnic group from being between three-quarters and four-fifths Catholic (in the Old Country) to being roughly 55 percent Protestant (in the USA) is way beyond the bounds of credibility. From mid-nineteenth century onwards, one of the great sources of pride of the Catholic church in the USA was its success in keeping the loyalty of Irish Catholics.

A third possibility is likely and is characterized by considerable explanatory power. I think that the most promising way of making sense of the religious pattern of Irish migration to the USA and of subsequent religio-ethnic history is to recall the basic distinction between migrants and the multi-generational ethnic cohort — and then to introduce the variable of time of arrival, which is a crucial determinate of the overall character of any ethnic group. By taking into account the differential times of arrival of the two major religious strands among Irish migrants, one can see a simple pattern: (1) That at some period in the pre-Famine migration to the USA (precisely what years is in doubt) the Protestant Irish migrants (both Anglo-Irish and Ulster Scots) significantly outnumbered the Catholic migrants and that (2) *it is almost certainly true that over the entire history of Irish migration to the United States, more individual Catholics than Protestants arrived.* The Catholics, however, in general came later. That pre-Famine (or at least, pre-1815) migration was tilted towards Protestant groups means that a multiplier existed. To use a simple example: a Catholic migrant from Munster in 1930 and an Ulster Protestant in 1830 are each single dots on the graph of migration flow, but in 1930 the Ulster migrant had scores of descendants within the Irish-descended group, but the newly-arrived Munster migrant was only one person in the group. That there was a significant difference along these lines is indicated by the NORC General Social Survey, which found that in its sample, 41 percent of Irish Catholics (as of the 1970s) were at least fourth generation in the U.S., while 83 percent of the Irish Protestants were.[6] (3) it is easy to accommodate within this framework the fact that a significant Protestant migration continued after the Great Famine. This was much smaller than the Catholic migration, but far from inconsequential. And (4) it is also easy to accept within this framework the suggestion that the Protestant migration to the USA was not an Ulster-Scots migration, but was broadly representative of the entire spectrum of Irish Protestantism, which included two major denominations (Presbyterian and Anglican) and several minor ones. Protestant migration had a wide geographical range, and did not stem merely from Ulster. Nor indeed, did origin in Ulster imply that the Protestant migrant was Presbyterian, for a considerable portion of the Ulster plantation was formed by Anglicans. Therefore one can accept the corollary of Protestant variation in the homeland, namely that the Protestant Irish in the USA took many forms.

Any serious, non-racist history of the Irish in the United States should spend as much time upon the Baptists (especially the Southern Baptists), Methodists, Anglicans, and Presbyterians, as it does upon the history of the Catholic Church. The life of William Bell Riley (the founding father of twentieth-century American fundamentalism) should be as well known as, say, that of Cardinal Spellman. And the career of Jimmie Rodgers (the father of American country music) deserves to be as widely known as that of the great tenor John McCormack. Only then will the historical study of the Irish in the USA have come of age.

(II)

The second surprising fact about the Irish in the USA is that, although there is a massive historical literature, detailed, and assertively self-confident, in fact *there is not and never has been accurate systematic demographic data on several of the most fundamental characteristics of the Irish in the United States.* There are hundreds of books that generalize about the Irish as an ethnic group, and even the most careful of local and community studies usually take for granted an assumed national context that in fact is unrelated to any verifiable data base.

Until 1969-70 none of the decennial censuses of the United States asked a question concerning the ethnicity of the individuals whom they were enumerating, and the census is the only potential source of such data. Granted, in the late 1920s, the American Council of Learned Societies tried to re-work the 1790 census data to give an indication of ethnicity at the end of the colonial period, but this effort failed miserably.[7] No further comprehensive attempt at dealing with ethnicity was made until 1969-70, when the Census Bureau asked an ethnicity question. Unhappily, the collection of the data was bungled and no firm conclusions came from it.[8] In 1980 and in 1990, the ethnicity question again was asked and again it was mishandled so as to be virtually useless.[9]

Even more extraordinary is that *never* have the United States census authorities collected information on the religious affiliation of specific individuals. The Census Bureau once, in 1957, asked a religion question of a voluntary sample group, but this met with so much opposition that the attempt was never repeated.[10] This refusal to deal with religious persuasion except by querying the various denominational authorities for their alleged total number of adherents, seems so perverse to non-American historians as to be almost pathological. But whatever the reasons for this refusal to enumerate individuals by religion,[11] it precludes the formulation by historians of any general statement, based on official census information, of the relationship of religion and Irish ethnicity.

Given that there are no comprehensive data either on Irish ethnicity or upon the religious persuasion of individuals of Irish background in the U.S., it follows that there are no cross-tabulations that relate either their ethnicity or their religious persuasion to such fundamental characteristics as their places of residence and occupation. Granted, there are several, indeed dozens, of valuable studies of the Irish in various cities of America, but in none of them is the matter of ethnicity and of religion defined for the entire population of the town or city with which the authors deal, and for none of them is it established where in the total context of the Irish in America their study-group fits. This is not the authors' fault: the census data are lacking. Unfortunately, however, because of the lack of data defining the entire Irish profile, ethnically and religiously, historians have studied the sub-groups on which data come most easily to hand — Catholics in large cities — and have given the impression that the characteristics of these easily-researched persons were universal among the Irish in America.

But, surely, there must be some pieces of comprehensive data about the Irish. There are. Beginning with the *1850* census of the United States, we know, at decennial intervals, the birth-place of everyone in the population.[12] This is useful indeed, as long as one remembers three points: first, that the data on the foreign-born in general, and on the Irish in particular, is information only on migrants, not on the bulk of the ethnic group; second, that the data on the Irish include both Catholics and Protestants, with no effort having been made to distinguish the respective proportions of each denomination; and, third, that the earliest data we have on the Irish reflect the situation *after* the extraordinary migration induced by the Great Famine had been several years in full spate. In other words, we have *no* demographic base line which allows us to determine what the character and extent of Irish migration to the United States were before the Famine. This is especially crippling, because, although it is quite clear that there was a heavy Irish migration to the United States before the Famine, the U.S. immigration statistics before 1855 are not trustworthy.

Manifestly, the material available on the number of Irish-born persons amongst the American population from

1850 onwards is much better than no information at all, but its limits are severe. Individuals with Irish parents or grandparents were counted simply as native Americans in the 1850, 1860, and 1870 censuses, which means that as far as the study of ethnicity is concerned, they ceased to exist. One genealogically-based study of a Wisconsin county indicated that in 1870 only about one-fifth of persons of Irish background were recorded as being Irish, since the U.S. census authorities tallied only the Irish-born.[13] The apparent impact of the Irish (particularly in frontier and farming regions where they settled early, often well before the Famine), is either lost or greatly diminished. That is apparent impact only: they were there; it is just that the U.S. records do not tally them as Irish.

In 1870 the census authorities asked all individuals whether or not they had foreign-born parents, but the information was elicited only in the form of a yes-or-no answer, not specifying what country the parents were from. The next census, that of 1880, asked the specific origin of those natives of the U.S. who had foreign-born parents and cross-tabulated this material in a refreshingly useful fashion. This quasi-ethnicity item was as close as the Census Bureau ever came in the last century to dealing with ethnicity in the true sense. As one authoritative study conducted in the early 1920s lamented, "The foreign stock can be traced back only one generation .... Beyond this the population must, in most cases be treated as an undifferentiated body of native stock."[14]

The problem, then, is that a *permanently invisible majority* of the Irish have been excluded from U.S. records. Up through the year 1849, there was no U.S. tally of place of birth, so all immigrant groups went unrecorded. Although the censuses of 1850-70 tallied the number of immigrants, this was at a time when most persons of Irish ethnicity were at least second generation, and so they left no mark on the demographic litmus paper. Then, from 1880 onwards, the first and second generations were tallied, but by that time many persons of Irish ethnicity were third generation (that is the grandchildren of Irish migrants) or later. And, if this was a probability in 1880 (the first such census), it certainly has been true throughout the twentieth century. Finally, in 1970, 1980, and 1990, attempts were made to measure multigeneration ethnicity, but with the fatal defects already mentioned.

In sum: (1) in census after census, most persons of Irish background have been excluded from U.S. demographic data that relate to ethnicity and (2) there is no direct indication in systematic census records of the religious persuasion of Irish immigrants and their descendants: only the non-government surveys conducted by NORC, Gallup and CUNY are of any use, and they are very recent.

These two facts explain why, although in the historical writing about the Irish in the USA there are many good local studies of immigrants, a few good first and second generation community studies, many useful biographies, and a good deal of institutional history (such as of political groups and of religious bodies, especially the Catholic church), there are no trustworthy documented historical studies of the Irish as a nationwide ethnic group, and none that define with reliable evidence the cultural characteristics (particularly the religious profile) of the full Irish group.

(III)

Perversely, framers of the U.S. historical literature on the Irish have refused to look to the one source of information that would help them out of many of their difficulties, namely the Canadian material. Indeed, *there is no history of the Irish in the U.S.; the history is of the Irish in North America*, and that is something very different indeed.

The necessity of dealing with North America as a unit is simply put. Until very recently (roughly the middle of the twentieth century) the U.S.-Canada border was a very permeable membrane. Despite ideological differences between the two nations, individuals and families moved across the border with relative ease. It was not at all uncommon for a person to spend part of his or her working life in, say, Toronto, and then move to Buffalo, later to Minneapolis, and then to Winnipeg. Branches of various Irish families spanned the border, half in Seattle, say, half in Vancouver. The Eastern Townships of Quebec contained many Irish families who had branches in Vermont. The border between Maine and Canada was in many places a figment, and the axis of movement between the Maritimes and the "Boston States" was a virtual highway. To segregate the Irish in Canada is to trepan the history of the Irish in North America, the largest of the New Worlds to which the Irish migrated. It is similar to someone truncating the history of Ireland by removing from the story the life histories of everyone from Connaught.

Secondly, in arguing the absolute necessity of dealing with the Irish in the U.S. within the context of North America, one should note that there are certain sources of crucial historical data for the Irish migrants and for the Irish ethnic group that are found only in Canada. For instance, some Canadian provinces conducted censuses of population well before the Great Famine. These allow the historian to establish a base line and thus permit the drawing of accurate generalizations about the nature of Famine migration, which is impossible to do if one is limited to U.S. sources.

Part of the American problem is that, until 1855, U.S. immigration statistics are much less help than one would expect. The immigration act of 1819, effective in 1820, required that all ships bringing migrants to the U.S. should prepare passenger lists or manifests giving the sex, age, occupation and the "country to which they severally belong," of all their passengers. The data thereby collected suffered by virtue of incomplete enforcement of the law (and, thus, undercounting) and by an ambiguity in the definition of nativity: it was not made clear whether it meant the country of birth, of citizenship, or of last long-term residence. These matters were corrected by the immigration act of 1855, but that is too late to throw light on the crucial dark ages of the Irish migration into America, the period from the end of the Napoleonic wars to the census of 1850.[15]

But even if the pre-1850 U.S. immigration data had been trustworthy, one still would need to adopt a wider, North American perspective. Why? Because before the mid-1840s, when changes in the navigation laws removed the price advantage of sailing to St. John's, Newfoundland, St. John, New Brunswick, or Quebec City, the cheapest way to get to the United States was by way of Canada. Hence, even had they been accurate, U.S. port-arrival data would seriously have underestimated the actual number of Irish-born persons who eventually fetched up in the States. One mid-nineteenth century authority estimated that in the 1820s (when most migrants from the British Isles to Canada were Irish), 67,993 immigrants came to the United States through Canada, and that in the 1830s the number was 199,130 (again, at a time when most migrants from the British Isles to Canada were Irish).[16] This same authority estimated that U.S. immigration totals should have been increased by 50 percent to allow for arrivals from Canada. A rather more conservative estimate made in the early 1870s suggested that the number of foreign-born persons coming to the United States via Canada was as follows:[17]

1815-20	12,157
1820-30	26,524
1830-40	56,364
1840-50	90,718

Given that from 1825 (when data become available) the Irish migrants comprised considerably more than half of the migrants from the British Isles to Canada, it is highly likely that most of the persons in this estimate were Irish-born.[18]

Were these individuals not recorded in U.S. immigration statistics? No. Efforts at recording land-border crossings into the United States began only in 1853, continued fitfully for a while, and were completely abandoned during the American civil war. The practice was reintroduced in 1865, but abandoned as being unsatisfactory and without a legal basis in 1885. The counting of migrants from Canada and Mexico to the United States did not begin again until the fiscal year 1908.[19] An indication of the data thus lost is found in a study showing that for the years 1879-85, the very incompletely recorded immigration from Canada and Mexico together totalled more than one-seventh (almost 14.6 percent) of all recorded immigration into the United States (99.4 percent of this Canadian and Mexican total was Canadian). Since the Irish were a larger proportion of the immigrant population in Canada than they were in the U.S.,[20] one can reasonably guess that more than one-seventh of the Irish immigrant flow was entering the U.S. unrecorded, and that at a very late date. Early in the process, before 1845, the proportion of flow from Canada must have been considerably higher, the Canadian flow comprising perhaps as much as one-quarter of the total Irish-born influx to the States.

Thus, if one is to make any headway in understanding the fundamental mysteries of pre-1850 Irish migration to the U.S., one must think in terms of a *North American* pool of migrants from Ireland: some sailed to Canada and stayed, others migrated directly to the U.S. and settled, yet others arrived in the U.S. and moved to Canada, while many more disembarked in Canada and subsequently moved on to the States.

In arguing that one can discuss sensibly the size and nature of the Irish migration to the U.S. in the nineteenth century (and, most especially, in the years before the first census of the foreign-born in 1850) only by adopting a North American context, I am of course discussing only the migrants, the so-called first generation. There is more to the point than that, however. Ultimately historians of the Irish in America would like to be able to deal not only with immigrants, but with the entire ethnic group. Hence, it is worth noting that, in all probability, of these second-and third-generation Irish in America a significant component were the children and grandchildren of migrants who had settled not in the U.S., but in Canada. In the absence of direct studies on this matter, the point has to be drawn inferentially from the facts that (a) the Canadian-born were a large element in the U.S. population—1,204,637 in 1910[21] and (b) that persons of Irish ethnicity composed the largest non-French ethnic group in Canada until the late 1880s or 1890s.[22] Hence, unless one wishes to postulate a much lower propensity-to-migrate for Canadians of native Irish ethnicity than for other groups, one has to infer that a significant proportion of the Irish-American ethnic cohort actually came, most recently, from Canada, and was of Canadian nativity.

Obviously, what the U.S. census data say about the Canadian-born and what they mean in terms of the Irish in America are two different things. Although the Canadian-born were tallied as foreign-born (and thus, as first-generation Americans), the fact is that they were at least second, and sometimes third or fourth generation *North*

Americans. Thus, they should be plugged into any explanation of the total ethnic pattern of the Irish in the U.S., not in the immigrant generation, but in the second and subsequent generations. Just as the path of the Irish migrants to the U.S. can only be understood as a forked one, some coming directly, others via Canada, so that of the second, third, and fourth generations can only be understood if one accepts their duality of nativity, Canadian and U.S. Manifestly, once one recognizes these facts, the permutations of immigration patterns and of ethnic mobility multiply and the accepted picture of the Irish in the USA as having stemmed from a simple, if cruelly uncomfortable, transatlantic passage to New York or Philadelphia or Boston, disappears.

In arguing the absolute necessity of dealing with the Irish in the U.S. (both the migrant generation and the entire ethnic group) within the overall context of North America, I have pointed out that there are certain censuses of Canadian provinces that were conducted before the Famine. Crucially, from the early 1840s onward, various Canadian enumerations inquired not only into nativity, but also into religion, something that has never done in the USA. And, most important, from 1871 onwards, the Dominion of Canada census authorities recorded not only each persons's religion and place of birth, but also his or her primary ethnicity, something that, again, has never been done in the USA.

Clearly, if one wishes to draw any valid generalizations about the Irish as an ethnic group — what, for example was their rate of social mobility? what occupational patterns emerged? in what sort of environment did they settle? how geographically mobile were they? how upwardly mobile economically were they? and how did religion affect these matters? — one would do well to use the Canadian information. Of course the situation in, say, Ontario in 1880 was not identical to that of, say, Illinois in the same year. No two social situations ever are identical. But careful experimental design can produce reliable results that are transportable across state and provincial borders.

The fact is, the historian of the Irish in any part of the U.S. who does not the Canadian data know, knows not the Irish in the USA.

Chapter 10

North America: The Big Case Part II: Specific Issues

(I)

If, because of the huge gaps in the historical record, we are at least a full generation away from being able to outline a general history of the Irish in the USA, we can nevertheless make some progress. We can pose several fundamental issues that need to be resolved, and we can make some tentative suggestions (sometimes with the help of the rich Canadian data) about the way that these issues are apt to be resolved.[1]

The first question is the hardest, and it is the one that historians will be able to answer only after most of the others are successfully dealt with. This is: what did it mean when a person said he or she was Irish? There is no question that from at least the mid-seventeenth century onwards, people in the geographic island of Ireland thought of themselves as being Irish. This held (and still holds) for Catholics and Protestants (not all Catholics and not all Protestants, but most), and for men and women of Ulster, Leinster, Munster, and Connaught. Yet, being Irish was only one of their several identities and what "Irish" meant changed over time, as well as being a different concept in different places.

John Kelleher once said he would like to meet his long-dead great-grandfather, a man of County Cork, and to ask him what he was. John guessed that he would say, first, that he was an "Eoghnacht," (meaning a descendant of the king of Munster), but which in practice meant "Catholic," the same way that the other contemporary term, "Sassenach" (Englishman) inevitably meant "Protestant." After that, John guessed, his great-grandfather would have said that he was a Munster man, and, if pushed, he might finally have said that he was an Irishman. But what that meant heaven only knows, because great-grandfather Kelleher almost certainly would have been incensed if told that he was of the same nation as somebody from Connaught. (That this is a shrewd guess is indicated by the fact that the pre-Famine migrants to the USA and to Canada often divided into vicious rival gangs according to their being Connaughtmen, Munstermen, or whatever).

A similar complexity exists to the present day. In what sense do present day persons in the USA who think of themselves as being Irish mean the term? Dealing with these and similar matters of *mentalité* will be the ultimate challenge for future historians of the Irish in North America.

(II)

A much easier issue to deal with is, to what extent did being Roman Catholic directly handicap Irish migrants who came to North America? Here I mean *causally*. A cultural deficiency that might have caused them to do poorly in North America is very different from discrimination against them because they were Catholics. The latter is something that is forced upon a set of people by outsiders and certainly it is not caused by their own culture.

In three societies that we have examined so far — Australia, New Zealand, and South Africa — it has been clearly demonstrated that Irish Catholicism was not a handicap for the Irish migrants in dealing with modernizing, expanding, societies of new settlement. Therefore, unless the USA for some reason received the damaged goods of the Irish diaspora, our expectation should be that Irish Catholic culture did not handicap the Irish migrants in the U.S. in a causal way.

It is true that there are some indications that the Irish migrants to the USA in the later periods were "the worst" of the Irish diaspora in terms of their preparation for a fast-modernizing society. Recall that Table 26 (in Chapter Five) indicated that in 1912-13 the occupational profile of Irish males migrating to the USA had a lower proportion of men in the skilled trades and in the professions and commerce, and a higher proportion of farm and general labourers, than was the case for any other diaspora lands. Further, David Fitzpatrick's emigration tabulations indicate that in the last quarter of the nineteenth century, Irish men and women who migrated to the USA "tended to come from counties which might be termed 'backward'."[2] We lack direct evidence for the years before 1876.

These differences between the USA and other countries should not be overstated. Except for the case of South Africa, the majority of male migrants to *all* destinations were labourers and the majority of women were farm or domestic servants. The differences, however, mean that we should be somewhat cautious in applying conclusions from elsewhere to the U.S. situation. It is possible that although being Catholic was no handicap elsewhere, the Irish Catholic migrants and their offspring fell below some important, if invisible, cultural level demanded in the U.S. and, therefore, that in a causal sense the Irish Catholic culture was a real impediment to their success.

Among scholars of the historical experience of the Irish immigrants in the USA, there are two opposed views on this matter. One school holds that, far from being a hindrance to coping with America in the age of frontier expansion and urban industrialization, Irish Catholicism actually helped. An exponent of this viewpoint is Dale B. Light, Jr.:

> Ethnic institutions and organisations were thus indispensable to the development of a separate Irish ethnic consciousness in nineteenth-century America, but, paradoxically, an examination of these organisations shows that they also embodied many values commonly associated with the dominant Protestant culture. Members of ethnic associations were exhorted to be diligent, temperate, patriotic, and thrifty, to submit to civil authority, to educate themselves and their children, to adopt clean and orderly personal habits, and to be devout Christians. *In other words they were urged to adopt the standards of behaviour and belief associated with exponents of the Protestant work ethnic and industrial discipline.* (italics mine) Ethnic organisations thus separated their adherents from the dominant culture while at the same time assimilating them to many of the most important elements of that culture.[3]

Most historians of the Irish migrants to America, however, accept the view that the cultural characteristics associated with Roman Catholicism in Ireland were an impediment to the migrants' adaptation to North American life. Fortunately, we possess an excellent test case of that conclusion. This is the *ne plus ultra* of the historiography of the Irish in the U.S., Kerby Miller's monumental *Emigrants and Exiles. Ireland and the Irish Exodus to North America.* The volume captured both the Merle Curti Award in American Social History and the Saloutas Memorial Book Award in American Immigration History. The study is at once an encapsulation of the majority of historical opinion on the Irish in the U.S. (up to the time of its writing) and the most forceful and expert articulation of what U.S. historians of the Irish believed they knew (again, at the time of its writing). The volume, therefore, is an appropriate and fair place to focus upon the historians' view of the Catholic culture of the nineteenth-century migrants, for it is the strongest statement available of the conventional wisdom.

The heart of the book, on which it must be judged, concerns the years 1815-1921, the era of the great Irish diaspora. Miller writes gracefully, and it is with an apologetic philistinism that one must wrench his argument from his prose and coldly outline his logic. To begin with, he has a phenomenon that he wishes to explain. This is his observed fact that nineteenth-century Irish emigrants were predisposed to perceive or at least to justify themselves not as voluntary, ambitious emigrants, but as involuntary, non-responsible "exiles" compelled to leave home by forces beyond individual control, particularly by British and landlord oppression.[4] Note that this observation involves only Irish Catholic emigrants, not Protestant. Miller pays considerable attention to Protestants, but his primary observation and his explanation of it concern only Roman Catholics.

To explain this primary phenomenon he introduces several causal factors. First, that beginning in the late 1820s, *relatively* [italics Miller's] poor Catholics from the three southern provinces constituted a major proportion of the movement overseas.[5] Second, the increasingly Catholic stream of emigrants was a river of reluctant exiles. According to Miller, much evidence indicates that Catholics throughout Ireland, not just in remote Irish-speaking areas, were much more reluctant to leave home than were their Protestant countrymen.[6] Third, for Catholics, emigration "posed severe social, cultural, and even psychological problems ..."[7]

As a link between his primary observed phenomena and these causal factors, Miller presents an intervening variable. He does not give the variable a name, but it can be dominated the *"Gaelic-Catholic Disability."* He says, concerning "traditionalist rural Catholics," that among those who emigrated, "their outlook on life ... was fatalistic and dependent, and their religious faith was usually neither generalized nor internalized, but instead was almost inseparable from archaic customs and landmarks rooted in particular locales now thousands of miles behind them."[8] He postulates "a Catholic Irish propensity to avoid individual responsibility for innovative actions such as emigration and to fall back on communally acceptable explanations embedded in archaic historic and literary traditions and reinforced by modern Irish political rhetoric.[9] Even the Irish language is fitted into this variable: the semantic structure of the Irish language itself reflected and reinforced an Irish world view which emphasized dependence and passivity.[10] Thus, "armed with a world view so shaped, the Irish experienced the socioeconomic changes associated with the modern commercial and industrial revolutions with certain psychological, as well as political and economic, disadvantages."[11] Such people perceived their movement into the then-modern world of nineteenth-century North America as banishment. As the century progressed and as a higher and higher proportion of emigrants came from western districts with strong Gaelic-Catholic cultures, the pervasive sense of exile increased.

A logical step is to ask: what are the implications of what I have called Miller's "Gaelic-Catholic Disability" variable? If that intervening variable is accurate and apposite, not only will it explain why the Irish Catholics wrote all those mournful exile songs and sent those tear-stained letters home, but it will permit us to draw hypotheses about the Irish Catholics in North America that can be empirically tested. If these hypotheses are confirmed, then the probability that Miller's Gaelic-Catholic Disability variable is valid will be greatly heightened. If, on the other hand, these hypotheses are disproved, then the validity of Miller's argument will have been shown to be so improbable as to be worthless.

Fortunately, the elegant simplicity of Miller's model permits a series of simple and effective tests. Since his position is that the Irish Catholic culture was both singular and a liability, then if it were found that the Irish Catholics (either in the migrant generation or among their immediate descendants) and Irish Protestants (who certainly did not share the Gaelic-Catholic culture) were fundamentally similar in behaviour, it will have been proved that the Gaelic-Catholic Disability was a chimera and that this interpretation of the Irish Catholic culture should not be adopted as part of the explanation of the history of the Irish Catholics worldwide.

It seems fair to suggest that from Miller's model of Gaelic-Catholic culture, and from his contrasts, both explicit and implicit, between Irish Protestants and Irish Catholics, one would predict in nineteenth-century North America: first, that, because of the communal and familial nature of their culture as described by Miller, Irish Catholics would be much less successful than Irish Protestants in operating in the isolated world of nineteenth-century North American agriculture; second, that Irish Catholics would have a significantly lower occupational profile than would Irish Protestants; and third, that Irish Catholics would show less rapid upward social mobility over time than would Irish Protestants.

But here we encounter a problem. Although it is easy to state in precise terms the implications of the Gaelic-Catholic Disability theory, there is no systematic data base in the United States covering any part of the nineteenth or early twentieth centuries that allows us to assess the behaviour of Irish Catholics as compared to Irish Protestants and to compare both to other faiths. It is at this point that Canada comes to the rescue. There exist Canadian studies that include wide-scale observations not only of the behaviour of Irish migrants but, better, of the entire ethnic group. Included in the Canadian data base is information on the religious affiliation of every person in the data set. These Canadian data deal with real behaviour, not with psychological presumptions, and the studies are capable of being replicated — that is, of being checked and repeated for accuracy. The most significant of the Canadian studies is the work of Gordon Darroch and Michael Ornstein.[12] This work is by far the most sophisticated research design yet adopted in North American ethnic historical studies, and it should serve as a model for what eventually must be done with the U.S. manuscript census data.

What Darroch and Ornstein did in substance was virtually to retabulate from original manuscript sources the 1871 Dominion of Canada censuses. This was done so as to permit the framing and answering of many questions that did not occur to the nineteenth-century enumeration officials. In particular, the nineteenth-century Canadian censuses are notoriously frustrating in that they contain data on several important variables, but do not provide cross-tabulations of those variables. To overcome such difficulties, Darroch and Ornstein drew from the 1871 dominion census a random group of 10,000 male heads of household, on each of whom there was data on several dozen characteristics. They followed up this massive sampling by linking a large body of their 1871 data to records on individuals who lived in central Canada during the third quarter of the nineteenth century. This allowed the tracing of several thousand randomly selected life patterns.

The fact that the major Canadian data base permits us to subject to systematic proof or disproof hypotheses about the Irish in North America is something that should make all historians of the Irish happy. However, anyone with a vested interest in leaving his or her hypotheses unchecked may wish to claim that the Irish Catholics who went to Canada were not comparable culturally to those who went to the United States. Now, although there were small differences in the last quarter of the nineteenth and early twentieth centuries between Catholic migrants to Canada and to the USA (the Canadian Catholics were slightly less working class), these Irish migrants were essentially the same people, whether they got off the boat in Montreal or in Philadelphia. Further, they (and their offspring) flowed back and forth across the U.S.-Canadian border with ease. And, moreover, it appears that earlier in the century — during the early years of the Famine — the least able, most sickly were dropped in New Brunswick and Quebec.[13]

Thus, the only remaining defence against using the Canadian data on Irish Catholics is to admit, yes, they were the same sort of people as the Irish Catholics who migrated to the USA, but some time after they arrived a selection process took place: the losers, the least able, went to the USA, "leaving behind a self-selected minority unrepresentative of Irish Catholics."[14] There is no evidence whatsoever of this having occurred. A large number of Irish Catholics moved from Canada to the USA (and fewer, but many, from the USA to Canada), but why it would be the losers who moved south and the winners who stayed north is an idea that defies explication; and indeed precludes credence.

What Darroch and Ornstein's studies revealed was, first, that Irish Roman Catholics were not disabled by their cultural background from entering the most important entrepreneurial occupation of the time — farming — either on the frontier or in already settled areas. Indeed, farming was the most common Irish Catholic occupation, as it was of the Irish Protestants. The Irish Catholics were only slightly less likely to go into farming — less than 10 percent below the national average — than was the average run of Canadians. The Irish Catholics were not ineluctably urban.

Further, Darroch and Ornstein show that, contrary to the hypothesis, Irish Catholics in Canada did not have a markedly lower economic profile than did persons of Irish Protestant ethnicity. The proportions of Irish Catholics and Irish Protestants amongst manufacturers, white-collar workers, and artisans were virtually identical in Canada in 1871. Catholics were under-represented in the professional class — only 3 percent of the total population, in any case — and were more likely than other groups to have labouring occupations, but not markedly so. Put simply, persons of Irish Catholic ethnicity did slightly less well than did persons of Irish Protestant ethnicity, but not enough to lend credence to the idea that Catholics were heavily handicapped by their cultural background. Strikingly, in rural areas it was found that the Irish Catholics had slightly greater proportions in the bourgeois occupations than did the Scots or Germans.[15]

Moreover, the data show that, contrary to the hypothesis, Irish Catholics did not evince significantly less upward mobility over time than did Irish Protestants. Amongst Irish-born persons — that is, Irish migrants —

linked by Darroch and Ornstein between 1861 and 1871, there was no dramatic difference either in occupational distribution or in occupational mobility between Irish Catholics and Irish Protestants. Irish Catholic immigrants started out over-represented somewhat in labouring occupations, but their rate of mobility out of labouring into more desirable occupations — and especially into the nation's most-desired way of earning a living, farm ownership — *exceeded* that of the Irish-born Protestants.[16]

What this adds up to is a crushing disproof of the validity of the idea that the Gaelic-Catholic culture was a heavy disability for individuals dealing with the modern world of nineteenth-century North America.

We must be absolutely clear about what that means. It directly disproves the idea that the Irish Catholic culture (and the social and linguistic features associated with it) were a cause of any collective lack of success on the part of Catholic migrants to North America and of their children during the second half of the nineteenth century. It does *not* mean that the Irish Catholics were as successful as every other North American group, or even as successful as the average. In fact, Irish Catholics met with frightful sectarian discrimination in the USA, and this, when combined with the ruthless economic structure characteristic of nascent capitalism, meant that many of them did very badly indeed. But this was discrimination, and not caused by something in their own cultural background. In the USA, the Irish encountered in the nineteenth century the most racist country in the English-speaking world and the one in which anti-Catholic discrimination was greatest. One finds them locked out of a whole range of jobs; they responded to this situation by adopting settlement and occupational patterns that helped them to cope with the greater, hostile society.

What the Canadian data prove is that in a relatively non-discriminatory society (far from perfectly so, but less so than the USA in the same period), the Irish Catholics were not hindered by their cultural background. Thus, when some historians argue that in the USA the occupational levels, the low rate of social mobility, and the heavy concentration in urban areas were the product of the Irish Catholic cultural heritage, they are confusing the victim with the oppressor. There was nothing in the Irish Catholics' background that made them do less well in the nineteenth century than other groups; it was the systematic discrimination, engrained racism and voracious emergent industrial capitalism of the contemporary U.S. society that did so.

(III)

The next issue, then, is when, as a group, did the Irish Catholics in the USA overcome the discrimination that they encountered in the nineteenth century?

The first reasonably clear window into this matter is found at the beginning of the twentieth century. In 1907, the United States Senate appointed a commission on immigration. Known as the "Dillingham Commission," after its chairman, Senator William P. Dillingham, this group produced forty-one volumes in the years 1907-10; these provide some insight (and considerable frustration) in chronicling the Irish in the USA.

Among the useful implications of the Dillingham data was that the Irish were experiencing inter-generational socio-economic mobility. That is, the second generation did better than the first. This was indicated by the commission's profile of male "breadwinners" for the year 1900:[17]

Agricultural:	First Generation	Second Generation
owners and managers	9.4 %	8.8 %
Agricultural:		
labourers and others	4.2	7.7
Professionals	1.9	3.7
Domestic and		
personal service	8.1	6.8
Unskilled labourers	22.3	10.2
Trade and Transport	21.6	28.4
Skilled building trades	5.9	6.9
Textile factory workers	2.0	2.1
Other factory workers	24.6	25.4
	100%	100%

Obviously, these data are limited,[18] but certainly the Irish were moving up, generation by generation. David Noel Doyle argues that the two generations surveyed in the 1900 data had rough parity in occupational levels with native Americans (that is, persons of third or subsequent generations), with one exception: New England remained a backwater for the Irish, a place of blocked occupational mobility.[19]

If, by 1900, the Irish were on the verge of being average, some time during the decade of the First World War Irish Catholics (considered as a multigenerational group) crossed that line and continued upwards. This conclusion comes from the ingenious work of Andrew M. Greeley who employed survey data collected by the National Opinion Research Center at the University of Chicago between 1972 and 1988. These were surveys of various aspects of ethnicity, religion, economic status and social attitudes. Greeley's breakthrough was to realize that the survey data on various individuals could be read as historical documents: if one has information on the careers of individuals who were born in, say, 1900, or 1910, then one can build up an assessment of the occupational profile of these people in the 1920s, the 1930s and so on. The key conclusion of this part of Greeley's work is that in the era of the First World War, persons of Irish Catholic ethnicity already slightly exceeded the U.S. national average on three major indices of occupational and social success: college attendance and graduation, professional careers, and white collar careers.[20]

From the 1920s onward Irish Catholics in the USA were above average socio-economically, and by the 1960s they were a privileged group. During the 1960s and 1970s, the University of Michigan Survey Research Center and the National Opinion Research Center generated large bodies of information on ethnicity, religion, and social variables. The Michigan composite base includes 17,770 persons, the NORC one 26,768, very large numbers for survey research. The data from these files dictate three unambiguous conclusions: (1) In the USA in the 1960s and 1970s, the ethnic group with the highest annual income was the Jews. The Gentile group with the highest annual family income was the Irish Catholics. Persons of British Protestant background (the "WASPs" of everyday conversation) were in the middle of the pack. (2) The ethnic group which had the highest average educational level was the Jews. The highest non-Jewish educational level was that of the Irish Catholics, with Protestants of English and Scottish ancestry slightly behind. And (3) in terms of occupational prestige ranked on standard scales, the highest status jobs (on average) were held by Jews, with — and this is significant — British Protestants coming second and Irish Catholics third.[21]

Why Irish Catholics, being the most privileged of the non-Jewish ethnic groups in the USA in terms of education and income, should be slightly below the old WASPs in terms of job prestige is hard to say. Prestige jobs are not necessarily those that pay the most, but are posts (such as book publishers, gallery curators, media personalities, research professors, artists) with social cachet. It may be that Irish Catholics still encounter discrimination in entrance into such areas, or it may be that the value-structure of the Irish Catholics (considered as a group) simply places more emphasis upon financial rewards than upon public prestige.

That is a sidebar. The central point is that the Irish Catholics as a multigenerational ethnic group were by the 1960s and '70s the second-most privileged ethnic group in the USA, behind the Jews, but slightly ahead of their old nemesis, the British-descended Protestants. It is hard to believe that the rise of the Irish Catholics could have occurred so swiftly (in less than a century-and-a-quarter from the Great Famine) if there had been some fundamental element in Irish Catholic culture which impeded the success of its adherents. Certainly, all of the Protestant groups that the Irish Catholics passed on their way up would not credit the existence of any such disability.

(IV)

But what about those Protestants in the larger ethnic group, persons who have in all probability been the majority of the Irish group throughout U.S. history? How did there come to be so many of them? When did they arrive? And how have they fared?

Those are easy questions to state, very difficult to answer.

The Irish Protestants in the USA stemmed from three sources: (a) Protestant migrants from Ireland who arrived in the American colonial period, before the Napoleonic Wars interrupted the migrant flow; (b) post-Napoleonic migrants, who began to arrive after 1815 and whose numbers became heavy in the 1830s; and (c) converts to Protestantism from Roman Catholicism. Because of the huge holes in the U.S. records (especially the complete lack of direct religious data) discussion of all three groups is necessarily anecdotal and circumstantial.

Consider the third group: converts from Catholicism. Even though it is not quantitatively measurable, this was a real phenomenon. David Noel Doyle, in making his own estimates of the number of the Irish ethnic group in twentieth-century America, notes that, simply put, there are too many Irish Protestants to be explained by differential immigration patterns and, therefore, part of the explanation of the large number of Irish Protestants is that "many of these must represent lapses from Catholicism."[22] This, of course, is speculation, but it is a sensible guess, if one accepts two qualifications.

The first of these is that although "lapses" undoubtedly have occurred throughout the history of the Irish in America, Catholic lapses were most apt to have happened in the pre-Famine era, when the Catholic church in the U.S. was still only a skeletal organization and, in many areas of Irish settlement, nonexistent. Secondly, it is crucial to realize that "lapses" from faith among Irish persons in that pre-Famine era occurred both ways: Irish Protestants turning Catholic and Irish Catholics turning Protestant. As a neutral example of this phenomenon (neutral in the U.S. context, as it comes from Nova Scotia) one notes the lament of the Rev. James MacGregor, a Presbyterian clergyman who in the early nineteenth century surveyed the religious situation on the Celtic fringe of Nova Scotia: Pictou, Antigonish, and Cape Breton. He reported to his synod that "they need not imagine that all Presbyterian emigrants continue Presbyterians. Multitudes of them settle among every other religious denomination, and in a few years become members of their churches."[23] Many, he said, became Roman Catholics.

The Rev. Mr. MacGregor's observation is salient because it highlights a fact of social history. Despite the level of animosity between Protestants and Catholics in the seventeenth and eighteenth centuries (especially in Ireland), there nevertheless existed such a strong commitment to folk religion (call it superstition, call it devotion, call it primitive Christianity, it matters not), that when placed in a New World, without their own form of Christianity conveniently to hand, simple people in hard circumstances turned for comfort to the next closest thing.[24] Thus, the Rev. Mr. MacGregor's recognition that his synod must sponsor more than church building, for otherwise the Presbyterians became Methodists, Baptists, Roman Catholics, whatever faith provided churches and clergy.

Up to the mid-nineteenth century, there almost certainly were more conversions of Catholics to Protestantism than vice versa. This had nothing to do with the relative spiritual power of the two faiths or of the level of devotion of clergy and people, but rather was the result of an asymmetrical situation. Everything was tilted against the Catholics. For example, at the outbreak of the American revolution, there were only fifty Roman Catholic churches in the entire thirteen colonies.[25]

This meant that when Catholics wanted to have a marriage, burial, or baptism conducted, in many areas (and in almost all of the frontier regions) they had to deal with Protestants. It was a short step from having one's child baptized by a Protestant minister to having a Protestant family.

Further, the asymmetry of conversion was accelerated by intermarriage. Here a simple "epidemiological model" is all that is required to explain things. That is, the Irish Catholics, being more likely to be surrounded by Protestants than vice versa (the population of the American colonies was overwhelmingly Protestant) contracted the "disease" of mixed marriage more often than did Protestants, who were likely to be protected by enclaves of other Protestants.

There was more to the process: systematic discrimination undoubtedly hurt the Catholics and caused many of them to change faith. It must be remembered that from the late seventeenth century until the 1790s, Catholics in Ireland were under a "penal code" that, though unevenly applied, impoverished large numbers of them and in many ways interfered with the operation of the Catholic church. Significant numbers of conversion to Protestantism occurred. This is not a subject much discussed: neither side in Ireland wants to know about it, for the abuse of state power during the penal era long has been an embarrassment to Protestant historians and the loss of faith by many Catholics an equal embarrassment to Catholic chroniclers. As late as the 1780s, one finds in contemporary Irish newspapers, announcements of Catholic conversion. For instance, the *Belfast News-Letter* of 30 December 1789 noted in its Dublin column that:

> On Sunday the 7th instant, the following persons embraced the Protestant religion in the church at Tarbert before the Rev. Ralph Wall and a full congregation, viz Francis Kelly, John Ware, John Fitzgerald, Michael Fitzgerald, Charles Connor, Jan Rea, Ann Ware, and Winifred Cuningham.

And from the town of Monaghan:

> Yesterday the following persons renounced the errors of the Church of Rome and embraced the Protestant religion, before the Rev. Dr. Warren: Francis Moynagh, Terence Duffy, and Peter McAtee.

The functional point is that even before leaving Ireland for the American colonies, a Catholic migrant had grown up in a society in which it was very clear that real economic and social benefits were to be gained by ceasing to be Catholic.

In Ireland, family and friends kept most waverers from changing faiths, but once out of Ireland and in America, the temptation to leave the old faith was reinforced. The social cost of being a Catholic — and thus an outsider — in colonial America was high. And what is often forgotten is that most of the American colonies had on their books legal instruments that were similar to (if weaker than) the Irish anti-Catholic penal code. Public mass was forbidden in Pennsylvania in 1707 and was not heard until 1729; in Maryland in the mid-eighteenth century, Roman Catholics were disarmed and excluded from the provincial militia; a New York act of 1700 forbade the entry into the colony of Catholic priests, and in 1741 a priest was hanged for breaking the ban; public worship by Catholics was not permitted in the New York colony until 1780. These and related enactments, though they often went unenforced, were a constant threat to Catholics and a continual reminder of their marginal position in this New World.[26]

Most of the American penal laws disappeared after the establishment of the federal constitution and the drawing of the Bill of Rights, but a surprising number of discriminatory state laws remained far into the nineteenth century. Public office in North Carolina was limited to Protestants until 1835; in New Jersey until 1844; and in New Hampshire until 1876.[27]

The one historian to deal directly with the issue of Catholic conversion to Protestantism in early America was the sedulous antiquarian Michael J. O'Brien, a much underrated figure in Irish historiography. Born in County Cork, O'Brien (1869/70-1960), emigrated to the USA in 1889. His daily living was earned as an accountant for the Western Union Telegraph Company, and this allowed him to travel all over the eastern United States. His real vocation, however, was the history of the Irish in the U.S., and he spent virtually all his spare time in cities, small towns, rural hamlets, hunting out and copying down the records of any organization that might have had anything to do with early Irish migrants and their descendants. These items were the basis of articles that he kept publishing right up to the time of his death at age ninety.[28]

Much of O'Brien's work was embarrassing to other persons of Irish Catholic descent. This stemmed from his continually repeating two themes. One of these was that he kept finding names in Baptist, Congregational, Presbyterian, and Anglican church records that he knew were Irish Catholic names. Conceivably, some of these individuals could have converted to Protestantism in the Old Country, but in other cases O'Brien possessed genealogical records which indicated that the conversions had occurred in America. O'Brien published this information for town after town. It gave him no pleasure to do so, for he was a devout Catholic himself. He believed that it was "a terrible misfortune ... that the early Irish [Catholic] immigrants had to abandon their faith, and it is mortifying to see so many persons bearing the grand old Gaelic names figuring in the records of Baptist, Methodist, and other churches, alongside the Puritans who hated them."[29]

The second theme that O'Brien continually articulated, again with the doleful sense of duty that characterized his work, was the large number of name changes from the Gaelic forms that are readily recognizable as "Irish" to cognates that sound like English or Scottish surnames, which presumably is what the person altering the name intended. Kirwans and MacKirwans became Whitcombs, MacTiernans became Masterson, O'Clerys became Clarkes, and so on. O'Brien did not like this phenomenon, but he did not flinch. His diagnosis was that descendants of Irish Catholics with Gaelic names had become "ashamed of their names and deliberately changed them by cutting off all semblance of their Irish origin."[30] Other investigators have noted the same phenomenon.[31]

Although such a change of name does not necessarily involve an abandonment of the old religion, that usually must have been done as well, either by the person making the name change or by his descendants: a person could hardly hide his Irish Catholic background if he changed his name, but kept the faith.

The conditions which led to numerous conversions of Irish Catholics to Protestantism in America did not continue after the Great Famine. Thereafter, the Catholic church in America became effective nationally in its ministry to its people. Further, because post-Famine migrants were much more urban than were their predecessors, the potential for intermarriage was cut down, especially since Irish women migrated in almost equal numbers to Irish men and thus family formation within the group was easy.

Although a great amasser of facts, Michael O'Brien was never able to quantify how large a portion of the colonial migration to America had been Irish Catholic, or what proportion of this group turned Protestant. Modern historians have not done much better, which is unfortunate, because the multiplier effect means that the early migrants to the Americas were very important in determining the character of the overall Irish ethnic group.

Recently, some very interesting heuristic speculations have been made by David Noel Doyle; these indicate that in 1790, the Irish ethnic population may be construed as follows:[32]

Of Irish Roman Catholic origin	139,400
Of Anglo-Irish origin	31,600
Of Ulster-Scots origin	<u>276,000</u>
Total of Irish ethnicity	447,000

It is instructive to compare the numbers of persons estimated to be of Irish Catholic origin (139,400) with the estimate of Father John Carroll, the first bishop of the United States, who in 1785 stated that the Catholic population of the United States was 25,000.[33] Even if the Catholic population (which, note, contained some non-Irish persons) was as high as 100,000,[34] the conversion rate certainly was significant. At minimum the number of Irish Catholics who turned Protestant appears to have equalled the number whose origins were Anglo-Irish (that is, Irish Protestants of "Anglican" background).[35]

As for guesses about what happened after 1790 (or effectively, 1815, given the hiatus in migration during the Napoleonic Wars) David Noel Doyle believes that four-fifths of Protestant Irish migration to the USA (Anglo-Irish and Scots-Irish combined) occurred after 1790.[36] He posits that a total of one-and one-quarter million Irish Protestants migrated to America in the period 1715-1940.[37] Protestant migration, one must emphasize, continued right through the Famine and into the mid-twentieth century. It was (at least from the 1830s onwards) a smaller stream than the Catholic, but not insignificant. Emigration data from the Irish side of the process implies that after 1815 the Anglo-Irish made up as large a part of the Irish Protestant stream as did the more-publicized Ulster-Scots.

All of the complex, and often wobbly, data suggest that the Protestants, who today make up the majority of the persons who cite "Irish" as their primary ancestry, stem from: (1) Ulster-Scots, who made up about 60 percent of the Irish migrants in the colonial period and probably one-tenth from the Napoleonic Wars onwards; (2) Anglo-Irish, who comprised perhaps 7 percent of the Irish migrants in the colonial era and roughly 10 percent thereafter; and (3) converts from Catholicism, most of whose roots go back to the pre-Famine era, and in most instances to the semi-penal era of colonial America. A reasonable set of bracketing figures is that they may have made up as little as 11 percent of the Irish ethnic population in 1790, or as much as 26 percent. (I suspect the lower figures are closer to the truth). Manifestly, the phenomenon warrants further study.

(V)

If that is where the Protestants of Irish descent in America came from, where did they go geographically and socio-economically?

The quick answer is: south, and down, in contrast to the Irish Catholics, who mostly went north and up. Irish Protestants tended to be over-represented in rural areas and in the middle states and the south. Persons of Irish Catholic background during the second half of the nineteenth century mostly stayed north (plus California) and were over-represented in urban areas. (Those, of course, are generalizations to which there were many individual exceptions).

An efficient summation of the socio-economic differences of the two major segments of the Irish ethnic group comes from the same NORC and University of Michigan data bases that I mentioned earlier in regard to Irish Catholic economic status. These data collections reveal that in the 1960s and 1970s, whereas persons of Irish Catholic ethnicity were the highest-ranking Gentile group in terms of income, education, and occupational prestige (and second overall, only to the Jews), persons of Irish Protestant descent in the USA were the *lowest* identifiable white group judged on the same criteria. They were lowest in terms of average family income, lowest in occupational prestige, and ninth out of twelve identifiable white groups in their educational level.[38]

This means that by the mid-twentieth century, the Irish ethnic group in the USA was polarized: between Catholics, 70 percent of whom lived in the northeast and north central United States, and Protestants, half of whom lived in the south. The Catholics were overwhelmingly urban and the Protestants, though by mid-twentieth century mostly urban as well, were nearly 30 percent rural. Most importantly, the segment of the Irish ethnic group that was of Catholic descent was a highly privileged group in U.S. society, while the segment of Irish Protestant descent was the least privileged among identifiable white groups.

An intriguing question follows from this information: when did the Protestant section of the Irish ethnic group slide below the Catholic segment? Andrew Greeley's estimate, based on his reconstruction of early twentieth-century sample cohorts, is that the Irish Protestants crossed beneath the national average (and simultaneously dropped below the Irish Catholics) in the 1930s.[39] Thus, the relative positions of Irish Protestants and Irish Catholics in the USA in the twentieth century could be graphed with a simple "X," the Protestant fortunes declining, the Catholic rising.[40]

(VI)

Words count, and no more so than in ethnic and multicultural studies. The mislabelling of individuals and of groups greatly inhibits understanding. That fact has been one of the chief implicit lessons of this primer.

When reading the historical literature about the Irish migrants and their descendants in North America, one should be especially watchful of the code use of "Irish" to refer only to Catholics, or only to refer to the immigrant generation of Catholics. When you catch that happening, you know that you are not reading history, but propaganda.

There are three other terms that warrant our attention: "Irish-American," "Anglo-Irish," and "Scotch-Irish."

The first of these, "Irish-American," should be banned from our vocabulary, for it is a code word. In almost every context in which it is used, it refers only to Catholics. It is a doubly dangerous term, because not only does it exclude, on sectarian or racist grounds, all Protestants from being "Irish," but it seduces the unwary reader into thinking that he or she knows more than is really the case: any generalization that concerns the "Irish-American" ethnic group (meaning the Irish Catholics) excludes more than half the ethnic group, the Protestants. In fact, there is a simple, accurate and unambiguous term for what is meant: "Irish Catholic." That is a proud and accurate term and should replace the mendacity of "Irish-American."

The second term, "Anglo-Irish," is one which is rarely used in American social history, but which should be, for it is a great aid in accurately analyzing the Irish migrants and their descendants. As suggested earlier, persons of Anglo-Irish origin probably composed slightly less than one-tenth of total Irish in-migration to the USA. Yet, they have been almost entirely ignored by historians, largely because they were part of a band that is aptly termed "invisible immigrants." They faced no heavy discrimination in the largely-Protestant USA, they spoke English fluently, and rather than settle in visible regional clusters, were highly mobile. In the long run, they will be the second-hardest segment of the Irish in the USA to chronicle (the pre-Famine Catholic converts to Protestantism will be the hardest). Nevertheless, by insisting that the term "Irish-Protestant" implies both Anglo-Irish and Ulster-Scots, one can avoid the error, common among U.S. historians, of believing that the great bulk of the Irish Protestants stemmed from Ulster and that they were almost universally of Presbyterian background.

As for the American neologism "Scotch-Irish," avoid it. This is not because the term does not refer to a certain historical reality, but because it has become such a lint ball of controversy, stereotyping, prejudice, and silliness, that its employment obscures many things that should be clear.[41]

Here is the problem. If today you ask persons in the USA whose ancestors came from Ireland and were of Presbyterian background, what their ethnicity is, overwhelmingly they will say "Irish," provided the structure of the questioning permits them to make it clear that they are not Irish Catholics (this pattern of identification was clearly established by the NORC, Gallup, and CUNY studies). And, if in, say, 1776, one had asked a similar question of Presbyterians from County Londonderry who were living in Pennsylvania, most likely they would have said "Irish Presbyterian" or simply "Irish." The Irish Presbyterians in colonial America stemmed from people who had lived in Ireland longer than most American colonists had lived in North America, and since their sense of being Irish preceded the development of the modern concept of Irish nationhood, their answer would have been perfectly accurate.[42] There is no doubt that contemporaries in North America in the eighteenth and early nineteenth centuries referred to such individuals as "Irish."[43]

But some time later, roughly between the Great Famine and World War I, the term "Scotch-Irish" arose to cloud the issue. Like many words that refer to social groups, "Scotch-Irish" originally had a pejorative meaning, but eventually the people to whom it referred themselves adopted the term and used it as a badge of pride. (In the history of the Irish homeland, the chief parallel is the word "Gaedhal," which in Old Welsh meant "woodsman," or, roughly, "bog-trotter": it became the prized "Gael."). "Scotch-Irish" seems to have first been used in the 1690s. It appears thereafter, although not frequently, in written works, such as topographical surveys and travel literature. The term was scarcely used in the later colonial era and after Independence it seems to have dropped out of use.[44] Later (some authorities say in the 1830s, others the 1840s,[45] others the 1850s[46]) the Ulster-Scots in the USA began to employ it to separate themselves from the Irish Catholics. The standard interpretation of the adoption of the term is that the Ulster-Scots assumed it "solely because of prejudice" on their part against the Catholic Irish.[47]

It was not as simple as that. For one thing, as I pointed out in Chapter Nine, this new nomenclature that was developing in the USA was a part of a larger phenomenon affecting the entire Irish diaspora. What occurred in the Irish homeland from the 1820s onward was an attempt (largely successful) to capture the term "Irish" for embryonic Catholic nationalism. This meant that non-Catholics, while thinking of themselves as being Irish, had to find another term that made it clear that they were not in favour of Irish Catholic nationalism. So, the adoption of the term "Scotch-Irish" by some persons of Ulster-Scots background in the USA was not simply a matter of their religious bigotry, although, of course, sectarian prejudice can be taken as pervasive in nineteenth-century American life. Further, it is not at all clearly documented that everyday people of Irish Presbyterian background referred to themselves as being Scotch-Irish with any degree of frequency. Nor has it been established that the term was very popular until a long time after the Famine. It was only in the 1870s that it began to have much currency and then it was found in learned histories and high-brow magazines.

The real expansion in use of the term seems to have occurred with the establishment in 1889 of the "Scotch-Irish Society of America," a group of ancestor-proud individuals, headed by clergy and upper middle class professionals. This body eventually published twelve volumes of hagiography that credited the Scotch-Irish with doing everything useful in

American history.[48] A good example of the tone of the group is found in the following book review by Ruth Dame Coolidge:

> When James I transplanted a colony of these lowerland Scotch, they crossed from the interior parts of Scotland to the northern counties of Ireland and settled there. The Gaelic language was commonly spoken and some of the immigrants in America knew no other language. But if they still retained this evidence of the Celt, and if, though very improbably, they intermarried with the native Irish, they were more strongly Anglo-Saxon; ... By the time these combined people had reached America they had already summed up in their composition the various elements which America is slowly fusing together today out of the various peoples that settle in her shores. They had already the daring of the Anglo-Saxon, and the inventiveness of the Celt, and these had united to produce the virile, practical, religious, persistent, independent and contentious Scotch Irishman.[49]

In response to such enthusiasms, a curious set of dualisms emerged. The American Irish Historical Society, and especially its chief writer, Michael J. O'Brien, continually insisted that the "Scotch-Irish" were simply Irish Presbyterians and should be designated as such. A person could be Irish and be non-Catholic, O'Brien and his associates argued, and this is exactly what the Presbyterians in Ireland had been.[50] Curiously, within Irish Catholic nationalism in the USA, an opposite idea prevailed in the same era, namely, that the Protestants in Ireland were not really Irish, and that, therefore, their descendants in the USA could not possibly be Irish.

This snarl might long ago have been sorted out, had it not provided professional historians of the second half of the twentieth century with an excuse for engaging in that great enemy of historical perspective, namely excessive academic specialization. By keeping Irish Protestants segregated from Irish Catholics in the American historical literature, it was much easier for historians to move confidently through what otherwise would have been a complicated landscape. For example, Wayland F. Dunaway, the first modern professional historian of the Ulster Scots in America (1944) quotes a proverb that "If a man is born in a stable, does that make him a horse?" "Really now," he asserts, "it is as simple as that," for he believed that the Irish Presbyterians were merely sojourning in Ireland, just passing through to the USA[51] (How the early Ulster-Scots knew that they would eventually end up in a New World argues a prophetic ability that Dunaway does not explain). Just as Dunaway was able to avoid dealing with Irish Catholics by his defining the Irish Presbyterians as day-trippers in Ireland, so most historians of the Irish Catholics in the USA have been able to ignore the Protestants in the Irish ethnic group by defining them as Ulster Presbyterians, and not Irish. Thus, for example, a recent study of the stereotyping of the Irish takes as its fundamental "fact" that the Irish in the USA were universally Catholic.[52] This study measures the "verbal image" of the Irish in America against a demographic baseline that is demonstrably false and, hence, the real nature of American prejudice against the Irish, both Protestant and Catholic, is lost.

All this helps to explain why the term "Scotch-Irish" should be abandoned. Like a badly tuned FM station, it carries too much static, so much so that hearing the real music is impossible. Because the connotations and associations of "Scotch-Irish" are too great to be erased, the word should be abandoned. A useful first step would be to adopt the term that is standard in Irish studies, "Ulster-Scot." The next would be to remember, always, the fundamental fact that neither in the history of the Irish homeland nor in any nation of the Irish diaspora, can one segregate from each other the three main components of post-Reformation Irish history, the Ulster-Scots, the Anglo-Irish, and the Irish Catholics.

(VII)

How many Irish migrants actually came to North America is, and always will be, a mystery. It is virtually a law of human behaviour that governments do not start to keep track of such things until it is too late. In the case of the Irish, good records of migrant patterns evolved only after the huge human flood engendered by the Great Famine had waned.

Summarized in Table 38 are estimates, derived from a consistent set of sources, of the migration to North America from 1825 to 1935.[53] Not all immigrants remained in North America, of course, and not all lived very long even when they did. The number of Irish-born persons actually living in the USA and Canada are indicated below:[54]

	USA (000s)	Canada (000s)
1841	n/a	122
1850-51	962	227
1860-61	1,611	286
1870-71	1,856	223
1880-81	1,855	186
1890-91	1,872	149
1900-01	1,615	102
1910-11	1,352	93
1920-21	1,037	93
1930-31	924	108
1940-41	678	86

The noteworthy point is how early Irish migration to North America tailed off. And, consequently, how swiftly the number of Irish-born persons in North America declined. From 1870-71 onwards, their total numbers dropped. The decline started sooner in Canada than in the USA. As a proportion of the total U.S. population, the Irish-born were at their peak in 1860, when they represented 5.12 percent of the U.S. population.[55] A parallel figure is impossible to give for the Canadas (because Confederation did not occur until 1867), but probably the Irish-born were at their apogee in proportional terms in the early 1850s when they were 5.8 percent of the Quebec population and 18.5 percent of the Ontario population.[56] The drop in the demographic significance of the Irish-born in the USA was precipitous. In 1900, the Irish-born were 2.13 percent of the U.S. population.[57] In 1960, the Irish-born (32 counties) were 0.05 percent.[58] In Canada in 1961, the Irish-born (32 counties) were 3.9 percent of the population.[59] In fact, the Irish-born proportion of the Canadian population was higher in 1961 than it has been at any time in the United States since 1870.

TABLE 38

Irish Emigration (32 Counties) to North America
1825-1935, inclusive

Time Period		U.S.A.	Canada	Total
1825-30	a. U.K. sources	22,775	60,204	82,979
	b. Irish sources	49,829	61,557	111,386
	c. Adams' formula	50,040	79,142	129,182
1831-40	a. U.K. sources	35,040	210,579	245,619
	b. Irish sources		Incomplete	
	c. Adams' formula	171,087	262,004	433,091
1841-50	a. U.K. sources	163,795	270,935	434,730
	b. Irish sources	822,675	329,321	1,151,996
	c. Adams' formula	908,292	362,738	1,271,030
1851-60	a. U.K. sources	636,636	106,303	742,939
	b. Irish sources	989,880	118,118	1,107,998
	c. with Adams' formula applied 1851, 1852	989,174	119,769	1,108,943
1861-70	U.K. and Irish sources	690,845	40,079	730,924
1871-80	U.K. and Irish sources	449,549	25,783	475,332
1881-90	U.K. and Irish sources	626,604	44,505	671,109
1891-1900	U.K. and Irish sources	427,301	10,648	437,949
1901-10	U.K. and Irish sources	418,995	38,238	457,233
1911-20	U.K. and Irish sources	172,490	32,857	205,347
1921-30	U.K. sources	231,319	66,787	298,106
1931-35	U.K. sources	3,004	1,881	4,885

Sources: For data and methods, and commentary on the sources, see: William Forbes Adams, *Ireland and the Irish Emigration to the New World from 1815 to the Famine* (New Haven: Yale University Press, 1932), appendix, pp. 410-28. Donald Harman Akenson, "Ontario: Whatever Happened to the Irish?" *Canadian Papers in Rural History* vol. 3, (1982), pp. 204-56; N.H. Carrier and J.R. Jeffery, *External Migration, A Study of the Available Statistics, 1815-1950* (London: HMSO, 1953), Table D/F/G(1), pp. 95-96; *Commission on Emigration and other Population Problems, 1948-1954* (Dublin: The Stationery Office, 1954), Table 26, pp. 314-16.

(VIII)

This brings us to Canada, the only portion of North America for which there are direct data on the ethnicity, place of birth, and religion of every one of its citizens, and this from the last one-third of the nineteenth century to the present. Unless an historian of the Irish in the United States is interested only in a single small community, knowledge of the Canadian information is absolutely necessary. The minute one attempts to generalize about the Irish or even to posit certain Irish attitudes to work, to economic systems, or to social order, then one has to look to Canada, for only there does a systematic and adequate data pool exist.

The Irish in Canada were drawn from the same general sources as were the Irish in the United States and until roughly the end of World War II were part of a North American ethnic group that flowed quite freely back and forth across the U.S.-Canadian border. The Irish in Canada were not identical with those in the U.S., any more than those in New York were identical with those in San Francisco, but one can design social observations that match up the two groups nicely. Thus, when one wants to learn, say, about the economic attitudes of Irish persons of the second and third generation in Buffalo, New York, upon whom there is very little direct data, one can draw inferences from parallel groups of Irish workers in, for example, Hamilton, Ontario, a city similar to Buffalo, where there exists a great deal of detailed information on ethnicity, religion, and occupational matters.[60]

As I mentioned in Chapter Nine, both the USA and Canada are anomalies within the Irish diaspora in one matter: the religious makeup of the multigenerational ethnic population. In both countries, the majority of the ethnic group is Protestant, a characteristic shared within the Irish diaspora only with South Africa. The norm for the Irish homeland and for the Irish diaspora is for the ethnic group to be roughly three-quarters Roman Catholic. However, as established in Chapter Nine, the Irish ethnic group in the USA in the mid-twentieth century was roughly 55 percent Protestant and almost certainly has been mostly Protestant throughout American history. Studies of the 1871 census of the Dominion of Canada indicate that in the original four provinces, Ontario, Quebec, Nova Scotia, and New Brunswick, approximately 60 percent of persons of Irish ethnicity were Protestant. If one adds the two other provinces of then-British North America (Newfoundland and Prince Edward Island), the Protestant proportion is about 54 percent.[61]

Where the USA and Canada differ, I think, is that the U.S. was what can be termed a double-anomaly within the Irish diaspora. The normal thing within the diaspora was for the religious characteristics of the multigenerational Irish ethnic group and of the Irish immigrants to be about the same at any given time. In New Zealand, for example, in 1910 not only were most members of the Irish ethnic group Roman Catholics, but so too were the immigrants, and in similar proportions. In Canada, at least from 1815 onwards, the majority of the Irish ethnic population was Protestant, as was the majority of the immigrants.

The USA, however, was different. Protestants among the Irish immigrants predominated during the colonial period, and this (together with the conversion of Catholics to Protestantism under early American conditions) meant that by, say, 1790, the Irish ethnic group was overwhelmingly Protestant. However, at some time in the nineteenth century — I suspect that the key decade was the 1830s — Catholic immigrants from Ireland began to outnumber Protestants. From 1846 onwards they outnumbered them heavily. So, from the 1830s, the USA has been characterized by the unusual situation of having a mostly-Protestant Irish ethnic group, but mostly Catholic Irish immigrants. (The immigrants, being visible and easy to study, are the ones on whom historians and social observers have concentrated, with inevitably misleading results).

The double anomaly in the U.S. historical situation — of having a mostly Protestant Irish ethnic group and of having the ethnic group and the immigrant generation forever dissonant — does not invalidate comparisons between the U.S. and Canada. Quite the opposite: The double anomaly explains why a comparison that at first looks *outré* (between a country where the Irish immigrants in, say, 1870, were mostly Catholic and one where they were mostly Protestant), actually works, provided one looks past the immigrants and instead studies the full ethnic group in each case. This is something we need to do in any event, because by 1870 the majority of persons of Irish background in both the USA and Canada were no longer immigrants, but second and third generation.

There is another way in which an apparent difference between Canada and the USA actually helps us to make valid cross-national generalizations. This is that Canada was (and still is) much more Irish than the USA. A favourite barroom argument of ethnic demographers (who hate arm wrestling and have to think of some other way to amuse themselves) is whether Australia or Canada is the more Irish country of the diaspora. Australia wins (unless one factors out Quebec), but not by much. The results of the first Dominion of Canada census of 1871 leave no doubt that at Confederation the Irish were the largest non-French ethnic group in the dominion. Specifically, the aggregate ethnic breakdown of the four provinces which comprised the Dominion of Canada in 1871 was as follows:[62]

French	31.1%
Irish	24.3%
English	20.3%
Scottish	15.8%
all others combined	8.5%
	100.0%

As Table 39 makes clear, in some jurisdictions (Ontario and New Brunswick in particular), the proportion of Irish persons in the general population was much higher than the national average. In fact, it is probable that those two provinces had a higher proportion of persons of Irish ethnicity in the nineteenth century than did any of the Australian colonies or the states of the American union: which is to say that Ontario and New Brunswick were the two demographically "most Irish" jurisdictions of any size, outside of Ireland. Thus, as in Australia, the Irish in Canada were virtually a "majority group." There were simply too many of them to push them around easily, and this held for the Catholics as well as for the Protestants. This fact concerning the Canadian situation helps us to escape from one of the most difficult problems in studies of the history of the Irish in the USA: the virtual impossibility of discerning if a given set of behaviours was a result of cultural

TABLE 39

Persons of Irish Ethnicity of Total Provincial Populations

Year	Ontario		Quebec		Nova Scotia		New Brunswick		Prince Edward Island		Manitoba	
	No.	%	No.	%	No.	%	No.	%	No.	%	No.	%
1871	559,442	34.5	123,478	10.4	62,851	16.2	100,643	35.2	N/A	N/A	N/A	N/A
1881	627,550	32.6	123,749	9.1	66,067	15.0	101,284	31.5	25,415	23.3	9,885	15.9
1891+												
1901	624,332	28.6	114,842	7.0	54,710	11.9	83,384	25.2	21,993	21.3	47,418	18.6
1911	614,502	24.3	103,720	5.2	54,612	11.1	77,839	22.1	19,987	21.3	60,583	13.1
1921	590,493	20.1	94,933	4.0	55,712	10.6	68,670	17.7	18,743	21.2	71,414	11.7
1931	647,831	18.9	108,312	3.8	56,453	11.0	66,873	16.4	17,698	20.1	77,559	11.1
1941	665,339	17.6	109,894	3.3	65,300	11.3	68,801	15.0	18,459	19.4	76,156	10.4
1951	723,888	15.7	110,189	2.7	76,479	11.9	71,750	13.9	19,019	19.3	77,802	10.0
1961	873,647	14.0	129,326	2.5	93,998	12.8	82,485	13.8	19,786	18.9	84,726	9.2
1971§												
1981§												

TABLE 39 (Continued)

Year	British Columbia		Northwest Territories		Saskatchewan		Alberta		Yukon		Newfoundland		Canadian Total*	
	No.	%	No.	%	No.	%	No.	%	No.	%	No.	%	No.	%
1871	N/A	N/A	N/A	N/A	N/A	N/A	N/A	N/A	N/A	N/A	N/A	N/A	846,414	24.3
1881	3,172	6.4	1,374	2.4	N/A	N/A	N/A	N/A	N/A	N/A	N/A	N/A	957,403	22.1
1891+														
1901	20,658	11.6	41	0.2	10,644	11.7	8,161	11.8	2,559	9.4	N/A	N/A	988,721	18.4
1911	43,831	11.2	135	2.1	58,069	11.8	40,668	10.9	897	10.5	N/A	N/A	1,074,738	14.9
1921	54,298	10.4	234	2.9	84,786	11.2	68,246	11.6	369	8.9	N/A	N/A	1,107,803	12.6
1931	71,612	10.3	296	3.0	104,096	11.3	79,978	10.9	198	4.7	N/A	N/A	1,230,808	11.9
1941	83,460	10.2	230	1.9	95,852	10.7	83,876	10.5	335	6.8	N/A	N/A	1,267,702	11.0
1951	124,098	10.7	619	3.9	84,811	10.2	96,549	10.3	1,097	12.1	53,334	14.8	1,439,635	11.0
1961	165,631	10.2	1,056	4.6	92,133	10.0	134,102	10.1	1,670	11.4	74,791	16.3	1,753,351	9.6
1971§														
1981§														

* For certain years small anomalies in the census processing resulted in the national total being slightly different from the column sums.

+ Ethnicity data not collected in compatible form in this census.

§ "Irish" no longer permitted as an ethnic category by federal census officials: Irish lumped with English, Scottish, and Welsh.

characteristics brought over from Ireland or was instead something that U.S. society forced upon the Irish. This problem is largely absent in the Canadian situation; Canada, therefore, is a much clearer historical window.

The point is reinforced if one looks at racism and at anti-Catholic discrimination. The Canadas, while far from perfect, were in the eighteenth and nineteenth centuries much less harsh in their treatment of immigrants and cultural minorities than was the USA. It is a telling fact that slavery was not proclaimed as abandoned in the USA until 1863. In contrast, when slavery was abolished in the British Empire in 1833, there were in fact only two slaves remaining in all of what is now Ontario. Directly related to the Irish is the fact that at the time of American Independence, none of the thirteen American colonies granted Roman Catholics full and equal civil and political rights; indeed, until the last quarter of the nineteenth century, some states still did not do so. In contrast, in 1774, Catholics were given full civil rights under the Quebec Act (which also applied to what is today called Ontario). These Catholic rights were confirmed in 1791.[63] Canada, during the late eighteenth and the nineteenth century, certainly had its share of anti-Catholicism, but nothing approaching the pressures that produced the numerous conversions in the colonial American colonies. Therefore, Canada can be used as a laboratory to determine how, if they had been given a reasonably fair chance, Irish persons (especially Irish Catholics), would have behaved in the USA. In other words, we can sort out cultural importations from New World exploitations.

While recognizing the value of nationwide Canadian demographic, religious, and ethnic data,[64] it is useful to realize that the country consists of several distinct regions and that Canada can usefully be looked at as a set of regional case studies. Since this primer is intended chiefly for U.S. audiences, here I shall simply point to the various cases and indicate (in the notes) some useful places to enter the historical literature.

Newfoundland has been called Ireland's oldest colony and only half in jest. Its links with Ireland began early; there was a particularly strong link between Newfoundland and the areas of Wexford and Waterford, on the southern Irish coasts. Early in the eighteenth century, the Irish became frequent seasonal migrants to the coast of Newfoundland, working in the fisheries for the summer and returning home in the fall. The seasonal migrants continued to come throughout the eighteenth century, but were gradually supplanted by long-term migrants who spent several years or an entire adult lifetime in Newfoundland. The early flow of migrants to Newfoundland was unusual in Canadian history in that it was embedded in a complex trade nexus, wherein the south of Ireland produced much of the pork, butter, salt beef, and tallow for the Newfoundland economy. Thus, the direct trade links between Newfoundland and Ireland, which weakened but did not fade entirely during the nineteenth century, kept alive a direct contact between the Old Country and the Irish emigrants and their descendants in Newfoundland; this close relationship, by reasons of geography, was precluded in most other parts of Canada. Of course the Irish were not the only group to settle in Newfoundland, and that is the problem. Because Newfoundland did not join the Dominion of Canada until after World War II, and because Newfoundland's census procedures were fairly rudimentary until after it joined Confederation, historians have yet to determine what proportion of the province's population was ethnically Irish at any specific date in the nineteenth century. As Table 39 indicates, in 1951, persons of Irish ethnic background comprised approximately 15 percent of the provincial population.[65]

Prince Edward Island provides an unusual opportunity for historians. It was highly Irish — 23.3 percent of its population was of Irish ethnicity in 1881, and 18.9 percent in 1961 — yet there is virtually nothing except local histories that discusses the Irish. In particular, PEI provides an opportunity to test the conventional wisdom about the adaptability to rural environments of Irish migrants and also to study the transfer and adaptation of potato culture back and forth across the Atlantic.[66]

Nova Scotia offers the chance to observe within the same legal jurisdiction three separate Irish complexes: rural settlers, mostly from the north of Ireland at the head of the Bay of Fundy; rural Catholics from the south of Ireland in Cape Breton; and an urban population, mostly Catholic, in Halifax. The Halifax population reached social maturity much sooner than occurred in smaller U.S. cities. By the 1860s the Irish ghetto had disappeared and the Irish were part of the local establishment.[67]

In New Brunswick, as in Nova Scotia, the large majority of the Irish ethnic group has its roots in pre-Famine Ireland. Thus, New Brunswick, like Nova Scotia, gives a clear picture of the emergence of pre-Famine Irish culture in a New World. This is especially valuable to historians of the Irish in the U.S., where one of the chief difficulties is to determine which aspects of the Irish cultural inheritance were long-term Irish characteristics, and which were products of the great trauma, the Famine. Moreover, there are three distinct Irish communities in New Brunswick, and these provide clear comparative cases: rural Catholics in the Miramichi River area in the north, rural Protestants in the south, and a large urban Irish community in Saint John.[68]

There are two regions of Canada for which we know very little about Irish settlement and adjustment: the Canadian west and Quebec.[69] In the case of the west this is understandable, as the west was not populated until long after the big waves of Irish migration to North America had passed. In Quebec, however, there was a significant Irish population (particularly in Montreal and in the Eastern Townships) from 1815 onwards. This Irish community in Quebec is potentially a very rewarding topic of study, for in the case of the Irish Catholics it lets us see how they behaved when they were part of the religious majority in the new society. One finds significant numbers of persons with Irish names who became monolingual Francophones (thus indicating that the Irish Catholics had in many cases assimilated with the French Catholic majority). On the other hand, the historical record is full of warfare within the Catholic church between French and Irish priests and between the laity of the two groups.

As Table 40 indicates, the heartland of the Irish population in Canada has been Ontario, and it is Ontario that offers the broadest range of comparative opportunities for U.S. historians. It is a good place to do laboratory work. This lab work is possible not only because of the high quality of the Canadian data base, but because Ontario itself is a large jurisdiction. In 1871, for example, its population was six-tenths that of New York City's. Ontario's population was

TABLE 40

Proportional Distribution of Persons of Irish Ethnicity in Canada
(Percentage)

Province	1871	1881	1901	1911	1921	1931	1941	1951	1961
Ontario	66.1	65.5	63.2	57.2	53.3	52.6	52.5	50.3	49.8
Quebec	14.6	12.9	11.6	9.6	8.6	8.8	8.7	7.7	7.4
Nova Scotia	7.4	6.9	5.6	5.1	5.0	4.6	5.1	5.3	5.4
New Brunswick	11.9	10.6	8.4	7.2	6.2	5.4	5.4	5.0	4.7
Prince Edward Island		2.7	2.2	1.9	1.7	1.4	1.5	1.4	1.0
Manitoba		1.0	4.8	5.6	6.4	6.3	6.0	5.4	4.8
British Columbia		0.3	2.1	4.1	4.9	5.8	6.6	8.6	9.5
Northwest Territories		0.1	0.1	0.0	0.0	0.0	0.0	0.0	0.1
Saskatchewan			1.1	5.4	7.7	8.5	7.6	5.9	5.3
Alberta			0.8	3.8	6.2	6.6	6.6	6.7	7.6
Yukon			0.1	0.1	0.0	0.0	0.0	0.0	0.1
Newfoundland								3.7	4.3
Total	100.0	100.0	100.0	100.0	100.0	100.0	100.0	100.0	100.0

Source: Akenson, Being Had, p. 87.

concentrated along the St. Lawrence River valley. On that strip there are numerous opportunities to observe both Irish Catholics and Irish Protestants in the nineteenth and early twentieth centuries living in their most characteristic environment, rural areas, and earning their living in the most common cases by farming. However, there were also several major cities — Toronto, Hamilton, and Kingston being the most important — where the Irish were either the largest, or nearly the largest, urban ethnic group. One can therefore study four important social types — urban Catholics, urban Protestants, rural Catholics, and rural Protestants — each with a data base large enough to permit verifiable conclusions to be drawn.

TABLE 41

Percentage of Persons of Irish Ethnicity in Canada who Lived in Rural Areas
(Percentages)

Year	Four Original Provinces				Entire Irish Pop. in Canada	Entire Canadian Pop.
	Ontario	Quebec	Nova Scotia	New Brunswick		
1871	77.8	63.9	81.2	73.1	75.3	79.6
1881	70.4	58.6	73.2	72.6	69.7	74.3
1901	58.4	48.7	60.3	66.3	60.0	62.5
1911	51.2	43.6	49.4	63.1	52.8	54.6
1921	45.7	38.8	46.9	62.1	49.2	50.5
1931	42.8	29.9	45.0	59.6	45.3	46.3

Source: Akenson, *Being Had*, p. 85.

Ontario, finally, provides the historian with the opportunity to ask a perpetually intriguing question and to receive a partial answer — what would the New World have been like if the Irish had been in charge? In spite of the mislabelling of Ontario as being "English" or "Scottish," the Irish in fact were the largest ethnic group, and had a direct impact greater than that of any other group in forming the institutional structure of the province, and probably a greater influence than in any other jurisdiction of comparable size throughout the Irish diaspora. If we take that as being the case and the year 1870 as our vantage point, a New World in which the Irish were prepotent would have been characterized by a tight sense of law and order, strong police services, an excellent system of public education, governmental financial support for Catholic schools, a strong sense of religious participation by both Protestant and Catholics, sectarian bickering between the two groups, an efficient agricultural economy and a rapidly modernizing urban sector, and a sense on the part of most persons of Irish ethnicity that it was a good thing that they (or their parents or their grandparents) had taken the heroic decision to leave Ireland and to create something new, half a world away.[70]

Chapter 11

Conclusion

The Irish diaspora, then, was a worldwide phenomenon, and can only be understood as such. What happened in the USA was related to what occurred in Australia, Canada, New Zealand, and South Africa, as well as to events in the Irish homeland. Potentially, when read with caution, each part of the diaspora helps us to understand every other part. Local studies, provincial studies, national studies, all are important, but unless they are read in the full international context of the diaspora the national, regional, or local historian of the Irish is apt to become like a young child who holds a piece of coloured glass to his eye and declares that all the world is blue, green, red, or orange. Context is crucial.

The Irish diaspora is itself a land of scholarly opportunity. In this primer I have mentioned enough topics for future research to fill a bookshelf, and that is only scratching the surface. There is, however, an order of priority. I think that the most pressing need is for serious historical research to be done on Irish women, in the homeland and the diaspora, especially from the end of the Napoleonic Wars (1815) to the Partition of Ireland (1920). That is the period in which the foundation of the Irish ethnic group worldwide was formed, and yet we know very little about one-half of that pioneer group. This holds for all women and girls, but most especially for the "religious" — that is, girls and women in Roman Catholic religious communities.

A commonplace observation concerning the twentieth century is that many of the most able females in local communities in Ireland, natural leaders, entered religious orders, and that frequently they emigrated. This had two simultaneous effects: it drained rural Ireland of some of its most talented females and at the same time helped transplant Catholic religious culture to various New Worlds. This was important for the "non-religious" (that is, secular) Catholic women who emigrated, for the church network in North America, Australia and South Africa helped them to adapt socially, to feel secure, and to keep their values: and this religious network was not simply a male creation, but one in which much of the fabric was established and maintained by nuns and sisters, person who are ill-chronicled historically, but nonetheless significant.

Secondly, despite the vast number of books and articles about the Irish, the situation in the USA remains a mystery. We do not know with confidence even the outlines of the Irish story in nineteenth-century America. This is because we have no reliable information on even the total number of Irish immigrants before 1850, and no direct data on the religion of the Irish in any generation, until the survey work of the NORC, Gallup, and CUNY studies of the second half of the twentieth century. Until a major study is conducted, based on nineteenth-century manuscript census records, and upon their linkage to religious and economic records, we will not know with certainty even the most elementary facts about the Irish. Such studies must be random, or at least representative of the entire nationwide context, not just studies of individual Irish communities. Local studies are fascinating, but they inevitably focus upon atypical concentrations.

Third, the worldwide relationship of the Irish and religious institutions is important. The Roman Catholic church has been well served: the development of the church, and the Irish part in that development in Australia, New Zealand, and the USA are well documented in the historical literature. What is almost totally ignored is the relationship of Irish Protestants to religious institutions. Yet the Irish Protestants were formative in many contexts worldwide. For example, it is clear that the "low" (meaning non-Catholic) tone of the Anglican church in Canada and in New Zealand was in considerable degree traceable to the influence of large numbers of Anglo-Irish laypersons in the Anglican churches of those two nations. Further, in each case, clergy whose intellectual roots were in Trinity College, Dublin reinforced this lay influence. The Ulster-Scots, though mostly Presbyterian in the Irish homeland, mutated religiously into a bewildering variety of beliefs. Under frontier conditions, they quickly became mainstays of the Methodist and Baptist churches. This happened all over the world, but was especially significant in the USA, where Irish Protestants became stalwarts of the major evangelical groups. This phenomenon, like the influence of the Anglo-Irish upon Anglicanism, has been little studied, and deserves immediate attention.

Fourth, a solid comparative investigation is required into what well may be the Irish Catholics' most important cultural legacy: separate (or denominational) education. In every nation in which they settled in significant numbers, they pressed hard, and at great personal sacrifice, for their own separate educational systems. In most places (Australia, New Zealand, Canada, and Great Britain) they were able to force the state to fund their schools, at least in part. Only in the USA did they fail, although it is possible that they may succeed in the future. The success or failure of the Catholic church in pressing for state-funded denominational segregation is a useful index of the relative power of the Irish Catholics as an ethnic group in each polity. Most important, in the second, third, and subsequent generations, the schools were the single most important instrument of preservation of the Irish Catholic identity.

Implicitly, this book has been a paean to the men, women, and children of the Irish diaspora, and especially to those of the migrant generation. In my view, they were heroes. They were not passive jetsam, but rather were individuals who collected information, weighed alternatives, and then took journeys to various New Worlds that were as far away from their previous experience as colonies on the moon would be for someone of our own age. They willed and survived, and ultimately their descendants prospered.

If I have emphasized the necessity of setting down "norms" and of drawing basic generalizations as a first step to understanding the Irish diaspora, the fun is to follow: historians can enjoy chronicling the terrific range of human experience that spreads out from these norms.

All over the world, the fate of Irish immigrants, their children, and grand-children, was to disappear. Identifiable "Irish" cultural strands still exist in every one of the diaspora countries, but the role of the children of the Irish immigrants was to become part of the white majority culture of whatever country in the English-speaking world they lived in. They joined the group which controlled things, and in every overseas nation — the USA, Canada, Australia, New Zealand and South Africa — they became privileged. By mid-twentieth century, they were better off than most other segments of that white community.

Like every ethnic group, the Irish have members who strongly wish to believe certain romantic or inaccurate generalizations about their own past: such as that they were all Catholic, that they were exiled from Ireland rather than that they left by choice, that the nineteenth-century immigrants were incapable of making it on the frontier and were unable to adapt quickly to modernizing industrial economies. Such misbeliefs have to be overcome, because they misrepresent those first generations and demean their skills and adaptability.

The belief state of some traditionalists is like that described by Max Ferguson, the Canadian musicologist and broadcaster, himself a man of strong Anglo-Irish roots:

> A man had an obsession that he was dead. His friends couldn't talk him out of it; he was convinced. It was a fixation. So they took him to a psychiatrist. With the cool aplomb of his trade, the psychiatrist turned to the patient and said, "Will you grant me one point?"
> "What is that?"
> "Do dead men bleed?"
> The man thought and said, "No, they don't."
> "Good." Removing a pin from the lapel of his coat, the psychiatrist then stuck it into the man's index finger. Blood spurted out, and he said, "And what do you say to that?"
> And the man with the delusion, the fixation, thought for a moment and rather crestfallenly said, "Well, I was wrong Doctor. Dead men do bleed."[1]

That is not what is required.

Notes

CHAPTER ONE

1 David Fitzpatrick, *Irish Emigration, 1901-1921* (Dundalk: Dundalgan Press Ltd., for the Economic and Social History Society of Ireland, 1984), p. 30.

2 Roy F. Foster, *Modern Ireland, 1600-1972* (London: Penguin, 1988), p. 345. Foster quite correctly notes that emigration statistics are "notoriously unreliable." In the usual case, they understate the actual degree of Irish out-migration.

3 Fitzpatrick, *Irish Migration*, p. 5.

4 See 1870-71 Dominion of Canada Census, reproduced in *Census of Canada, 1931, Summary*, vol. 1, p. 710.

5 Ibid., pp. 710-23.

6 Sean Connolly, *Religion and Society in Nineteenth-Century Ireland* (Dundalk: Dundalgan Press Ltd., for the Economic and Society History Society of Ireland, 1985), p. 29.

7 See the special issue on sectarianism of the *Canadian Journal of Irish Studies* vol. 15 (Dec. 1989).

8 *Commission on Emigration and other Population Problems, 1948-1954* (Dublin: Stationery Office, 1954).

9 John A. O'Brien (ed.), *The Vanishing Irish. The Enigma of the Modern World* (London: W.H. Allen, 1954).

10 Bruce Elliott, *Irish Migrants in the Canadas. A New Approach* (Kingston and Montreal: McGill-Queen's University Press, and Belfast; Institute of Irish Studies of the Queen's University of Belfast, 1988).

11 See, for example: L.W.B. Brockliss and P. Ferte, *Irish Clerics in France in the Seventeenth and Eighteenth Centuries: A Statistical Study* (Dublin: Royal Irish Academy, 1987); Bill Foley, "The Irish in Argentina," *Irish Family History*, vol. 6 (1990), pp. 5-13; J.G. Simms, "The Irish on the Continent, 1691-1800," in T.W. Moody and W.E. Vaughan (eds.), *A New History of Ireland*, vol. IV, *Eighteenth-Century Ireland, 1691-1800* (Oxford: Clarendon Press, 1986), pp. 629-56; Pat Clifford O'Donovan, *The Irish in France* (London: De Beauvoir Books,

1991); Liam Swords, *The Green Cockade: The Irish in the French Revolution, 1789-1815* (Dublin: Glendale Press, 1989).

12　For a stimulating discussion of early migration into Ireland see Nicholas Canny, "Migration and Opportunity: Britain, Ireland, and the New World," *Irish Economic and Social History* vol. 12 (1985), pp. 7-32.

13　The 6 percent figure is from Fitzpatrick *Irish Migration*, p. 7, citing the work of J.D. Gould. The 10 percent figure is found in the M.A. thesis of Marjolein 'T. Hart, "Heading for Paddy's Green Shamrock Shore: The Returned Emigrants in Nineteenth Century Ireland," (M.A., Rijks universiteit Groningen, 1982), summarized by Hart in *Irish Economic and Social History* vol. 10 (1983), pp. 96-97.

14　The entire volume repays study: R.A. Burchell, *The San Francisco Irish, 1848-1880* (Manchester: Manchester University Press, 1979).

CHAPTER TWO

1.　*Canadian Journal of Irish Studies*, vol. 17 (July 1991), p. 109.

2　David Fitzpatrick, *Irish Emigration, 1801-1921*, (Dundalk: Dundalgan Press, for the Economic and Social History Society of Ireland, 1984), p. 1.

3　The vulnerability to stereotypes and to modern agendas is well illustrated by the Irish short story writer Ciaran J. Bryne in a review of the fradulent book. "This book is a timely reminder of the famine which struck Ireland in the middle of the last century. Reading it one realizes why the Irish have been among the first to come to the aid of famine victims in modern times. Those whose forebears have suffered famine know what it is like... It is engraved upon their souls." (*Sunday Tribune* 11 August 1991).

The Canadian edition of 1982 was published by Carraig Books, Ste-Foy, Quebec, and was explicitly stated by James Mangan, F.S.C. (editor and re-writer of the piece) to have been "fictionalized." In fact, however, it was not fictionalized from an old diary as Brother Managan claimed, but from a novel. For an amusing commentary on the entire affair, see Jim Jackson, "The Making of a Best Seller," *Irish Review*, no 11 (Winter 1991-92), pp. 1-8.

4　For a summary of the debate, as of the beginning of the 1980s, see J.M. Goldstrom, "Irish Agriculture and the Great Famine," in J.M. Goldstrom and L.A. Clarkson, *Irish Population, Economy and Society. Essays in Honour of the late K.H. Connell* (Oxford: Clarendon Press, pp. 155-71.) For instances of the swing towards a re-emphasis on the Famine see the Ó Gráda and the Mokyr books cited below, note 5.

5　Considering the importance of the event, the curious point about Irish historiography is how little scholarly work was done on the Famine until the 1980s. Before that decade the only two books of a professionally competent level were published: R.D. Edwards and T.D. Williams (eds) *The Great Famine: Studies in Irish History* (Dublin: 1956), and Cecil Woodham-Smith, *The Great Hunger: Ireland, 1845-49* (London: 1962).

The acceleration of work in the 1980s is exemplified by: Mary E. Daly, *The Famine in Ireland* (Dundalk: Dundalgan Press, for the Dublin Historical Association, 1986); Joel Mokyr, *Why Ireland Starved: A Quantitative and Analytical History of the Irish Economy, 1800-1850* (London: George Allen and Unwin, 1983); Cormac Ó' Gráda, *The Great Irish Famine* (London: MacMillan, 1989). There are several relevant essays in W.E. Vaughan (ed), *A New History of Ireland*, vol. V, *Ireland Under the Union, Part I, 1801-70* (Oxford: Clarendon Press, for the Royal Irish Academy, 1989).

6　Moykr, pp. 265-66.

7　Ó Gráda, *Great Irish Famine*, p. 76.

8　Ibid., p. 9.

9　Patrick O'Farrell, "Whose reality? The Irish Famine in history and literature," *Historical Studies* (Melbourne) vol. 20 (April 1982), pp. 1-13.

10　A particularly unfortunate Irish American example is Thomas Gallagher's, *Paddy's Lament. Ireland 1846-1847. Prelude to Hatred* (New York: Harcourt Brace Jovanovich, 1982).

11　David Fitzpatrick, "The Disappearance of the Irish Agricultural Labourer, 1841-1912," *Irish Economic and Social History*, vol. 7 (1980), pp. 66-92.

12　The terms of reference for the debate on pre-Famine family structure were determined by the pioneering work of Kenneth Connell, and anyone reading his work can only be impressed with the skill and verve with which he navigated through an area that was, before his explorations, *terra incognita*. See especially his: *Irish Peasant Society* (Oxford: Clarendon Press, 1968), pp. 113-63; "The Colonisation of Waste Land in Ireland, 1780-1845," in *Economic History Review*, rev., 2nd ser. vol. 2 (1950), pp. 44-71; "Some Unsettled Problems in English and Irish Population History, 1750-1845," *Irish Historical Studies*, vol. 7 (Sept. 1951) pp. 225-34; "The History of the Potato," *Economic History Review*, 2nd ser. vol. 3 (1951): 388-95; "The Land Legislation and Irish Social Life," *Economic History Review,* 2nd ser. vol. 11 (1958), pp. 1-7; "Peasant Marriage in Ireland: Its Structure and Development Since the Famine," *Economic History Review*, 2nd ser. vol. 14 (1962), pp. 502-23; *The Population of Ireland, 1750-1845* (Oxford: Clarendon Press, 1950); "The Population of Ireland in the Eighteenth Century," *Economic History Review*, 1st ser. vol. 16 (1946), pp. 111-24.

13 The classic studies on the manner in which the Irish stem family system operated are: Conrad M. Arensberg and Solon T. Kimball, *Family and Community in Ireland* (Cambridge: Harvard University Press, 1940), and Conrad M. Arensberg, *The Irish Countryman: An Anthropological Study* (New York: MacMillan, 1937).

14 On the sources of data on the age of marriage, see Robert E. Kennedy, Jr., *The Irish Emigration, Marriage, and Fertility* (Berkeley: University of California Press, 1973), pp. 193n-140n. Data on the marriage age of women are illuminating. In 1864, 18 percent were under twenty-one when first married; the figure for 1911 was 5 percent. In 1864, 71 percent of women were under twenty-five when first married; by 1911, the figure was down to 51 percent. (See Connell, "Catholicism and marriage in the Century After the Famine," in *Irish Peasant Society*, 113n3).

15 Ibid., pp. 140-45.

16 Ibid., pp. 113-61.

17 The controversial relationship between celibacy and mental illness in modern Ireland is discussed in Nancy Scheper-Hughes, *Saints, Scholars and Schizophrenics: Mental Illness in Rural Ireland* (Berkeley: University of California Press, 1979). For comparative diagnostic data, some of them dating back to 1911, see pp. 65-74. Scheper-Hughes' study has not been well-received in Ireland. Nor has the work on sexual repression in certain Irish "museum areas" on the west coast, conducted by John Messenger. See Messenger's comments on both the character of repression and on the resistance of Irish scholars to acknowledge its existence in his "Sex and Repression in Irish Folk Communities," in Donald S. Marshall and Robert C. Suggs, eds., *Human Sexual Behaviour: Variations in the Ethnographic Spectrum* (Philadelphia: Basic Books, 1971), pp. 3-37. Findings of scholars such as Scheper-Hughes and Messenger often are mistakenly taken as an attack on the churches. However, as Joseph Lee notes, "it seems probable that only the consolation offered by the Churches to the celibate victims of economic man prevented lunacy rates, which quadrupled between 1850 and 1914, from rising even more rapidly." (Joseph Lee, *The Modernisation of Irish Society* (Dublin: Gill and MacMillan, 1973, p. 6).

18 Irish marital fertility was at a high of 307 legitimate births per 1,000 married women aged from 15 to 44 years in 1871.

Fertility declined thereafter until 1946 (in southern Ireland) when it levelled off. Even so, in 1961 the southern Irish marital fertility rate was as high as that of El Salvador, Panama, and Chile, nations that exhibited at that time some of the highest population growth rates in the world. Kennedy, pp. 174-76 and Brendan M. Walsh, *Some Irish Population Problems Reconsidered* (Dublin: Economic and Social Research Institute, 1968) pp. 5-7.

19 Walsh, p. 9.

20 Kennedy, p. 3.

21 Kurt Bowen, *Protestants in a Catholic State. Ireland's Privileged Minority* (Kingston and Montreal: McGill-Queen's University Press, 1983), p. 83.

22 Ibid., pp. 89-94.

23 Donald Harman Akenson, *Small Differences. Irish Catholics and Irish Protestants, 1815-1922. An International Perspective* (Kingston and Montreal: McGill-Queen's University Press, 1988).

24 Karl Marx, "Forced Emigration," orig. pub. *New York Daily Tribune* 22 March 1853, reprinted in *Marx, Engels,, Ireland and the Irish Question* (Moscow: Progress Publishers, 1971), p. 67.

25 For a sensibly modest attempt to use economic context as an explanatory variable for Irish migration, see J.G. Kennan, "Irish Migration, All or Nothing Resolved?" *Economic and Social Review*, vol. 12 (April 1981), pp. 169-86.

26 Carrier and Jeffery, p. 33.

27 Peter Lyon, "On Diasporas — the Jewish, the British and some others." *Collected Seminar Papers*, no. 31. *The Diaspora of the British* (London: University of London, Institute of Commonwealth Studies, 1982), pp. 72-80.

28 Oliver MacDonagh, "The Economy and Society, 1830-1945," in Vaughan (ed), p. 234.

29 For a compendium of the data on nineteenth-century language preferences, see Donald Harman Akenson, *The Irish Education Experiment. The National System of Education in the Nineteenth Century.* (London: Routledge and Kegan Paul, 1970), pp. 378-80.

30 Mokyr, pp. 183-84.

31 Akenson, *Irish Education Experiment*, p. 376.

32 See Fitzpatrick, "Emigration, 1801-70," in Vaughan, p. 613, Table 6. The figures in this table somewhat understate the number of literate persons, because people who could read, but not write, are included in it as "illiterates."

33 Richard A. Easterlin, "Immigration: Economic and Social

Characteristics," in Stephan Thernstrom (ed.), *Harvard Encyclopedia of American Ethnic Groups* (Cambridge: Harvard University Press, 1980), Table 2, p. 478.

34 Fitzpatrick, in Vaughan, p. 578.

35 *Commission on Emigration and Other Population Problems, 1948-1954*, (Dublin: Stationery Office, 1954), Table 90, p. 120.

36 Carrier and Jeffery, Table H, p. 102.

37 Ibid., Table I, p. 109.

38 Fitzpatrick, in Vaughan, p. 608.

39 See John Mannion, "The Waterford Merchants and the Irish Newfoundland Provisions Trade, 1770-1820" in Donald Harman Akenson (ed.), *Canadian Papers in Rural History*, vol. 3 (1982), pp. 178-203.

40 Daly, p. 36.

41 Fitzpatrick, "Irish Emigration in the Later Nineteenth Century," pp. 128-32; Fitzpatrick, *Irish Emigration 1801-1921*, p. 11.

42 Fitzpatrick, in Vaughan, pp. 575-76; *Commission on Migration and Other Population Problems, 1948-1954*, p. 127.

43 Fitzpatrick, "Irish Emigration in the Later Nineteenth Century," p. 129.

44 See Carrier and Jeffery, Tables N/O (3), N/O (4), and N/O (5), pp. 116-21.

45 Ibid., Table 11, p. 57.

46 Cormac Ó Gráda, "Did Ulster Catholics Always Have Larger Families?" *Irish Economic and Social History*, vol. 12 (1985), pp. 79-86.

47 Fitzpatrick, in Vaughan, pp. 579-87,

48 Kennedy, p. 119.

49 For religious figures on Northern Ireland, see *Ulster Year Book, 1966-68* (Belfast: HMSO, 1967), p. 10.

50 For reglious figures on Southern Ireland. see *Statistical Abstracts of Ireland, 1966* (Dublin: Stationery Office, 1966), pp. 52, 350, 358.

51 There is no trustworthy modern accounting of the losses in the 1920-22 period in Belfast. A well-informed, but not entirely unbiased work is *Fifty Years of Ulster, 1890-1940* (Belfast: The Irish News, 1941) by T.J. Campbell, sometime editor of the *Irish News*, Belfast's leading Catholic newspaper. See esp. pp. 25-30, 116-17. The estimate of 9,000 Catholics forced from employment was put forward by Michael Collins to the United Kingdom government on 27 March 1922 (ibid., 117).

52 Patrick J. Buckland, "Southern Unionism, 1885-1922," (Ph.D. thesis, Queen's University of Belfast, 1969), pp. 585, 589. This excellent thesis is in some ways more serviceable than the two-

volume published version. For reports of outrages during the period 1920-22, *The Church of Ireland Gazette* is particularly useful. See especially 16 June 1922, 1 December 1922, and 12 January 1923. See also the condemnation by Daniel Cohalan, Roman Catholic bishop of Cork, on the murder of Protestants in his diocese (*Irish Catholic Directory*, 1923, entry for 30 April 1922), pp. 566.

On Protestant insecurities, see Patrick J. Buckland, *Irish Unionism, 1885-1923. A Documentary History* (Belfast: Her Majesty's Stationery Office, 1973), pp. 366-67, 378, 383.

53 This decline of about 32.5 percent of the Protestant population occurred at a time when the Catholic population of the twenty-six counties was declining by only 2.2 percent (Patrick J. Buckland, *The Anglo-Irish and the New Ireland*, (Dublin: Gill and MacMillan, 1972, pp. 285.)

Free State politicians and their historians have tried to argue that this sharp decline in the Protestant population was almost entirely ascribable to persons who had "garrison" positions leaving Ireland. However, research has clearly established that, at most, the withdrawal of the British garrisons and its dependents accounted for only one-quarter of the Protestant decline. See Bowen, pp. 20-25.

54 See William Forbes Adams, *Ireland and the Irish Emigration to the New World from 1815 to the Famine* (New Haven: Yale University Press, 1932), esp. pp. 410-28.

55 "Some aspects of Nineteenth-Century Irish Migration," in L.M. Cullen and T.C. Smout, *Comparative Aspects of Scottish and Irish Economic and Social History, 1600-1900* (Edinburgh: John Donald Publishers Ltd., 1978), p. 65.

56 Cormac Ó Gráda, "A Note on Nineteenth-Century Irish Emigration Statistics," *Population Studies* vol. 29 (no. 1, 1973), pp. 143-49.

57 Ibid., pp. 145, 148.

CHAPTER THREE

1 The study of the Irish in New Zealand is in the early stages of development. A pioneering volume is Richard P. Davis, *Irish Issues in New Zealand Politics, 1868-1922* (Dunedin: University of Otago Press, 1974). The most revealing book about the Irish in New Zealand is Patrick O'Farrell's Vanished Kingdoms. Irish in Australia and New Zealand (Kensington: New South Wales University Press, 1990). It is an amazing, high-risk book that works: an interlayering of personal memories, family history, big historical questions and reflections on the Irish in the antipodes.

Sadly embarassing, on the other hand, is the journalistic work of David McGill, *The Lion and the Wolfhound. The Irish Rebellion on the New Zealand Goldfields* (Wellington: Grantham House, 1990). Most of the material for this primer's chapter on New Zealand is taken from Donald Harman Akenson, *Half the World from Home. Perspectives on the Irish in New Zealand, 1860-1950* (Wellington: Victoria University Press 1990, dist. outside Australasia by Langdale Press, Gananoque, Ont., Canada). See also Akenson, "Immigration and Ethnicity in New Zealand and the U.S.A. — The Irish Example," in Jock Phillips (ed.), *New Worlds? The Comparative History of New Zealand and the United States* (Wellington: NZ-US Education Foundation and the Stout Research Centre of Victoria University, 1989), pp. 28-57, and Akenson, "Letters from the Irish Emigrant. Texts from Real Life," in *Migration and New Zealand Society* (Wellington: Stout Research Centre of Victoria University, 1990), pp. 1-17.

2   See the letters in Akenson, "Letters from the Irish Emigrant," cited above, note 1.

3   "New Zealand," *Dublin University Magazine* vol. 26 (Oct. 1845), p. 405.

4   As in "Traditions, Customs and Superstitions of the New Zealanders," ibid., vol. 47 (Feb. 1856), pp. 221-35.

5   "The Homes of the South," ibid., vol. 52 (Sept. 1858), p. 306.

6   *Report of the Select Committee of the House of Lords on Colonization from Ireland*, p. 383, queries 3757-8, H.C. 1847 (737), vi.

7   This tradition, of relating Ireland to New Zealand, continued well into the twentieth century. See Leslie Symons, "The Pastoral Economy of New Zealand and some comparisons with Ireland," *Statistical and Social Inquiry Society of Ireland, Journal* 114th session (1960-61), pp. 94-131.

8   William Pember Reeves, *The Long White Cloud. Ao Tea Roa* (London: George Allen and Unwin, fourth ed., 1950), p. 26.

9   J.S. Marais, *The Colonization of New Zealand* (Oxford: Clarendon Press, 1927), p. 46n6.

10   W.D. Borrie, "Immigration to New Zealand, 1854-1880," *Journal of the Royal Australian Historical Society*, vol. 30 (1944), p. 314.

11   Davis, p. 30n16.

12   Ibid., pp. 25-50.

13   Memorandum by William Rolleston; 4 March 1883, reproduced in *Appendix to the Journals of the House of Representatives of New Zealand* 1883, A-1, p. 18.

14   For methods and definitions, see Akenson, *Half the World*, Appendix A, pp. 205-15.

15   For my method of calculating ethnicity, see *Half the World,* Appendix C, pp. 219-23.

16   For methods of determining religious breakdown of the multigenerational Irish group, see ibid., pp. 65-66.

17   In the text that follows, quotation of lengthy passages is by kind permission of the owners of copyright. Short quotations are employed under the fair usage provisions of the Copyright Acts of Canada and of the United States of America and the associated international copyright conventions of which the United Kingdom, the Republic of Ireland, and the government of New Zealand are parties

18   The Willams ms is found in the Alexander Turnbull Library, Wellington, N.Z., Ms 2035.

19   The Quinn letters are found in the Public Record Office of Northern Ireland, T1552/1-15, and cover the period from October 1890 through June 1907. The Quinns are discussed in their Australian aspect in Patrick O'Farrell, *Letters from Irish Australia, 1825-1920* (Sydney: New South Wales University Press and Belfast: Ulster Historical Foundation 1984), pp. 54-55.

20   William Quinn to Mrs. Eliza Quinn, 7 October 1890, PRONTI T1552/1.

21   William Quinn to Mrs. Eliza Quinn, 3 December 1895, PRONTI T1552/8.

22   Patrick Quinn to John Quinn, 9 October 1900, PRONTI T1552/11.

23   Oliver McSparron to Archibald McSparron, 18 Nov. 1865, PRONI, T2724/2/1.

24   Oliver McSparron to Archibald McSparron, 26 May 1869, PRONI, T2743/2/3.

25   Oliver McSparron to Archibald McSparron, 16 May 1880, PRONI, T2743/2/5.

26   Oliver McSparron to Archibald McSparron, 1 August 1882, PRONI, T2743/2/5.

27   William Quinn to _____Quinn, 23 March 1906, PRONI, T1552/14.

28   Patrick Quinn to John Quinn, 29 January 1906, PRONI, T1552/13.

29   Mrs. Elizabeth McCleland to Ann McCleland, 1 October 1840, PRONI, T3034/1.

30   Hugh Rea to William McCance, 6 November 1905, PRONI, D965/1.

31   J.N. Armstrong to Miss Marian Armstrong, 25 August 1859, PRONI, T1978/1.

32   J.N. Armstrong to Miss Marian Armstrong, 6 May 1865, PRONI, T1978/3.

33   For a discussion of the nature of this "sample" see *Half the*

World, Appendix B, pp. 216-218.
34   Derived from *Results of a Census ... 1921 General Report Birthplaces*, p. 9.
35   Derived from *Report on the Results of a Census, 1916*, p. 9.
36   *Results of a Census ... 1921. General Report*, p. 130.

CHAPTER FOUR

1   Patrick O'Farrell's monumental pioneering volume is indispensable: *The Irish in Australia* (Kensington: New South Wales University Press, 1987). It supplements, but does not significantly duplicate the material in his *The Catholic Church and Community: An Australian History* (Kensington: New South Wales University Press, new ed., 1985). One should also consult his richly evocative, *Vanished Kingdoms. Irish in Australia and New Zealand* (Kensington: New South Wales University Press, 1990). Other material by O'Farrell that is of especial value includes: "Irish-Australia at an End," *Papers and Proceedings. Tasmanian Historical Research Association* 21 (Dec. 1974), pp. 142-60; "Irish-Australian Diplomatic Relations," *Quadrant* (March 1980), pp. 11-20; "The Irish in Australia: Some Aspects of the Period, 1791-1850," *Descent* 7 (March 1975), pp. 43-56.
2   Richard Reid, "Tracking the Immigrants," in Eric Richards, Richard Reid and David Fitzpatrick, *Visible Immigrants. Neglected Sources for the History of Australian Immigration* (Canberra: Australian National University, 1989, p. 32.
3   On the strengths of the Australian assisted migrant records, see Eric Richards, "Annals of the Australian Immigrants," in Richards, Reid, and Fitzpatrick pp. 7-22; Richard Reid, "Tracking the Immigrants," ibid., pp. 23-46; Richard Reid, "Emigration from Ireland to New South Wales in the mid-nineteenth century," in Oliver MacDonagh and W.F. Mandle (eds) *Irish-Australian Studies: Papers Delivered at the Fifth Irish-Australian Conference* (Canberra: Australian National University, 1989), pp. 304-17.
4   O'Farrell, *Irish in Australia*, p. 1. For basic background information on the general topic of nineteenth century migration to Australia, see Helen R. Woodcock, *Rights of Passage: Emigration to Australia in the Nineteenth Century* (London: Tavistock Publications, 1986).
5   Geoffrey Bolton, "The Irish in Australian Historiography," in Colin Kiernan (ed.), *Australia and Ireland, 1788-1988. Bicentenary Essays* (Dublin: Gill and MacMillan, 1986), p. 15.
6   Stephen Nicholas and Peter Shergold, "British and Irish Convicts," in James Jupp (ed.), *The Australian People. An Encyclopedia of the Nation, its People and their Origins* (North

Notes

Ryde, NSW: Angus and Robertson, 1988), p. 25.
7   Patrick O'Farrell, "The Irish in Australia and New Zealand, 1791-1870," in W.E. Vaughn (ed.), *A New History of Ireland. V. Ireland under the Union, part I, 1801-70* (Oxford: Clarendon Press, 1989), pp. 660-61; O'Farrell, "The Irish in Australia," pp. 43-45. For a valuable discussion both of the shortcomings of many previous estimates of the character of the convict force, see James Waldersee, *Catholic Society in New South Wales, 1788-1860* (Sydney: Sydney University Press, 1974).
8   O'Farrell, "The Irish in Australia," p. 45. For related analysis, see Manning Clark, "The Origins of the Convicts Transported to Eastern Australia, 1787-1852, Part I," *Historical Studies* 7 (Melbourne, May 1956), pp. 121-35; and Part II, Ibid, vol. 7 (Nov. 1956), pp. 314-27.
9   R.J. Schultz, "Immigration into Eastern Australia, 1788-1851," *Historical Studies* 14 (Melbourne, April 1970), pp. 228 and 281, tables IV and V.
10   *General Report on the Eleventh Census of New South Wales* (Sydney: 1894), p. 90.
11   Oliver MacDonagh, "The Irish in Victoria, 1851-91: A Demographic Essay," in T.D. Williams, (ed.), *Historical Studies* (Dublin: Gill and MacMillan, 1971), vol. 8, p. 82.
12   Neil Coughlan, "The Coming of the Irish to Victoria," *Historical Studies* (Melbourne, Oct. 1965), p. 73.
13   John Knott, "Settlement, 1851-1880," in Jupp, pp. 52, 54.
14   For information on the various schemes, see Alan Atkinson, "Free Settlers before 1851," in Jupp, pp. 37-42; Allan Martin, "Public Policy before Federation," in Jupp, pp. 71-77; Geoffrey Sherington, "Settlement 1881-1914," in Jupp, pp. 83-88; Robert J. Schultz, "The Assisted Immigrants, 1837-1850," (Ph.D. thesis, Australian National University, 1971); Robert J. Schultz, "Immigration in Eastern Australia, 1788-1851," *Historical Studies* (Melbourne), vol. 14 (April 1970), pp. 273-83.
15   Richards in Richards, Reid, and Fitzpatrick, p. 16.
16   Schultz, "The Assisted Immigrants, 1837-1850," p. 42.
17   James Jupp, "The Making of the Anglo-Australian," in Jupp, p. 58.
18   David Fitzpatrick, "Irish Emigration in the later nineteenth century," *Irish Historical Studies*, vol. 22 (Sept 1980), p. 131.
19   David Fitzpatrick, *Irish Emigration, 1801-1921* (Dundalk: Dundalgan Press, for the Economic and Social History Society of Ireland, 1984), p. 18.
20   Fitzpatrick, "Irish emigration in the later nineteenth century," p. 131.
21   Richards in Richards, Reid, and Fitzpatrick, p. 21.

22   The nineteenth century immigration data for all the Australian colonies is collected in James J. Fenton, *Victorian Yearbook 1895-98, containing a digest of the statistics of Victoria, with reference to the statistics of the other Australasian colonies and other countries* (Melbourne: Government Printer, 1901), tables in frontispiece. For comments on the data quality, see E.T. McPhee, "Australia — its Immigrant Population," in vol. II (1969 supplement) to Walter F. Wilcox, *International Migrations* (New York: Gordon and Breach), pp. 169-70.

23   This is not to deny the fact that significant (if, by historical standards, small) numbers of Irish persons continue to migrate to Australia to the present day. For a revealing study, see Seamus Grimes, "Postwar Irish Immigration in Australia: The Sydney Experience," in Seamus Grimes and Gearoid O'Tuathaigh (eds.) *The Irish-Australian Connection* (Galway: University College, Galway, 1989), pp. 137-59.

24   O'Farrell, in Vaughan, pp. 674-75.

25   Fitzpatrick in Kiernan, p. 140.

26   Paula Hamilton, in Jupp, p. 567.

27   Fitzpatrick, "Irish emigration in the later nineteenth century," p. 137.

28   Carrier and Jeffery, Table H(1), p. 102.

29   *Census of the Commonwealth of Australia taken for the night between the 2nd and 3rd April 1911*, vol. I, p. 147.

30   Ibid., p. 153.

31   Ibid., p. 152. The reader may wish to refer to the almost-classic misinterpretation of the Australian situation — "that the Catholic and Irish communities can be treated as substantially synonymous" — by Oliver MacDonagh in *Historical Studies,* vol. 8 (Dublin: Gill and MacMillan, 1971), pp. 67-92. Patrick O'Farrell has dismissively referred to this sort of effort as being a "takeover bid for sole possession of the identity of being Irish by Catholic forces..." Patrick O'Farrell, in Oliver MacDonagh and W.F. Mandle, *Ireland and Irish-Australia: Studies in Cultural and Political History* (London: Croom Helm, 1986), p. 226. O'Farrell sees this as being mostly a nineteenth-century process.

32   Fitzpatrick, in Vaughn, Table 7, p. 614.

33   Richard Reid, in Jupp, p. 583.

34   Ibid.

35   Schultz, "The Assisted Immigrants, 1837-1850," p. 65.

36   Fitzpatrick, "Irish emigration in the later nineteenth century," p. 132n13.

37   Carrier and Jeffery, Table N/O (5), pp. 120-21.

38   Fitzpatrick, "Irish emigration in the later nineteenth century," p. 137.

Notes

39   O'Farrell, "Emigrant Attitudes and Behaviour ...", p. 126.

40   O'Farrell, in Vaughan, p. 672.

41   David Fitzpatrick, "Irish Immigrants in Australia: Patterns of Settlement and Paths of Mobility," *Australia 1888*, vol. 1 (Feb. 1979), p. 50.

42   Reid, in Jupp, p. 585.

43   MacDonagh, "The Irish in Victoria ...", p. 75.

44   See Australia Census, 1911, vol. 2, pp. 188-89. If anything, the nearly 80 percent figure understates the length of residence of these people, for there were 9,119 persons whose length of residence was unspecified and some, probably most of these, would have been in the twenty-plus years residence group.

45   Derived from ibid., pp. 128-29, 296-97.

46   David Fitzpatrick, "The Settlers: Immigration from Ireland in the Nineteenth Century," in Colm Kiernan, (ed.), *Ireland and Australia* (Cork: Mercier Press, 1984), p. 28.

47   Derived from data in Australia Census, 1911, vol. 2, pp. 128-29, 296-97.

48   Fitzpatrick, "Irish Immigrants in Australia: Patterns of Settlement and Paths of Mobility," *Australia 1888*, vol. 1 (Feb. 1979), p. 52.

49   Fitzpatrick, "Irish emigration in the later nineteenth century," p. 136.

50   Chris McConville, "Catholics and Mobility in Melbourne and Sydney, 1861-1891," *Australia 1888*, vol. 1 (Aug. 1979), p. 56.

51   See Malcolm Campbell, "The Kingdom of the Ryans: Aspects of Irish-Australian society in south west New South Wales, 1816-1890," (Ph.D., University of New South Wales, 1989); Malcolm Campbell, "The Irish in Southwest New South Wales: the validity of a regional approach," in MacDonagh and Mandle, pp. 25-41.

52   Derived from *Results of a Census of New South Wales, 1901*, pp. 770-76.

53   Derived from Ibid., pp. 786-93. In using the Catholic population as a surrogate for the multigenerational group, one somewhat blurs reality. This is because (to take a representative year) in 1891, roughly 17.5 percent of the Roman Catholic population was not of Irish origin (Akenson, *Small Differences*, p. 62).

54   Eric Richards, "The Importance of Being Irish in Colonial South Australia," in John O'Brien and Pauric Travers (eds.), *The Irish Emigrant Experience in Australia* (Swords Co. Dublin: Pool beg Press, 1991), pp. 94-95.

55   For a succinct summary of Price's methods, see Charles A. Price, "The Ethnic Character of the Australian Population," in Jupp, pp. 121-22.

56   This theme runs through much of O'Farrell's work. It is

particularly clearly articulated in "The Irish and Australian History," pp. 17-21, and in *The Irish in Australia*, pp. 10-15.

57   The spectrum I am describing is an articulation of a dualism found in David Fitzpatrick's "'That beloved country, that no place else resembles,': connotations of Irishness in Irish-Australian letters, 1841-1915," *Irish Historical Studies*, vol. 27 (Nov. 1991), p. 326.

58   Ibid., pp. 324-51.

59   O'Farrell, in Vaughan, p. 674.

60   Fitzpatrick, "Irish Immigration, 1840-1914," in Jupp, p. 563.

61   For an impressive (indeed, brilliant) essay on the Irish immigrant situation in Australia and on the need for sophistication in approaching criminality records, see Mark Finnane, "Irish and Crime in the late nineteenth century: a statistical inquiry," in MacDonagh and Mandle, pp. 77-98.

The only historical study of which I am aware that successfully takes into account ethnic prejudice in a judicial system against the Irish-born, and the Irish Catholics as a group, is John Weaver, "Moral Order and Repression in Upper Canada: The Case of the Criminal Justice System in the Gore District and Hamilton, 1831-1851," *Ontario History*, vol. 87 (September 1986), pp. 176-207.

62   O'Farrell, *The Irish in Australia*, p. 169.

63   Fitzpatrick, "Irish Immigration, 1841-1914," in Jupp, p. 563.

64   See studies cited in Nancy Scheper-Hughes, *Saints, Scholars and Schizophrenics. Mental Illness in Rural Ireland* (Berkeley: University of California Press, 1979), pp. 72-73.

65   Ibid., pp. 66-68.

66   See Scheper-Hughes, pp. 163-85.

CHAPTER FIVE

1   N.H. Carrier and J.R. Jeffery, *External Migration. A Study of the Available Statistics, 1815-1950* (London: HMSO, 1953), Table H (1), p. 102.

2   Ibid.

3   On Irish out-migration see Donald Harman Akenson, *Occasional Papers on the Irish in South Africa* (Grahamstown: Institute of Social and Economic Research, Rhodes University, 1991), Table 2, p. 56 and Table 3, p. 61.

4   Compiled from Carrier and Jeffery, pp. 117-23.

5   Ibid. For an indication of why an Irish girl would do well to avoid being a domestic in South Africa, see Charles Van Onselen, "The Witches of Suburbia. Domestic Servants of Witwatersrand, 1890-1914," in Charles Van Onselen, *Studies in the Social and Economic History of the Witwatersrand 1886-1914* (London: Longman, 1982), pp. 1-66.

6   The raw data on which this assertion of religious background is made are found in South Africa's *Fourth Census ... 1926. Report*, pp. 46-47, 72-75, 121-22.   My analysis of these data is found in Akenson, *Irish in South Africa*, pp. 69-72.

7   Donal McCracken, *The Irish Pro-Boers, 1877-1902* (Johannesburg: Perskor Books, 1989); Donal McCracken (ed.) *The Irish in South Africa, 1795-1910* and the Committee for Southern African-Irish Historical Studies, *Southern African-Irish Studies*, vol. 1 (1991).

8   E. Morse Jones, *Role of the British Settlers in South Africa, Part I.   Up to 1826* (Cape Town: A.A. Balkema, second ed., 1971).

9   Harold E. Hockly, *The Story of the British Settlers of 1820 in South Africa* (Cape Town and Johannesburg: Juta and Co., second ed., 1957).

10   John Clark, *Natal Settler-Agent, The Career of John Moreland: Agent for the Byrne Emigration-Scheme of 1849-51* (Cape Town: A.A. Balkema, 1972).

11   Such as J.P.R. Wallis's *One Man's Hand: the Story of Sir Charles Coghlan and the Liberation of Southern Rhodesia* (London: Longmans, Green and Co. 1950).

12   For a useful guide to the immigration literature, see Kathleen M. Cox, Immigration into South Africa, 1940-67: A Bibliography (Cape Town: University of Cape Town Libraries), 1970).

13   Fundamental is Gustave Saron and Louis Hotz, (eds.), *The Jews in South Africa. A History* (Cape Town: Oxford University Press, 1955).   Among the large number of other studies, the following are especially useful: Taffy Adler, "Lithuania's Diaspora: The Johannesburg Jewish Workers' Club, 1928-1948," *Journal of Southern African Studies*, vol. 6, (April 1980), pp. 70-92; Steven E. Ascheim, "The Communal Organization of South African Jewry," *Jewish Journal of Sociology*, vol. 12 (1970), pp. 204-31; Daniel J. Elazar, with Peter Medding, *Jewish Communities in Frontier Societies, Argentina, Australia, and South Africa* (New York: Holmes and Meier, 1983); E. Feit, "Community and 'Aparteid'," *Race*, vol. 8 (April, 1967), pp. 395-408; Riva Krut, "The Making of a South African Jewish Community in Johannesburg, 1886-1914," in Belinda Bozzoli, (ed.), *Class Community and Conflict, South African Perspectives* (Johannesburg: Ravan Press, 1987), pp. 134-78; Sergio Della Pergola and Allie A. Dubb, "South African Jewry: A Sociodemographic Profile," *American Jewish Year Book 1988* (New York: American Jewish Committee and Philadelphia: Jewish Publications Society, 1988), pp. 59-140; Ziona Strelitz, "Jewish Identity in Cape Town, with special reference to out-marriage," *Jewish Journal of Sociology*, vol. 13 (1971), pp. 73-93.

14   As, for example, Jean Jacques van-Helten and Keith William,

"'The Crying Need of South Africa': The Emigration of Single British Women to the Transvaal, 1901-10," *Journal of Southern African Studies*, vol. 10 (October 1983), pp. 18-38.
    15   See, for instance, Robert A. Huttenback, *Racism and Empire: White Settlers and Colored Immigrants in the British Self-Governing Colonies, 1830-1910* (Ithaca: Cornell University Press, 1976).
    16   For a vigorous attack on the concept of ethnicity from a structural Marxist view, see Dan O'Mara, *Volkskapitalisme, Class, Capital and Ideology in the Development of Afrikaner Nationalism, 1934-1948* (Johannesburg: Ravan Press, 1983).
    17   Alan H. Jeeves, "The 1820 Settlers to South Africa," M.A., Queen's University, Ontario, 1965).
    18   Arthur Keppel-Jones, (ed.) *Philips, 1820 Settler* (Pietermaritzburg: Shuter and Shooter, 1960).
    19   Dorothy E. Rivett-Carnac, *Thus Came the English in 1820* (London: Bailey Bros. and Swinfen Ltd., 1961).
    20   Isobel E. Edwards, *The 1820 Settlers in South Africa, A Study in British Colonial Policy* (London: Longmans, Green and Co., 1934).
    21   Alan F. Hattersley, *The Natal Settlers, 1849-1851* (Pietermaritzburg: Shuter and Shooter, 1949), and, *The British Settlement of Natal. A Study in Imperial Migration* (Cambridge: Cambridge University Press, 1950).

CHAPTER SIX

    1   Ronald Robinson, "Non-European foundation of European imperialism: sketch for a theory of collaboration," in Roger Owen and Bob Sutcliffe (eds.), *Studies in the Theory of Imperialism* (London: Longman, 1972), pp. 117-42.
    2   Ibid., p. 124.
    3   David Fitzpatrick, "'A peculiar tramping people': the Irish in Britain, 1801-70," in W.E. Vaughan (ed.), *A New History of Ireland*, V, *Ireland under the Union*, I, *1801-70* (Oxford: Clarendon Press, 1989), p. 641.
    4   H.J. Hanham, "Religion and Nationality in the Mid-Victorian Army," in M.R.D. Foot (ed.) *War and Society. Historical essay in honour and memory of J.R. Western, 1928-71* (London: Paul Elek, 1973), p. 162.
    5   Terence Denman, "The Catholic Irish soldier in the First World War: the 'racial environment,'" *Irish Historical Studies*, vol. 28 (Nov. 1991), p. 354.
    6   See Donal McCracken, *The Irish-Pro-Boers* (Johannesburg: Perskor Books, 1989).
    7   Donal McCracken "The Irish in Colonial South Africa: An

Overview," *South African-Irish Studies* vol. 1 (1991), p. 32.
8   Patrick O'Farrell, *The Irish in Australia* (Kensington, New South Wales University Press, 1987), p. 142.
9   Scott B. Cook, "The Irish Raj: Social Origins and Careers of Irishmen in the Indian Civil Service, 1855-1919," *Journal of Social History*, vol. 20, no. 3 (1987), pp. 510 and 525*n*27.
10   Ibid., table 2, p. 516.
11   Ibid., p. 507.
12   Ibid., p. 527*n*46.
13   See Table 33.
14   Ibid.
15   *Commission on Emigration and other Population Problems, 1948-1954* (Dublin: The Stationary Office, 1954), Table 95, p. 126.
16   For a discerning discussion of mid-nineteenth century seasonal migration, see Ruth-Ann Harris, "Seasonal Migration between Ireland and England prior to the Famine," in *Canadian Papers in Rural History*, vol. 7 (1990), pp. 362-83.
17   Sean Glynn, "Irish Immigration to Britain, 1911-1951: Patterns and Policy," *Irish Economic and Social History* vol. 8 (1981), p. 51.
18   *Commission on Emigration...* Table 95, p. 126.
19   Donald MacAmhlaigh, "Britain's Irish workers," *The Tablet* 18 March 1978, pp. 260-62.

CHAPTER SEVEN

1   Robert E. Kennedy, Jr. *The Irish. Emigration, Marriage and Fertility* (Berkeley: University of California Press, 1973).
2   David Fitzpatrick, "'A share of the honeycomb': Education, Emigration and Irishwomen," *Continuity and Change* vol. 2, no. 1 (1986), p. 220.
3   David Fitzpatrick, "Review article: Women, gender and the writing of Irish history," *Irish Historical Studies* vol. 27 (May 1991), p. 272.
4   Janet A. Nolan, *Ourselves Alone. Women's Emigration from Ireland 1885-1920* (Lexington: University of Kentucky Press, 1989), p. 29.
5   Ibid., p. 32.
6   Ibid., p. 42.
7   For background information on Irish women's history, see (in addition to the items cited elsewhere in this chapter) the following: Jenny Beale, *Women in Ireland. Voices of Change* (London: MacMillan, 1986); Malcolm Campbell, "Irish Women in Nineteenth Century Australia: A More Hidden Ireland?" in *Irish Australian Studies* (ed. Phililp Bull, Chris McConville and Noel

McLachlan), (Melbourne: La Trobe University, 1991), pp 25-38; Sheelagh Conway, *A Woman and Catholicism* (Toronto: Paperjacks Ltd., 1987); Art Cosgrove (ed.), *Marriage in Ireland* (Dublin: College Press, 1985): Pauline Jackson, "Women in 19th Century Irish Emigration," *International Migration Review,* vol. 18 (Winter 1984), pp. 1,005-1,020; Maria Luddy and Cliona Murphy, *Women Surviving* (Dublin: Poolbeg, 1989); Margaret MacCurtain and Donncha O'Corrain (eds.), *Women in Irish Society. The Historical Dimension* (Westport, Conn: Greenwood Press, 1979), p. 40; Magaret MacCurtain, Mary Dowd and Maria Luddy, "An Agenda for Women's History in Ireland, 1500-1900," *Irish National Studies,* vol. 28 (May 1992), pp. 1-37; Eilean Ni Chuilleanain, *Irish Women: Image and Achievement. Women in Irish Culture from Earliest Times* (Dublin: Arlen House, 1985); Margaret Ward, *Unmanageable Revolutionaries. Women and Irish Nationalism* (Dublin: Pluto Press, 1983).

    In the Luddy and Murphy volume there are two particularly good studies which go beyond the usual generalizations and provide precise data on women's position in the familial-based economy: Mary Cullen, "Breadwinners and Providers: Women in the Household Economy of Labouring Families, 1835-36," pp. 85-116, and Monica Hearn, "Life for Domestic Servants in Dublin, 1880-1920," pp. 148-79. To this should be added several pioneering studies by Joanna Bourke, especially "Women and Poultry in Ireland, 1891-1914," *Irish Historical Studies* vol. 25 (May 1987), pp. 293-310. Although this sounds like a récherché topic, it actually is crucial, for control of the "egg money" was one of the matters that determined a wife's degree of economic independence within the farm unit.

8   The classic, if somewhat idealized descriptions of the post-Famine match is found in Conrad M. Arensberg and Solon T. Kimball, *Family and Community in Ireland* (Cambridge: Harvard University Press, 1940).

9   David Fitzpatrick, "The modernisation of the Irish Female," in Patrick O'Flanagan, Paul Ferguson, and Kevin Whelan (eds.) *Rural Ireland 1600-1900. Modernisation and Change* (Cork: Cork University Press, 1987), pp. 162-63.

10   On women's life in the Belfast textile industry, see Betty Messenger, *Picking Up the Linen Threads. A Study in Industrial Folklore* (Belfast: Blackstaff Press, 1975).

11   Joanna Bourke, "'The Best of all Home Rulers': The Economic Power of Women in Ireland, 1880-1914," *Irish Economic and Social History,* vol. 18 (1991), p. 34.

12   Ibid., pp. 39-47.

13   John Revans, *Evils of the State of Ireland. Their Causes and*

Notes

their Remedy — *A Poor Law* (London: John Hatchard, second edition., 1837).

14   The best discussion that I have encountered of the marginal status of pre-Famine Irish women is Andrea Ebel [Brozyna], "Illegitimacy in Pre-Famine Ireland: Women, Marginality, and Alternative Modes of Family Formation," (M.A. Queen's University, Kingston, Ontario, 1989), esp. pp. 49-74.

15   Jackson, Table 3, p. 1,013, citing *Commission on Emigration and Other Population Problems* Table 57, p. 72.

16   Jackson, Table 1, page 1,007, derived from *Commission on Emigration and Other Population Problems*, Table 28, p. 318. These data (as explained in Chapter Two) suffer from undercounting, but I think that on gender ratios they are representative of the somewhat larger real picture.

17   Fitzpatrick, "A share of the honeycomb," p. 225.

18   William Forbes Adams remains the only scholar who has gone carefully through the primary sources on Irish migration to British North America (the largest pre-Famine overseas destination) and to the United States. See his *Ireland and the Irish Emigration to the New World from 1815 to the Famine* (New Haven: Yale University Press, 1932). Some material in Adams' statistical appendix (esp. p. 411) concerning the migration to British North America is useful, for it provides us with the largest possible sample. Adams noted that in shipping records of migrants to BNA, children were sharply undercounted, being counted either as one-half an adult, one-third, or not counted at all. He concluded that the pre-Famine BNA total numbers had to be increased by 20 percent because of this undercounting of children. Assuming that what Adams was correcting was a two-thirds undercount of children among the emigrants (this is his median case, children being counted as one-third an adult), this means that the Irish migrant flow prior to the Famine was composed of one-quarter juveniles, three-quarters adults. Now, for the sake of argument, assume two children per family and two parents per family (which is not unrealistic, given that emigration by and large was an activity of young families, not of older couples with completed families), then one-quarter of the emigration flow consisted of married adults. If the gender ratio had been equal among the unmarried adults, then one-quarter were single adult females (or, considered as a proportion of females, one-half would have been unmarried). However, anecdotal sources suggest that single females were less represented than they were later to become, so probably somewhat fewer than half of the females were single adults.

One point is certain: the pre-Famine emigration was different from post-Famine for the reason that pre-Famine Ireland

293

was a vastly different social and economic context as compared to post-Famine. Therefore, on that ground alone, one would not accept assertions that there was a continuity — a long tradition of economically independent females dominating Irish emigration — between the pre-Famine exodus and late Victorian female emigration.

19   Derived from N.H. Carrier and J.R. Jeffery, *External Migration. A Study of the Available Statistics, 1815-1920* (London: HMDO, 1953), Table VI, p. 104. The reader who is familiar with Janet Nolan's *Ourselves Alone* will note that Carrier and Jeffery's percentages indicate a somewhat different married/unmarried ratio in the entire emigration population than is implied by the cohort data (for ages 15-34) in her Table 6, p. 51. This is because Nolan uses only data for overseas sailings from Irish ports, whereas the Carrier and Jeffery data are more comprehensive, being gathered from all UK emigration ports. (Incidentally, the reader of Nolan's book should correct the headings on her Table 6, as it is the heart of her study. The table does not, as the heading suggests, give the percentage of unmarried female emigrants who were between ages 15 and 35. Rather, it gives the percentage of female emigrants aged 15 to 35 who were unmarried, something totally different.)

20   Derived from Carrier and Jeffery, Table 1(1), p. 104.

21   Carrier and Jeffery, p. 54.

22   Widows with children made up 1.7 percent of the Vogel sample in 1876. See Akenson, *Half the World from Home. Perspectives on the Irish in New Zealand, 1860-1950* (Wellington: Victoria University Press, 1990). See Table 10, p. 44.

23   See ibid., pp. 45-46, for Vogel sample.

24   Ibid.

25   Carrier and Jeffery, Table K(1), p. 106.

26   See ibid. This is the average proportion in the five-year age groups that are composed solely of dependent single females (that is, the groups up to age 15) and this can be taken as the normal proportion of females-emigrating-in-family: which is to say that roughly 71 percent of the 15-19 (inclusive) age group consisted of young women emigrating on their own.

27   The distribution of the unmarried non-dependent females (59.0 percent of the total female outflow) as between those of marriage age and those over that age is done by using the age-data for female emigrants, found in Carrier and Jeffery, Table K(1), p. 106.

28   Carrier and Jeffery, p. 54.

29   Fitzpatrick, "The modernization of the Irish female," Table 8:7, p. 174.

30   Ide O'Carroll, *Models for Movers. Irish Women's Emigration to America* (Dublin: Attic Press, 1990), p. 18.

31   Brenda Collins, reviewing Hsia Diner's "Erin's Daughters in America," in *Irish Economic and Social History* vol. 12 (1985), p. 144.

32   Memorandum by William Rolleston, 14 March 1883, reproduced in *Appendix to the Journals of the House of Representatives of New Zealand, 1883,* A-1, p. 18.

33   Allan Martin, "Public Policy before Federation," in James Jupp (ed.), *The Australian People. An Encyclopedia of the Nation, its People and Their Origins* (North Ryde, NSW: 1988), p. 71.

34   Eric Richards, "The importance of being Irish in Colonial South Australia," in John O'Brien and Pauric Travers (eds.), *The Irish Experience in Australia* (Dublin: Poolbeg, 1991), pp. 75-81; "Irish life and progress in colonial South Australia," *Irish Historical Studies* vol. 28 (May 1991), pp. 223-27.

35   Alexander Gordon McClure to Anna, Emily, and Charlotte McClure, 28 May 1868, Public Record Office of Northern Ireland, D. 1746/3/1.

36   James McClure to Anna, Emily, and Charlotte McClure, 24 June 1860, PRONI, D1746/5/1.37   James M. McClure to Miss Emily McClure, 17 September 1865, PRONI, D1746/5/2.38 David Fitzpatrick, "Emigration, 1801-79," in W.E. Vaughan (ed.), *A New History of Ireland,* V, *Ireland under the Union, I, 1801-70* (Oxford: Clarendon Press, 1989), p. 601.

39   Ibid., citing the work of Arnold Schrier.

40   Chris McConville, "The Victorian Irish: Emigrants and Families, 1851-1891," *Australia 1881* (Sept. 1982), Table 4, page 72.

41   On the commitment of Irish women to staying home, see Hsia R. Diner, *Erin's Daughters in America. Irish Immigrant Women in the Nineteenth Century* (Baltimore: Johns Hopkins University Press, 1983), pp. 51-52.

42   Nolan, Table 14, p. 82, citing the Dillingham Commission of 1907-10.

43   Niles Carpenter, *Immigrants and their Children, 1920* (Washington D.C.: Government Printing Office, 1927 p. 290.

44   Sharon Morgan, "Irish Women in Port Phillip and Victoria, 1840-60," in Oliver MacDonagh and W.F. Mandle, *Irish-Australian Studies* (Canberra: Australian National University, 1989), pp. 240-45.

45   Nolan, p. 76.

46   Diner, p. 46. See also pp. 47-53.

47   Chris McConville, "The Victorian Irish: Emigrants and Families, 1851-1891," in Patricia Grimshaw, Chris McConville,

and Ellen McEwen (eds.) *Families in Colonial Australia* (Sydney: 1985), p. 5, cited in Morgan, p. 246*n*30.

48   *Census of the Commonwealth of Australia Taken for the Night between the 2nd and 3rd April 1911* vol. I, p. 151. It is worth noting that the comparative figures for the English-born and Scots-born were higher, being 61.5 percent and 57.1 percent, respectively. Those relative data are useful, but one should not ignore the fact that most Irish females over age 15 were married, and if one could factor out those below the usual marriage age (say, age 25), then the absolute majority married would be seen to be quite high.

49   Derived from ibid., vol. II, pp. 774-75.

50   David Fitzpatrick, "'That beloved country, that no place else resembles:' Connotations of Irishness in Irish-Australian letters, 1841-1915," *Irish Historical Studies* vol. 27 (Nov. 1991), pp. 334-35.

51   For inhibitions on religiously mixed marriages in the Irish homeland, see Akenson, *Small Differences*, pp. 109-15.

52   Paula Hamilton, "'Tipperarifying the moral atmosphere,' Irish Catholic immigration and the state, 1840-1860," in Sydney Labour History Group (ed.), *What Rough Beast? The State and Social Order in Australian History* (Sydney: George Allen and Unwin, 1982), p. 23.

53   Pastoral quoted in Patrick O'Farrell and Deirdre O'Farrell (eds.) *Documents in Australian Catholic History, 1788-1884* (London: Geoffrey Chapman, 1969), vol. I, pp. 350-51.

54   McConville, "The Victorian Irish ..." p. 71.

55   Derived from Australian Census of 1911, vol. I, pp. 106, 271, 272. The calculation of percentages is done upon a base of the total number of marriages for which the religion of both husband and wife is known and only for instances where both husband and wife were residing together at the time of the census.

56   McConville, "The Victorian Irish ...", p. 71.

57   Derived from Australian Census of 1911, vol. I, p. 269.

58   Liam Ryan, "Irish Emigration to Britain Since World War II," in Richard Kearney, (ed.), *Migrations. The Irish at Home and Abroad* (Dublin: Wolfhound Press, 1990), Table 4, p. 63. The source is the U.K. Registrar General's Statistical Review of England and Wales for 1970. This is the first year for which such inter-marriage figures are available.

59   Ryan, p. 63.

60   The temptation to be avoided on this matter is to turn to the various available studies of various ghettoized Irish migrant women and then to try to draw conclusions from that information about the entire female migrant group (as, for example, does Diner, pp. 50-51). Studies of ghettos and of heavy urban concentrations (such as New York) automatically excluded those Irish women who decided to live

their lives totally outside of the extant ethnic group. The lives of Irish women in, say, rural Iowa, are just as important as those in, say, an Irish ghetto such as Lowell, Massachusetts. It is bad method to exclude from the female picture those women who were most emancipated from the ethnic and religious definition of correct behaviour set down in the Old World.

61   Elizabeth McCleland to Ann McCleland, 1 October 1840, PRONI T3034/1.

62   Ann McCleland's movements are documented in PRONI, T3034/4 -17, which cover the years 1843-62. T3034/18 is a useful commentary by one of her descendants.

CHAPTER EIGHT

1   Liam Ryan, "Irish Emigration to Britain since World War II," in Richard Kearney (ed.), *Migrations. The Irish at Home and Abroad* (Dublin: Wolfhound Press, 1990), p. 45.

2   Ibid., p. 46.

3   I am grateful to Dr. Roger Swift of the Institute of Irish Studies, the University of Liverpool, for sharing with me a good deal of information on the Irish in Great Britain. One should call to the reader's attention Dr. Swift's recent succinct introductory pamphlet, *The Irish in Britain, 1815-1914* (London: The Historical Association, 1990).

4   R.F. Foster, *Modern Ireland, 1600-1972* (London: Penguin Press, 1988), p. 356.

5   Reference to these books and also to several of the more outstanding essays are found in the citations below.

Respect should be paid to earlier, more discursive works. Chief among these is John Denvir, *The Irish in Britain from the earliest times to the Fall and Death of Parnell* (London: Kegan Paul, French, Trubner and Co., 1892).   Also valuable is J.E. Handley, *The Irish in Scotland, 1798-1845* (Cork: Cork University Press, 1943) and his *The Irish in Modern Scotland* (Cork: Cork University Press, 1947).   A very serviceable survey is John A. Archer, *The Irish in Britain* (London: Routledge and Kegan Paul, 1963).

The one indispensable government document is the *Report on the State of the Irish Poor in Great Britain* found in the British Parliamentary Papers, H.C., 1836, (34) xxxiv.

For a bibliography, see Maureen Hartigan and Mary J. Hickman, *The History of the Irish in Britain. A Bibliography* (London: Irish in Britain History Centre, 1986).

The only single-authored history of the Irish in Britain to appear during the second half of the twentieth century is Graham

Davis's valuable, *The Irish in Britain, 1815-1914* (Dublin: Gill and MacMillan, 1991).

6   For an attempt in one local area to get around the absence of ethnicity data, see W.J. Lowe, "The Lancashire Irish and the Catholic church, 1846-71: the social dimension," *Irish Historical Studies*, vol. 20 (Sept. 1976), p. 141*n*49.

7   Ryan, p. 48.

8   The period 1876 offers the best opportunities for obtaining an indication of the numbers using Great Britain as a stepwise migration platform. In that period (and only for that period) one has two separate sources of migration data: (a) that compiled by the Registrar General on migrants to various overseas destinations from Irish ports and (b) information collected by United Kingdom Board of Trade authorities on Irish persons leaving for overseas from anywhere in the United Kingdom. By subtracting "a" from "b" one would have a rough estimate of the number of Irish persons using British ports. That is useful data, but note what it provides: it yields the proportion of Irish migrants from the British Isles to, say, the USA, who used Britain as a staging point. What it does not tell us is: what portion of persons who migrated to Britain during any given time period eventually used Britain as a staging point.

9   I am grateful to Dr. Harris for providing me with a pre-publication copy of her book, *The Nearest Place that Wasn't Ireland: A Study of the Pre-Famine Seasonal Migrants of the Irish People to Britain.* Due to be published by the Iowa State University Press in 1993, this is the most sophisticated historical study yet done on Irish transient labour in Great Britain. Unless otherwise noted, my data on transient labour come from this source.

Some of Harris's conclusions are found in "Seasonal Migration between Ireland and England prior to the Famine," in Donald H. Akenson (ed.), *Canadian Papers in Rural History*, vol. 7, (1990), pp. 363-86.

10   Sarah Barber, "Irish Agricultural Labourers in Nineteenth Century Lincolnshire," *Saothar*, vol. 8 (1982), pp. 10-23.

11   David Fitzpatrick, "A curious middleplace: the Irish in Britain, 1871-1921," in Roger Swift and Sheridan Gilley (eds.) *The Irish in Britain, 1815-1939* (London: Pinter Publishers, 1989), Table 1:3, p. 17.

12   Ibid.

13   David Fitzpatrick, "Irish emigration in the later nineteenth century," *Irish Historical Studies* vol. 22 (Sept. 1980), p. 130*n*6.

14   Fitzpatrick, "A curious middle place," pp. 12 and 52*n*1.

15   B.C. Cormac Ó Gráda, "A Note on Nineteenth-Century Irish Emigration Statistics," *Population Studies*, vol. 29 (1973), pp. 143-49.

16 See *Commission on Emigration and other Population Problems, 1948-1954* (Dublin: The Stationary Office, 1954), Table 96, p. 128.

17 Chris Craig, "Sources for courses: the facts behind the faces," *Fortnight* (supplement to no. 295, May, 1991), pp. 4-5.

18 For backgrounds on the Irish settlement pattern, see: Colin Holmes, "The impact of immigration on British Society, 1870-1980," in Theo Barker and Michael Drake (eds.), *Population and Society in Britain, 1850-1980* (New York: New York University Press, 1982), pp. 172-95; M.A.G. O'Tuathaigh, "The Irish in nineteenth-century Britain: Problems of Integration," *Transactions of the Royal Historical Society*, 5 ser., vol 31 (1981), pp. 149-73; E.D. Steele, "The Irish Presence in the North of England, 1850-1914," *Northern History*, vol. 12 (1976), pp. 220-41.

Among the published studies (why, one wonders, have so few of the Ph.D. theses on the Irish in Britain been published?), the following stand out: Brenda Collins, "Irish Emigration to Dundee and Paisley during the first half of the nineteenth century," in J.M. Goldstrom and L.A. Clarkson (eds.), *Irish Population, Economy, and Society* (Oxford: Clarendon press, 1981), pp. 195-212; Frances Finnegan, *Poverty and Prejudice. A Study of Irish Immigrants in York, 1840-1875* (Cork: Cork University press, 1982); R. Lawton, "Irish Immigration to England and Wales in the mid-Nineteenth Century," *Irish Geography* no. 1 (1959), pp. 35-54 (despite its title, Lawton's study deals mostly with Liverpool); Lynn H. Lees, *Exiles of Erin. Irish Migrants in Victorian London* (Ithica: Cornell University Press, 1979), and "Mid-Victorian Migration and the Irish Family Economy," *Victorian Studies* vol. 20 (Autumn 1976), pp. 25-43; R.D. Lobban, "The Irish Community in Greenock in the Nineteenth Century," *Irish Geography*, vol. 6 (1971), pp. 270-81; W.J. Lowe, "Social Agencies among the Irish in Lancashire during the mid-nineteenth century," *Saothar* vol. 3 (1977), pp. 15-20; Roger Swift, "The Outcast Irish in the British Victorian City: Problems and Perspectives," *Irish Historical Studies*, vol. 25 (May 1987), pp. 264-76; John Werly, "The Irish in Manchester, 1832-49," *Irish Historical Studies*, vol. 18 (March 1973), pp. 345-58.

Two volumes edited by Roger Swift and Sheridan Gilley contain a number of essays on specific communities. See Swift and Gilley (eds.) *The Irish in the Victorian City* (London: Croom Helm, 1985), which contains essays on Bristol (David Large), York (Frances Finnegan), Glasgow and Liverpool (Tom Gallagher), Edinburgh (Bernard Aspinwall and John McCaffrey, and Stockport (Pauline Millward). See also Swift and Gilley (eds.), *The Irish in Britain, 1815-1939* (London: Pinter Publishers, 1989) which contains an essay on Stafford (John Herson).

19   *Census of England and Wales for the Year 1861 General Report*, pp. 160-61, H.C., 1863 [3221], liii, part i.
20   *Census of Great Britain. Population Tables, Scotland*, p. 1038, H.C. [1691-II], 1852-53, lxxxviii, part II.
21   David Fitzpatrick, "'A peculiar tramping people': the Irish in Britain, 1801-70," in W.E. Vaughan (ed.), *A New History of Ireland*, vol. V, *Ireland under the Union, part I, 1801-70* (Oxford: Clarendon Press, 1989), p. 634.
22   Colin G. Pooley, "Segregation or integration? The residential experience of the Irish in mid-Victorian Britain," in Swift and Gilley (1989), p. 60. The entire essay (pp. 60-83) is worth close attention.
23   *Census of England and Wales for the Year 1871, General Report*, vol. 4, p. 70, H.C. 1873 [c.872-I], lxxi, part II.
24   Swift and Gilley (1989), p. 3.
25   Harris, "The Nearest Place ...", p. 4:40.
26 *Eighth Decennial Census of the Population of Scotland*, vol. II, p. xxxiv, H.C., 1873 [C.84], xxiii.
27   Ryan, p. 48.
28   Henry Mayhew, *London Labour and the London Poor* (London: 1864), vol. II, p. 130, quoted in Jackson, p. 90.
29   Pooley, in Swift and Gilley (1989), p. 80.
30   *Observer* 14 Dec. 1928, notice reproduced in Kevin O'Connor, *The Irish in Britain* (London: Sidgwick and Jackson, 1972), p. 69.
31   Ryan, p. 54.
32   Lees, "Mid-Victorian Migration and the Irish Family Economy," p. 42.
33   Indeed, as the case here being discussed illustrates, not only can competent scholars come to divergent views of the usefulness of a given data-set, but a single scholar can, at various points in his or her career, have different opinions. For example, in 1980, that most conscientious of diaspora scholars, David Fitzpatrick, took the 1876-1920 data about migration to Britain to be an understatement, but a balanced one — that is a "sample" — from which he concluded that "the permanent emigrants" tended to leave regions with comparatively large non-agricultural labour sectors ("Irish emigration in the later nineteenth century," p. 130.) After re-examining these data, he concluded (in 1989) that "one should beware of drawing inferences from the official emigration returns ..." because they were woefully inadequate as especially concerning Leinster and Connaught ("A curious middle place ..." p. 20.)
34   Fitzpatrick, "A peculiar tramping people," pp. 629-30.
35   For an example of an ingenious attempt to break out of the mid-twentieth century's lack of information on British religious patterns, see A.E.C.W. Spencer, "Catholics in Britain and Ireland:

Regional Contrasts," in D.A. Coleman, *Demography of Immigrants and Minority Groups in the United Kingdom* (London: Academic Press, 1982), pp. 213-43.

36 Sean Glynn, "Irish Immigration to Britain, 1911-1951: Patterns and Policy," *Irish Economic and Social History* vol. 8 (1981), p. 52.

37 For discussions of this Protestant emigration from Southern Ireland, see Glynn, pp. 50-69; Kurt Bowen, *Protestants in a Catholic State. Ireland's Privileged Minority* (Kingston and Montreal: McGill-Queen's University Press, 1983), pp. 20-46; Robert E. Kennedy, Jr., *The Irish. Emigration, Marriage, and Fertility* (Berkeley: University of California Press, 1973), pp. 110-38.

38 Craig, pp. 4-5.

39 Fitzpatrick, "A peculiar tramping people," p. 630. This is not in any way to denigrate work that has been done on intra-Irish sectarians in Great Britain, merely to suggest that it has to be kept in perspective. For excellent studies see, for example, Tom Gallagher, "A Tale of Two Cities: Communal Strife in Glasgow and Liverpool before 1914," in Swift and Gilley (1985), pp. 106-29; Frank Neal, *Sectarian Violence. The Liverpool Experience, 1819-1914. An Aspect of Anglo-Irish History* (Manchester: Manchester University Press, 1988). Strongly recommended is Alan Bleasdale's amazing film *No Surrender* which puts everything into perspective.

40 Ryan, pp. 59-60.

41 The argument between L.P. Curtis (the "hard" side) and Sheridan Gilley ("soft") is summarized in O'Tuathaigh, in Swift and Gilley, (1985), pp. 20-21.

42 Ryan, p. 63.

43 Spencer, pp. 237- 41.

44 Gerard Connolly, "Irish and Catholic: Myth or Reality? Another sort of Irish and the Renewal of the Clerical Profession among Catholics in England, 1791-1918," in Swift and Gilley (1985), pp. 225-32.

45 Ibid., pp. 232-35.

46 See, for example, *Commission on Emigration and other Population Problems, 1948-1954* (Dublin: Stationary Office, 1954).

47 Ryan, pp. 66-67.

48 Nesca A. Robb, *An Ulsterwoman in England 1924-1941* (Cambridge: Cambridge University Press, 1942), p. 1.

CHAPTER NINE

1 This is North American usage. Confusingly, British Isles usage sometimes employs "first generation" to mean the first generation born in the new homeland. In this book North American

usage is adopted.

2   Andrew M. Greeley, "The American Irish: A Report from Great Ireland," *International Journal of Comparative Sociology*, vol. 29 (1979), pp. 67-81; Greeley, "Ethnic Minorities in the United States: Demographic Perspectives," *International Journal of Group Tensions*, vol. 7 (1977), pp. 84-97; Greeley, *Ethnicity in the United States: A Preliminary Reconnaissance*, John Wiley and Sons, New York, 1974 pp. 35-89; Greeley, "The Success and Assimilation of Irish Protestants and Irish Catholics in the, United States," *SSR*, vol. 72, no. 4 (July 1988), pp. 229-36; Fred Boal, "Who Are the `Irish Americans'?," *Fortnight*, no. 155, (Oct. 1977), pp. 4-5.

3   George Gallup, Jr. and Jim Castelli, *The People's Religion. American Faith in the 90s*, (New York: MacMillan, 1989), pp. 119-22.

4   Barry Kosmin, et.al., *Research Report. The National Survey of Religious Identification, 1989-90. Selected Tabulations*, (CUNY Graduate Center, 1991), p. 14.

5   D.G. Boyce, "Sense and Sensibility," *Irish Literary Supplement*, (Fall, 1990), p. 28.

6   Greeley, "Success and Assimiliation", p. 229.

7   See Donald H. Akenson, "Why the Accepted Estimates of the Ethnicity of the American People, 1790, Are Unacceptable," *William and Mary Quarterly*, 3rd Ser., vol. 41 (Jan. 1984), pp. 102-19.

8   The problem was that persons returning more than one ethnic origin were lumped into an "other" category which embraced roughly half the population! See Charles A. Price, "Methods of Estimating the Size of Groups," in Stephen Thernstrom (ed.), *Harvard Encyclopedia of American Ethnic Groups*, (Cambridge: Harvard University Press, 1980), pp. 1033-34. The reader should be especially cautious of the Census Bureau's misleading presentation of these data, as, for example in *Statistical Abstract of the United States, 1981* (Washington, D.C.: U.S. Bureau of Census 1981), Table 42, p. 35.

9   Once again, individuals were allowed to list multiple ancestries, rather than a single dominant one, so that 55 percent listed two or more in the 1980 census. Thus, one individual might leave a single mark on the ethnic canvas, while others could designate a dozen or more ethnicities.   The data on ethnicity therefore cannot be related to any other variable, nor, in fact, can it serve as anything but the basis for the crudest guessing about what the real ethnic composition of the country actually is.

10   Price in Thernstrom (ed.), p. 1040.

11   For a fascinating discussion of this fear of collecting religious data and especially of the trouble which arose when it was proposed

to include religion in the 1960 census, see William Petersen, "Religious Statistics in the United States," *Journal for the Scientific Study of Religion*, vol. 1 (1965), pp. 165-78. This article also discusses the Census Bureau's suppression (!) of the data it had collected in the 1957 voluntary-sample study.

12   A very useful version of that census was compiled by J.D.B. Debow, superintendent of the U.S. census, *A Statistical View of the United States...*, Beverley Tucker, Senate Printer, Washington, D.C., 1854.

13   Joseph A. King, *The Irish Lumberman-Farmer. Fitzgeralds, Harrigans, and Others* (Lafayette, Cal: privately printed, 1982), Appendix D, pp. 228-29.

14   Niles Carpenter, *Immigrants and their Children. A Study based on Census Statistics relative to the Foreign born and the Native Whites of Foreign or Mixed Parentage*, (Washington, D.C.: Census Monographs VII, Government Printing Office, 1927), p. 2.

Although the U.S. Census Bureau's collections of ethnic data went no further than the migrants and their offspring, it is of course possible to do extrapolations of the gross number of persons in the third generation. This was attempted by the Census Bureau for the 1920 census (See Carpenter, p. 92) and, further, amateur demographers were always willing to try to establish the total strength of the Irish ethnic group from the limited knowledge available concerning the first two generations in the United States. Michael J. O'Brien, historiographer of the American-Irish Historical Society, surveyed some of the early attempts and shrewdly, if tiredly, remarked that "to form any reliable estimate of the numerical strength of the Irish and their descendants in the United States would, I believe, be a hopeless task and while several have attempted to do so, I am of the opinion that all such estimates should be discarded as mere conjecture." Michael J. O'Brien, "The Irish in the United States," in *The Glories of Ireland*, Phoenix, ltd., (Washington, D.C., 1914), edited by Joseph Dunn and P.J. Lennox, p. 208.

15   E.P. Hutchinson, "Notes on Immigration Statistics of the United States," *American Statistical Association Journal*, vol. 53 (December 1958), pp. 968-79.

I am here leaving aside entirely the problem involved with the counterflow from the U.S. to various foreign countries. Net migration data are what one requires, but in the absence of records on alien departures from the U.S., there is no way of measuring net immigration before 1908. (Carpenter, p. 3).

16   Estimate found in J.D.B. DeBow, *The Industrial Resources Statistics etc. of the United States*, (New York: Appleton, third ed., 1854), vol. 3, pp. 396, 424, cited in Hutchinson, p. 975.

17   Edward Jarvis, "Immigration," *Atlantic Monthly*, vol. 29 (April 1872), p. 456, quoted in Hutchinson, p. 976.

18   I am here avoiding the virtually insoluble question of how great was the counter-flow of British Isles-born persons who shipped to the U.S. and came from thence to Canada. Undoubtedly, it was much less than the flow from Canada into the U.S., but whether it was 2 percent or 20.3 percent or 30 percent, no one really knows (see Hutchinson, p. 976).

19   Ibid., pp. 974-81.

20   Computed from ibid., p. 981.

For instance, the Irish-born constituted 4.81 percent of the U.S. population in 1870, while in 1871 the Irish-born constituted 6.2 percent of the Canadian population. Compare the text above, with *Seventh Census of Canada, 1931* (Ottawa: Kings Printer, 1936), vol. I, p. 517.

21   Leon E. Truesdell, *The Canadian Born in the United States. An Analysis of the Statistics of the Canadian Element in the Population of the United States, 1850 to 1930* (New Haven: Yale University Press, 1943), pp. 10, 19, 30, 32.

22   The precise date is problematical. The Irish were the largest Canadian ethnic group in 1881, but the English had surpassed them by 1901. Unfortunately, the 1891 census did not yield ethnicity data in a form comparable to that provided by the censuses of 1881 and 1901, so one necessarily must be vague. For the data, see *Seventh Census of Canada, 1931*, vol. I, p. 710.

CHAPTER TEN

1   For entry into the large body of historical writing on the Irish in the USA, see: R.A. Burchell, "The Historiography of the American-Irish," *Immigrants and Minorities*, vol. 1, no. 3 (Nov. 1982), pp. 281-305; David Noel Doyle, "The regional bibliography of Irish America, 1800-1930: a review and addendum," *Irish Historical Studies*, vol. 23, no. 91 (May 1983), pp. 254-83; Seamus P. Metress, *The Irish-American Experience. A Guide to the Literature*, University Press of America, Inc., (Washington, D.C.: 1981); Seamus P. Metress and Kathleen R. Annable, *The Irish in the Great Lakes Region: a Bibliographic Survey* (Toledo, Ohio: Great Lakes Irish Studies, 1990).

2   David Fitzpatrick, "Irish emigration in the later nineteenth century," *Irish Historical Studies* vol. 22 (Sept 1980), p. 129.

3   Dale B. Light, Jr., "The role of Irish-American organizations in assimilation and community formation," in P.J. Drudy (ed.), *The Irish in America: Emigration, Assimilation and Impact* (Cambridge: Cambridge University Press, 1985), p. 114. The

entire essay (pp. 113-41) is important.

4   Kerby A. Miller, *Emigrants and Exiles. Ireland and the Irish Exodus to North America*, Oxford University Press, New York, 1985, p. 556.

5   Ibid., p. 198.

6   Ibid., p. 238.

7   Ibid., p. 240.

8   Ibid., p. 259.

9   Ibid., p. 277.

10   Ibid., p. 119.

11   Ibid., p. 8.

12   Gordon Darroch, "Class in nineteenth-century, central Ontario: a reassessment of the crisis and demise of small producers during early industrialization, 1861-1871," in Gregory S. Kealey (ed.), *Class, Gender, and Region: Essays in Canadian Historical Sociology* (Committee on Canadian Labour History, St. John's, Nfld., 1988), pp. 49-72; A. Gordon Darroch and Michael Ornstein, "Ethnicity and Class. Transitions over a Decade: Ontario, 1861-1871," Canadian Historical Association, *History Papers, 1984*, pp. 111-37; A. Gordon Darroch and Michael D. Ornstein, "Ethnicity and Occupational Structure in Canada in 1871: the Vertical Mosaic in Historical Perspective," *Canadian Historical Review*, vol. 61, no. 3 (Sept. 1980), pp. 305-33. A wide-ranging book, expanding their research design, is in press.

13   Oliver MacDonagh, "The Irish Famine Emigration to the United States," *Perspectives in American History*, vol. X (1976), p. 410.

14   Thus, Kerby Miller in *The Journal of Religion*, vol. 70 (January, 1990), pp. 105-106.

15   Darroch and Ornstein, "Ethnicity and Occupational Structure ...", p. 320-25.

16   Compare the table in Darroch and Ornstein, "Ethnicity and Class ...", pp. 121-22.

17   Derived from *Report of the Immigration Commission. Occupations of the First and Second Generations of Immigrants in the United States* (Washington: Government Printing Office, 1911), Table 2, p. 12.

18   The limits are: (1) occupational categories which are not entirely revealing; (2) Protestants of Irish background are not separated out, and they probably comprised about one-fifth of each generation; (3) absence of comparative data for the entire U.S. population; and (4) a curious definition of "second generation."

This included all persons born in the United states who had one *or* both parents born outside of the United States. That meant (a) that double-counting occurred; a person, born in New York, for example, of an Italian mother and an Irish father fit the commission's definition both of an Irish person of the second generation and of an Italian person of the second generation. Further (b), a person born of, for example, an Irish-born mother and a "native American" (that is, of a person of third generation) well might have assumed all the ethnic attributes of the "native American" side of the family, and yet was included in the Irish second generation totals. This was not a mere technicality: intermarriages of Irish Catholics with Catholic Francophones (particularly in Maine, Vermont, New Hampshire, and western Massachusetts) were frequent, as were marriages with German Catholics in the mid-west.

19   David Noel Doyle, *Irish Americans, Native Rights and National Empires: the structure, divisions and attitudes of the Catholic minority in the decade of expansion, 1890-1901* (New York: Arno Press, 1976), pp. 49-63.

20   Andrew Greeley, "The success and Assimilation of Irish Protestants and Irish Catholics in the United States," *SSR*, vol. 72, no. 4 (July, 1988), pp. 229-35.

21   The points outlined in the text are documented in detail in three publications by Andrew M. Greeley: *The American Catholic. A Social Portrait* (New York: Basic Books, 1977); "Ethnic Minorities in the United States: Demographic Perspectives," *International Journal of Group Tensions*, vol. 7 (1977), pp. 64-97; *Ethnicity, Denomination, and Inequality* (New York: Sage Research Papers in the Social Sciences, 1976).

22   David Noel Doyle, "Catholicism, politics and Irish America since 1890: some critical consideration,: in P.J. Drudy, *The Irish in America: Emigration, Assimilation, and Impact* (Cambridge: Cambridge University Press, 1985), p. 192.

23   George Patterson (ed.), *A Few Remains of the Rev. James MacGregor, D.D.* (Edinburgh: William Oliphant and Co., 1859), p. 259.

24   For an assessment of the state of Catholic folk religion in the late eighteenth century and in the first half of the nineteenth, see S.J. Connolly, *Priests and People in Pre-Famine Ireland, 1780-1845* (Dublin: Gill and MacMillan, 1982).

25   W.W. Sweet, *The Story of Religion in America* (New York: 1930), cited in Audrey Lockhart, *Some Aspects of Emigration from Ireland to the North American Colonies between 1660 and 1775*

(New York: Arno Press, 1976), p. 143.

26 Francis S. Curran, *Catholics in Colonial Law* (Chicago: Loyola University Press, 1963), passim; Lockhart, pp. 139-43.

27 David Noel Doyle, "The Irish in North America, 1776-1845," in W.E. Vaughan (ed.), *A New History of Ireland*, Vol V. *Ireland under the Union, part i, 1801-70* (Oxford: Clarendon Press, 1989), p. 697.

28 For a shrewd appreciation of O'Brien, see Margaret E. Fitzgerald and Joseph A. King, *The Uncounted Irish in Canada and the United States* (Toronto: P.D. Meany Publishers, 1990), pp. 147-78.

29 Michael J. O'Brien, "An Authoritative Account of the earliest Irish pioneers in New England," orig. pub. 1919, reprinted in Michael J. O'Brien, *Irish Settlers in America. A Consolidation of Articles from the Journal of the American Irish Historical Society (in two volumes)*, (Baltimore: Genealogical Publishing Co., 1979), vol. I, p. 433.

30 "How the descendants of Irish settlers in America were written into History as `Anglo-Saxons' and `Scotch-Irish'," orig. pub. 1919, repub. ibid., I, p. 424.

31 "*List of Persons Whose Names have been changed in Massachusetts* (Baltimore: Geneological Publishing Co., 1972) shows almost invariable changes from Irish to Anglo names." Dennis Clark, *Hibernia America. The Irish and Regional Cultures* (New York: Greenwood Press, 1986), p. 46n7.

32 David Noel Doyle, *Ireland, Irishmen and Revolutionary America, 1760-1820* (Dublin and Cork: Mercier Press, 1981), pp. 52, 61, 71, 73, 74. I have distilled Doyle's estimates from his prose, I hope accurately. Doyle, "The Irish in North America, 1776-1845," in Vaughan, p. 692, gives a second, somewhat different set of figures.

33 Thomas D'Arcy McGee, *A History of the Irish Settlers in North America, from the earliest period to the census of 1850* (Boston: Patrick Donahoe, 1852), pp. 75-76.

34 McGee, it should be noted, disagreed with John Carroll's estimate, and thought that "100,000 Catholics" [including the non-Irish] would be nearer the mark. Even if this is the case, a significant proportion of Irish Catholics had changed religion.

35 The limit to the credibility of such estimates is whether or not one accepts the 1790 ethnicity estimates. The 1790 census left behind a fairly full set of names of the heads of households (whites

only). From those names several attempts have been made to calculate the ethnicity of the U.S. population in 1790: by the U.S. Census Bureau early in the twentieth century, by the American Council of Learned Societies in the late 1920s and early 1930s; by David Noel Doyle in the 1980s (see *Ireland Irishmen* ..., pp. 75-76) and at about the same time by Forrest McDonald and Ellen Shapiro McDonald ("The Ethnic Origins of the American People, 1790" *William and Mary Quarterly* 3rd ser., vol. 41, 1984, pp. 85-101).

For reasons that I explain in detail in "Why the Accepted Estimates of the Ethnicity of the American People, 1790, are Unacceptable," (*William and Mary Quarterly*, 3rd ser., vol. 41, Jan. 1984, pp. 102-19), none of the various uses of surnames as proxies for ethnic identifiers works, and this despite heroic amounts of effort spent on the task by the individuals named above. Sadly, this lesson has been ignored in the recent work of Aaron Fogelman, "Migrations to the Thirteen British North American Colonies, 1700-1775: New Estimates," *Journal of Interdisciplinary History*, vol. 22 (Spring 1992), pp. 691-709.

36   Doyle, "Catholicism, politics, and Irish America since 1890," p. 217*n*6.

37   Ibid., p. 192.

38   These statements are based on the same sources as are cited in notes 20 and 21 above.

39   Greeley, "The Success and Assimilation of Irish Protestants and Irish Catholics in the United States," pp. 229-30.

40   The student may wish to follow a fascinating scholarly by-way which, for want of space, I have not been able to discuss: this is the "Celtic thesis" concerning the Irish and the American south. This is an attempt to do two things simultaneously: (a) to break out of the usual narrow national categories in immigration-cultural studies, and to aggregate as a social force the various Celtic groups, Irish Catholics, Ulster-Scots, Cornish, Welsh, Scots, Manx, and (b) to explain some of the nineteenth-century South's social and economic patterns by reference to the southern settlement pattern of these groups. For an introduction, see: Forrest McDonald and Grady McWhiney, "The Antebellum Southern Herdsman: A Reinterpretation," *Journal of Southern History,* vol. 41 (May 1975), pp. 147-66; Forrest McDonald, "The Ethnic Factor in Alabama History: A Neglected Dimension," *Alabama Review,* vol. 31 (1978), pp. 256-65; Forrest McDonald, "The Celtic South," *History Today,* vol. 30 (July 1980), pp. 11-15.

41   For rigorous scholarly discussions of central episodes in the early settlement of the Ulster-Scots in Ireland, see: Raymond

Gillespie, *Colonial Ulster. The Settlement of East Ulster 1600-1641* (Cork: Cork University Press, 1985); Michael Perceval-Maxwell, *The Scottish Migration to Ulster in the Reign of James I* (London: Routledge and Kegan Paul, 1973).

42   On the demonstrably Irish aspect of the Irish Presbyterian's identity, see, Clark, *Hibernia-America*, p. xv; Doyle, "The Irish in North America, 1776-1845," in Vaughan, p. 692; O'Brien, "Some Examples of the 'Scotch-Irish' in America," (orig. pub. 1915), reprinted O'Brien, (1979), vol. I, p. 259.

43   James G. Leyburn, "The Scotch-Irish," *American Heritage*, vol. 22 (Dec. 1970), p. 31.

44   For a survey of early usage of the term, see James G. Leyburn, *The Scotch-Irish. A Social History* (Chapel Hill: University of North Carolina Press, 1962), Appendix 1, pp. 327-34. See also the *Oxford English Dictionary*.

45   Maldwyn A. Jones, "Scotch-Irish," in Stephan Thernstrom (ed.) *Harvard Encyclopedia of American Ethnic Groups* (Cambridge: Harvard University Press, 1980), p. 906.

46   Leyburn, p. 331.

47   Ibid.

48   Jones, p. 907.

49   Ruth Dame Coolidge, "The Scotch-Irish in New England," *New England Magazine* new ser., vol. 42 (1910), pp. 747-48. Less hagiographical, and, indeed, valuable in parts, were two products of the same era, namely, Charles A. Hanna, *The Scotch-Irish or the Scot in North Britain, North Ireland, and North America* (New York: G.P. Putnam's Son, 1902), 2 vols; Henry Ford Jones, *The Scotch-Irish in America* (Princeton: Princeton University Press, 1915).

50 For example, Michael J. O'Brien, "Historical items Obtainable from the Newspapers," orig. pub. 1928, repub. (1979) in O'Brien, vol. II, esp. p. 520.

51 Wayland F. Dunaway, *The Scotch-Irish of Colonial Pennsylvania* (orig. pub. Chapel Hill: University of North Carolina Press, 1944, reprinted, Hamden Conn: Archon Books, 1962), p. 5.

For more recent studies, see E.R.R. Green, (ed.) *Essays in Scotch-Irish History* (London: Routledge and Kegan Paul, 1969); R.J. Dickson, *Ulster Emigration to Colonial America, 1717-1775* (London: Routledge and Kegan Paul, 1966). There is a good deal of relevant material in the classic *Ireland and Irish Emigration to the New World from 1815 to the Famine* by William Forbes Adams (New Haven: Yale University Press, 1932). A recent volume aimed at a popular audience is Rory Fitzpatrick, *God's Frontiersmen. The Scots-Irish Epic* (London: Weidenfeld and Nicolson, 1989).

52   Dale T. Knobel, *Paddy and the Republic. Ethnicity and*

Nationality in Antebellum America (Middleton: Wesleyan University Press, 1986).

53   The data in Table 38 are from U.K. and Irish sources which permits the creation of a longer time-series and for all of North America, not just the USA. On the recipient side, the U.S. Department of State under an act of 1819, collected information upon incoming immigrants, but up to 1868, when the Bureau of Statistics took over, the returns are open to serious questions. See E.P. Hutchinson, "Notes on Immigration Statistics of the United States," *American Statistical Association, Journal* vol. 53 (Dec. 1958), pp. 968-79.

On the failure of pre-Famine U.S. immigration statistics, and of the eccentric attempts by U.S. officials to compensate for undercounting, see Charlotte Erickson, "Emigration from the British Isles to the U.S.A. in 1831," *Population Studies* vol. 35 (July 1981), pp. 180-81.

For a comparison of the actual numbers reported for the major series data on Irish migration to the U.S.A. for 1852-1910, see Cormac Ó Gráda, "Note on Nineteenth Century Irish Emigration Statistics," *Population Studies* vol. 29 (1973), Table 1, p. 144. Ó Gráda believes that from 1852 onwards the U.S. immigration data are more accurate than the U.K. out-migration data, as far as the Irish are concerned. Actually, the two sources are fairly close in total migrants, but vary considerably in some individual years.

54   *Commission on Emigration and other Population Problems, 1948-1954* (Dublin: The Stationery Office, 1954), Table 95, p. 126.

55   Arnold Schrier, "Ireland and the American Emigration, 1850-1900," (Ph.D., Northwestern University, 1956), p. 231.

56   See *Census of Canada, 1870-71*, vol. IV, *Censuses of Canada, 1665-1871*, pp. 132-362.

57   Schrier, p. 231.

58   *Historical Statistics of the United States. Colonial Times to 1970* (Washington, D.C.: Bureau of the Census, 1975), Table C228-295, p. 117.

59   M.C. Urquhart and K.A.H. Buckley, *Historical Statistics of Canada* (Cambridge: Cambridge University press, 1965) Series A170-199, p. 20.

60   A badly-needed modern history of the Irish in Canada has recently appeared: Cecil J. Houston and William J. Smyth, *Irish Emigration and Canadian Settlement: Patterns, Links, and Letters* (Toronto: University of Toronto Press, 1990). A helpful brief introduction is David Wilson, *The Irish in Canada* (Ottawa: Canadian Historical Association, 1989), for which I provided the substantive material. The two-volume set *The Untold Story: The*

Irish in Canada, edited by Robert O'Driscoll and Lorna Reynolds (Toronto: Celtic Arts, 1988) is a wide-ranging collection of articles. The classic older study is Nicholas Flood Davin, *The Irishman in Canada* (London: Sampson Low, Marston and Co., 1977).

61   Darroch and Ornstein, "Ethnicity and Occupational Structure in Canadian 1871," Table 1, p. 312; Cecil J. Houston and William J. Smyth, *Irish Emigration ...*, p. 226.

62   *Census of Canada, 1931* vol. I, *Summary*, p. 710.

63   Sheldon J. Godfrey, "Brief submitted to the Special Joint Committee on a Renewed Canada on behalf of the Ontario region of the Canadian Council of Christians and Jews," (Oct. 1991), pp. 3-4.

64   Any serious look at the social history of Irish in Canada must be based upon the Canadian census data, first in its aggregate form, and secondly upon the individual manuscript census returns. The 1931 census of Canada reprinted earlier data in a convenient form. The work of Darroch and Ornstein, based upon the manuscript census material, is of interest not only to historians of the Irish in Canada, but to ethnic historians of any sort.   It is the most sophisticated research design and analysis done in ethnic studies any place in the English-speaking world. See the items cited above, (note 12).

On recent ethnicity data, see Sheila T. McGee and Victoria M. Esses, "The Irish in Canada: A Demographic Study Based on the 1986 Census," *Canadian Journal of Irish Studies* vol. 16 (July 1990), pp. 1-14.   The nature of the Canadian data on the Irish (as well as the character of the U.S. data) is discussed in detail in Donald Harman Akenson, *Being Had: Historians, Evidence, and the Irish in North America* (Toronto: P.D. Meany Publishers, 1985).

65   The Irish in Newfoundland provide a great opportunity for the historian of North America. They need a full history. For background, see John Mannion's, "The Waterford Merchants and the Irish-Newfoundland Provisions Trade, 1770-1820," *Canadian Papers in Rural History*, vol. 3 (1982), pp. 178-203, and his evocative *Point Lance in Transition: The Transformation of a Newfoundland Outport* (Toronto: McClelland and Stewart, 1976).

Because of the vigorous Folklore Department at the Memorial University of Newfoundland in St. John's, there is more Irish folklore collected for Newfoundland than for the rest of Canada combined.   See the department's various publications.   Historical geography as a field is also strong. For a brilliant study of a 300 year-old Irish fishing village, see Gerald L. Pocius, *A Place to Belong: Community Order and Everyday Space in Calvert, Newfoundland* (Montreal and Kingston: McGill-Queen's University Press, 1991).

66   Some material on Prince Edward Island is found in Terrence Murphy and Cyril J. Byrne, *Religion and Identity. The Experience of Irish and Scottish Catholics in Atlantic Canada* (St. John's, Nfld: Jesperson Press, 1987).
67   Much of the work on Halifax has been done by Terence M. Punch: "The Irish in Halifax, 1836-71, A Study in Ethnic Assimilation" (M.A., Dalhousie University, 1976); *Irish Halifax: The Immigrant Generation, 1815-1859* (Halifax: Ethnic Heritage Series, 1981); and many articles in genealogical publications. See also J.S. Martell, *Immigration to and Emigration from Nova Scotia, 1815-1838* (Halifax: Public Archives of Nova Scotia, 1942); Herbert L. Stewart, *the Irish in Nova Scotia. Annals of the Charitable Irish Society of Halifax (1786-1836)* (Halifax: Charitable Irish Society, 1949); Douglas F. Campbell (ed.) *Banked Fires. The Ethnics of Nova Scotia* (Halifax: Scribbers' press, 1978) is industrious amateur work, as is A.A. MacKenzie's *The Irish in Cape Breton* (Antigonish: Formac Publishing, 1979).
68   Until recently, the historiography of the Irish in New Brunswick has been largely a footnote to the industry of Peter M. Toner. See especially his "Occupation and Ethnicity: the Irish in New Brunswick," *Canadian Ethnic Studies* vol. 20 (1988), pp. 155-65, and his editing of *Historical Essays on the Irish in New Brunswick: New Ireland Remembered* (Fredericton: New Ireland Press, 1988).
       A very useful set of essays, which includes new work on New Brunswick is Thomas P. Power (ed.), *The Irish in Atlantic Canada. 1780-1900* (Fredericton: New Ireland Press, 1988). There are a number of important observations about the Irish in New Brunswick (and elsewhere) in Margaret E. Fitzgerald and Joseph A. King, *The Uncounted Irish in Canada and the United States* (Toronto: P.D. Meany Publishers, 1990).
69   The historical literature on the Irish who settled west of Ontario is severely limited. See, however, "Some Irish Figures in Colonial Days," by Margaret A. Ormsby, *British Columbia Historical Quarterly*, vol. 14, nos. 1 and 2 (1950), pp. 61-82, and Bruce Proudfoot, "Irish Settlers in Alberta," *Ulster Folklife*, vols. 15-16 (1970), pp. 216-23. See also the articles on the Irish in Western Canada in O'Driscoll and Reynolds (eds.) vol. I, pp. 381-450.
       On the Irish in Quebec see ibid., pp. 253-305, especially the article by Marianna Gallagher, "The Irish in Quebec," pp. 253-61.
70   An important breakthrough in the method of North American immigration studies is made in Bruce S. Elliott, *Irish Migrants in the Canadas. A New Approach* (Kingston and Montreal: McGill-Queen's University Press, 1988). Also useful is Donald

Notes

Harman Akenson, *The Irish in Ontario. A Study in Rural History* (Montreal and Kingston: McGill-Queen's University Press, 1984). Material culture in Ontario, New Brunswick, and Newfoundland is discussed in John J. Mannion, *Irish Settlements in Eastern Canada. A Study of Cultural Transfer and Adaptation* (Toronto: University of Toronto Press, 1974). This work, however is flawed by the fact that "Dr. Mannion finds it unnecessary to explain that by Irish he means Irish Catholic." (*Irish Historical Studies*, vol. 19, March 1975, p. 358).

On the Irish in urban areas, there is relevant material in Michael Katz's well-known *The People of Hamilton, Canada West. Family and Class in a Mid-Nineteenth Century City* (Cambridge: Harvard University Press, 1975). Readers should recognize, however, that Katz has confused Irish immigrants with the Irish ethnic group, so his conclusions must be taken with a good deal of skepticism. More solid is Barrie Drummond Dyster, "Toronto, 1840-1860: Making it a British Protestant Town," (Ph.D., University of Toronto, 1970).

Various aspects of Canadian Orangeism have been analyzed in several articles by Hereward Senior and synthesized in *Orangeism: The Canadian Phase* (Toronto: McGraw-Hill-Ryerson, 1972). A very valuable recent study of the Order is by Cecil J. Houston and William J. Smyth, *The Sash Canada Wore: A Historical Geography of the Orange Order in Canada* (Toronto: University of Toronto Press, 1980). See also the heuristic biography of the founder of Canadian Orangeism: D.H. Akenson, *The Orangeman. the Life and Times of Ogle Gowan* (Toronto: James Lorimer, 1986).

Of more specialized studies, four deserve special mention: John Irwin Cooper, "Irish Immigration and the Canadian Church before the Middle of the 19th Century," *Journal of the Canadian Church Historical Society*, vol. 2 (May 1955), pp. 1-20; R. Cole Harris, et al., "The Settlement of Mono Township," *Canadian Geographer*, vol. 19 (1975), pp. 1-17; J. Richard Houston, *Numbering the Survivors: A History of the Standish Family of Ireland, Ontario, and Alberta* (Agincourt, Ontario: 1979); and the excellent chapter on the Orange Order in Gregory S. Kealey, *Toronto Workers Respond to Industrial Capitalism, 1867-1892* (Toronto: University of Toronto Press, 1980).

CHAPTER ELEVEN

1   Max Ferguson, "My Irish Humor," in Robert O'Driscoll and Lorna Reynolds, (eds.), *The Untold Story: The Irish in Canada* (Toronto: Celtic Arts of Canada, 1988), vol. II, p. 733.

Irish Diaspora

Index

Irish born, 198; occupations, 200-203; provincial origins, 203-07; religion, 208-11, ethnicity, 210-14
Greeley, Andrew M., 243-44, 251-52

Hanham, H.J., 143
Harris, Ruth-Ann, 192-94
Henderson, R.H., 133
Hattersley, A.F., 137
Hockly, Harold, 133, 137
Humphreys, Emily, 176

Ideal type, as concept, 52-53, 61, 218-19
Indian Civil Service, 145-46
"Irish," as concept, 6-10, 15-16, 218, 221, 233-34, 252, 254
Irish-born, as concept, 9-10, 218-19
Irish language, 39-40
Irish national system of education, 40-41
Irish-American, as concept, 252
Italians, 14

Jeeves, Alan, 137
Jews, 35-36, 243-44, 251, 289n13
Jones, E. Morse, 133, 137
Joyce, James, 7

Kati-Kati, 7-8
Keegan, Gerald, 16
Kelleher, John, 59-60, 61, 141-42, 233-34
Kelly, Ned, 94
Kennedy, Robert E., Jr., 159-61
Keppel-Jones, Arthur, 137
Kosmin, Barry A., 219-20

Larikanism, 94
Latin America, 13
Light, Dale Jr., 235
Literacy, 39-41, 279n32
Lost Persons column, 75

MacAmhlaigh, Donald, 149
McCleland, Ann, 187
McCleland, Elizabeth, 77-78
McClelland, David, 34
McClure, Alexander, 176-77
McClure, James, 176-77
McConville, Chris, 177-78, 183
McCormack, John, 224
McCracken, Donal, 133
MacDonagh, Oliver, 39, 286n31
MacGregor, James, 245-46
McSparron, Oliver, 75-76
"Malthusian," 19
Marx, Karl, 36-37
"Match," 163
Matched-twin studies, 60
Mayhew, Henry, 200
Mental illness, 119, 122, 278n17
Mexico, 13
Methodist, 224, 248, 273. *See also* Protestants.
Michigan University Survey Research Center, 243-44, 251
Migration from Ireland, total, 5-6
Migrant generation, concept, 9-14
Miller, Kerby, 34, 236-42
Missionaries, 146-48
Mitchel, John, 19-20
Mixed marriages, 184-86. *See also* Conversions
Mokyr, Joel, 40
Moravians, 41
Moreland, John, 133
Multicultural studies, 4, 5, 214

Index

Revans, John, 165
Richards, Eric, 91, 98, 111-12
Robb, Nesca A., 215
Robinson, Mary, 15-16
Robinson, Ronald, 142
Rodgers, Jimmie, 224
Roman Catholic. *See* Catholic
Ryan, Liam, 189, 211, 213

Sandburg, Carl, 14
Sassenach, 234
Scandinavians, 41
Scheper-Hughes, Nancy, 119, 122, 278n17
"Scotch-Irish," as concept, 252-56. *See also* Ulster-Scots
Shaw, Savil, and Co., 70
Scotland. *See* Great Britain
Seasonal labour, 192-94
Small Differences, 34
Soldiers, Irish in UK army, 143-44
South Africa, 5, 48-49, 56, 59, 168, 174, 234, 235: gender ratio, 123-24; occupations, 124-30; religion, 129-30; historiography, 130-38; provincial origins, 131-32; Irish-born, 134; ethnic composition, 135, 136
South America, 13
Spanish empire, 4
Spellman, Francis, Cardinal, 224
Spencer, A.E.C.W., 213
Stem family, 25-26, 278n13 *See also* European family pattern

Tasman connection, 73
Tawney, R.H., 34
Trinity College, Dublin, 273

Ulster-Scots, 28, 221, 222, 249, 253-56
United States of America, 4-5, 8, 9, 12, 14, 20, 47-49, 56, 59, 60, 94, 124, 128, 150-51, 168, 173, 174, 180-81, 257-58, 272; religious composition, 219-24; 302-03n11; lack of data, 225-28, 302n9, 302-03n11, 303n14; North American context, 228-32; Catholics, 234-44; Protestants, 244-52

The Vanishing Irish, 10
Volgel, Sir Julius. *See* Vogel scheme
Vogel scheme, 64, 79-83, 168, 169

Weber, Max, 34
Williams family, 70-73
Women: "surplus" women, 20; as desirable migrants, 64-65; New Zealand, 84; South Africa, 123-24, 128-30; volitional migrants, 159; disadvantaged in Ireland, 159-61; Irish family, 161-63; vocational alternatives, 164-66; types of emigrants, 166-73; governmental policies, 173-76; families and emigration, 176-80; occupations, 180-82; marriage patterns, emigrants, 182-86; occupations in Great Britain, 201-03; need for study, 271-72. *See also* Gender ratios